D1273093

Word Wealth

revised edition

WARD S. MILLER
John Marshall High School
Rochester, New York

NEW YORK
HENRY HOLT AND COMPANY

PRINTED IN THE
UNITED STATES OF AMERICA

TO THE TEACHER
A Plan for Teaching Vocabulary

For several years educators have expressed increasing concern over the vocabulary deficiencies exhibited by pupils in high schools and colleges. Pupils themselves bewail their inadequacy in this respect.

This condition is not surprising in view of the fact that English teachers have taught grammar, punctuation, spelling, letter writing, outlining, news writing, and etiquette systematically, but never vocabulary. Somehow we have naïvely assumed that it should be caught rather than taught, or else we have contented ourselves with a few spasmodic measures which have amounted to very little. In any event, it was a phase of English too vast to treat until and unless it were somehow delimited.

Enrichment of the curriculum — and of our national life — at every point has made this traditional neglect of vocabulary no longer tolerable. Some comprehensive solution is necessary, however bewildering and complex the problem of finding for the English language a common denominator that can and should be inculcated in high school.

This book is an attempt to provide a tested and efficient technique as well as a list of words comprehensive enough to integrate the teaching of vocabulary throughout the English department of a high school. It consists of three parts, each of which contains ten units of twenty-five words.

Practically all are words often encountered in newspapers, magazines, books, radio programs, movies, churches, clubs, and conversations of our day. They are words which a high-school graduate should at least be able to recognize meaningfully. They are so arranged that each Part is more difficult than the preceding one. Determination of the relative difficulty of words is based upon certain considerations which will be explained later.

How the Words Were Selected

Although the English language is said to contain between two and three million words, a college-size dictionary includes only about 50,000 on its basic list, and the number of words of *general* vocabulary in common use probably does not exceed 25,000. These may be divided into seven classes:

1. Those which an average elementary-school graduate knows.

2. Words not in Class 1 the meaning of which becomes self-evident for one of the following reasons:

(*a*) They are compounded of familiar elements.

Examples: *irreparable, irrevocable, query, insuperable, machinations, quizzical, innumerable, insupportable, imperturbable, liquidate*

(*b*) They are onomatopoetic — or in some way obvious from the sound.

Examples: *sonorous, truckle, swashbuckling, insipid, reverberate*

(*c*) They are used for emphasis or rhythm more than for meaning.

Examples: *veritable, inordinate*

(*d*) The context usually and necessarily defines them accurately when they appear.

3. Words which, if taught, enter a pupil's vocabulary through the study of Latin, or which the study of Latin unlocks. This includes prefixes which provide a reliable clue to dozens of words such as *premature, prescience, postlude, retrospect.*

4. Words which are taught indirectly through the study of Greek, French, German, or Spanish. This is rather small for any one language.

5. Archaic or obsolete words which occur only in books.

Examples: *seneschal, pillion, trencher*

TO THE TEACHER

6. Words limited to technical use.

Examples: *carburetor, hormone, thrombosis*

7. Unfamiliar words which have a specific meaning that is not obvious. This, of course, excludes most words which belong to some specialized hobby, skill, occupation, or any special interest more than to general vocabulary.

Most of the words which may profitably be taught in high school by means of a book like this belong to Class 7. If the noun, adjective, verb, and adverb or other variant forms be taught and counted as one word, *the total number of words which should be included does not exceed* 1500 *and can easily be reduced to* 1000.

With the problem thus simplified, it remains only to stratify the words to some extent according to difficulty and frequency. Thus, the words in Part One tend to be less complicated in form and meaning than those in Part Two, and nearly all occur within Thorndike's first 10,000 in frequency. They are words of which the use is chiefly literal rather than figurative, and they are selected (this does not apply to material in small type) with reference to the everyday life and maturity of the pupil. It should be noticed that perfect adherence to the *double* standard of difficulty and frequency, even if it were attainable — and there are several reasons why it is not, practically, and need not be — would tend to make later units too formidable. As the arrangement stands, words in Part Three are, in many cases, no more difficult than words in Part One, but they are usually words which occur less frequently than those in Part One. *Secede*, for example, is not a difficult word, but it is not so common as it seems in the schools, where it has reference chiefly to a single event in American history.

How to Use This Book

One unit a month is a satisfactory rate of progress. An average class spending twenty to twenty-five minutes a day can complete a unit in six days. These do not need to be consecutive.

A suggested procedure follows:

First Day: The pretest is given and scored.[1] Pupils record their scores for later reference. They read over the words in concert and individually for ear familiarity.

Second Day: They pronounce the words and compose sentences using the words on the first half of the unit. The teacher may demonstrate by references to school life, current affairs, celebrities, and literature.

Third Day: Same procedure for second half of unit.

Fourth Day: First sentence set is used.

Fifth Day: Second sentence set is used, if necessary. Creative exercise is undertaken or gone over if assigned outside.

Sixth Day: Final test is given.

More time is needed for slow pupils, who will average up to 40 per cent on the pretest, less time for accelerated pupils. Those who score above 80 per cent on the pretest may omit one or more steps as a class or as individuals. The notes and queries in small type provide extra experience for such, and the supplementary tests are provided to measure the extent to which superior pupils (who make nearly perfect scores on the pretests) master this surplus material. Such pupils, however, even those who have from the start an almost perfect recognition-knowledge of the basic words in a unit, profit from experience in using these words and their variant forms while other pupils are gaining only a recognition-knowledge.

The sentence sets are designed for practice work. In using them, the pupil writes down a meaning of each word that is appropriate in the sentence. They may be dictated if the teacher wishes to emphasize the spelling of the words. Such emphasis is undoubtedly worth while with superior pupils. For a helpful discussion of the teaching of spelling, see Ap-

---

[1] The appetizers belong logically at the end of the unit but psychologically at the beginning where they appear. Any very thorough attempt to solve them before the unit is studied will prove futile in most cases. The fact that some answers are debatable is an intentional challenge to class discussion, some of which can scarcely fail to be humorous.

pendix Two, pp. 323–325. This essay, contributed by Ethel M. Dunn, a colleague of the author, is a summary of a recent study of the teaching of spelling which she made.

The division tests provide a convenient pretest as well as a final examination for each of the three parts of the book. They measure meaningful recognition of the words apart from a context and should, therefore, guarantee meaningful recognition in reading, or in speech if the pronunciation has been practiced sufficiently. Given as a pretest, they help a teacher determine whether Part One should be used with a particular grade, or whether Part Two would be a better starting point for that grade.

Keys are provided to facilitate self-education on the part of pupils. Thus the units may be used individually, each pupil setting his own rate of progress and checking the extent of his mastery as he goes along.

Though pupils tend to consider vocabulary building more practical and valuable than grammar work, punctuation, or even letter writing, their progress should be dramatized as much as possible. That is why pretests are included for each unit. Each pupil may make a graph of his pretest percentages and his final percentages. It is desirable to give a standardized vocabulary test [1] at the beginning of a year and again at the end, graphing the results against the norms for the grade and comparing progress with the "horse-and-buggy" rate at which vocabulary is "caught."

For pupils who do not take Latin, it is wise to start with a few lessons in word building. At least twenty-five common Latin or Greek prefixes should be taught and an equal number of the commonest roots, such as –spect– and –pel–puls–. For this purpose Appendix One is provided, pp. 263–322. Use of the first three lessons is strongly recommended as a prerequisite to any part of the book unless a majority of the class takes Latin. These lessons will help pupils remember by logical asso-

[1] Inglis Forms X and Y are excellent and may be used comparatively, but they are not hard enough for superior pupils beyond the tenth grade. Forms A, B, and C should be used for such pupils.

ciation many of the words which appear or recur in the main units.

Older and cruder methods of teaching vocabulary which have been used successfully have a limited use in conjunction with this book. The list below may be helpful:

1. Incidental method. The teacher suggests or demands that the pupil look up those words in his reading which he does not know.

2. Individual dictionary method. Pupils are given a list of words to look up, with due attention to meaning, pronunciation, and derivation. Teachers should beware of selecting them unintelligently in terms of difficulty and frequency.

3. Socialized dictionary method. Committees in rotation look up words in the reading and present them.

4. Socialized synonym approach. Pupils compile a class list of all possible synonyms for such concepts as *go, say, fight,* and differentiate shades of meaning. This is a fine tonic the day before themes are due.

5. " Felt-need " method. Pupils find and use new words as they need them to fill gaps in thinking, feeling, writing, or in sets of sentences which have been skillfully contrived for the purpose. This has real though limited value for maturer minds.

6. Independent method. A single student makes a hobby of collecting and looking up unfamiliar words, or he joins a group dedicated to such an undertaking. It *has* been done.

7. Direct teaching of words. A few words from or not from reading to be done are presented each day or each week by the teacher, cut out, nailed down, and clinched. The least efficient technique is to write them on the board and have students copy them.

The last is the method out of which this book has grown. It is foolproof because it cannot be escaped, evaded, dodged, avoided, eluded, side-stepped, or outwitted except by illness, death, or genius. It advances the democratic ideals of education because it is scientific and efficient. The use of non-topicalized units increases their versatility in application and their imaginative appeal.

The technique embodied in this book is evolved from attempts to meet as well as possible eight requirements:

1. It must enlist the interest of the pupil in his own progress — and dramatize that progress. (Hence the use of some standardized test of general vocabulary before and after a year of study, particularly with deficient pupils, is recommended.)

2. It must be efficient and practical.

3. It must be easy to use, for both pupil and teacher.

4. It must adapt itself readily to individual differences within the class.

5. It must be positive and definite.

6. It must be objective and self-educative.

7. It must not replace use of the dictionary.

8. It must encourage creativeness.

It is for the pupils and teachers who use this book to decide how perfectly these ideals have been achieved. The "paragraph provocations" and other new material which has been added in this edition will, it is hoped, further enhance the utility and popularity with which the book has been credited increasingly by its many thousands of users.

W. S. M.

Rochester, New York
March, 1948

ACKNOWLEDGMENTS

The writer wishes to thank all who had a part in making this book what it has become, particularly James M. Spinning, Elmer W. Snyder, and the late Elizabeth LeMay Wright for helpful criticism of the earlier stages of the project. To Mrs. Wright the writer owes his dawning realization of the importance of teaching the vocabulary of our own language.

Mrs. Caro F. Spencer, Philip Jenkins, Kenneth Fulkerson, Miss Lulu Bartholomew, Miss Eulalie Richardson, Miss Grace Leader, Miss Katherine Monaghan, Miss Ethel Dunn, Mrs. Marguerite Mahoney, Miss Susan McCowan, Mrs. Jane Jones, Miss Catherine Combs, Mrs. Mary Murphy, Mrs. Florence Toolan, Lewis Whitbeck, William A. Howe, Claude Westburg, and W. D. Cummings voluntarily participated in testing and improving the technique on which this book is built and in the experimentation which was carried on. Their assistance was of the utmost value.

It would be unfair to overlook several hundred pupils who participated in the experiments, many of . them with such enthusiasm that they all unwittingly encouraged this project and motivated the improvement of methods and technique which took place over a period of nearly three years before a book-length manuscript was compiled and offered for publication.

Appreciation is hereby expressed to the G. and C. Merriam Company for permitting the author to use their system of respelling for pronunciation in connection with the list of basic words at the back of the book. Its exactness will add to the usefulness of the list.

CONTENTS

APPENDIXES

TO THE PUPIL

Just a Minute ... ! Do You Know What It's All About?

"An extensive knowledge of the exact meanings of English words accompanies outstanding success in this country more often than any other single characteristic which the Human Engineering Laboratory has been able to isolate and measure." [1] That makes vocabulary sound pretty important, doesn't it? It is. Scientific experiments have demonstrated over and over again that if a pupil increases his vocabulary systematically, he improves his standing — slowly — in all of his subjects.

Now you know why a book like this came into being, why it was published, and why you are now in possession of a copy. In studying a foreign language one must learn ten or fifteen words a day for weeks at a time. Because of the start you got at home and in earlier years of school, twenty-five words a month will suffice for your own language at present. Some of them you half know already. At that, it isn't easy, though you would think so if you had studied a few of these units with the pupils who had them in John Marshall High School during their experimental stages — and liked them. At first there were no study guides and no examples. Many of the words were too rare and too bookish to be retained anywhere in the present set of units.

The words in this book are words you need to know because you see or hear them often both in school and outside. If you can *use* them as well as recognize them and know what they mean, you will not be like Herb M. He was really clever and he had good ideas, but he couldn't get them across. His talk was always rather hazy. He just couldn't express himself very well.

[1] O'Connor, Johnson, director of Human Engineering Laboratory, Stevens Institute of Technology, Hoboken, New Jersey.

No, it wasn't *all* a matter of a small vocabulary, but that had a lot to do with it. It was a definite handicap socially and in conversation with his friends when they were having a "real" session.

Herb tried to improve, but he didn't know just how. One day he fumbled for fifteen seconds or more — that's a long time, you will discover, if you try it on your watch — trying to say that what he had just seen in a movie could easily occur in real life. The word *plausible* just wasn't in his vocabulary. Such synonyms as *bewildering* and *perplexing* for *puzzling* were beyond his reach. The only word anyone had ever heard him use to indicate a state of mental uncertainty was *puzzled*.

This got by well enough in high school. It passed for bashfulness and modesty. It was, partly. But Herb was ambitious, and he knew it would hinder him and lessen his chances for promotion in any kind of work where he would have to meet people very much or express ideas so that they would "go across."

*　　*　　*

Perhaps, when you finally come to that warm evening in June and that impressive ceremony on a flower-decked platform, you may decide that a good vocabulary is more important than any other technical phase of English. Don't say it, though. Comparisons are odious. Each part contributes to the perfect whole.

What makes a good vocabulary? Plainly, it is not rare and uncommon words like *poltroon* (coward) and *catholicon* (a panacea or cure-all), because these are not as useful as their more familiar equivalents. Rather, it is words commonly used in newspapers, magazines, radio programs, movies, and conversation which are either vague or completely meaningless to the average student.

The number of these words is not so large as one would imagine. The units in this book include fewer than a thousand basic words, but these have been selected with such care that they go far toward covering the margin between those which everyone should know and those which no one knows except highly educated persons or specialists in particular branches of knowledge. Each basic word is the key to four or five others, as vocabularians count them, and "A Secret Process" in Appendix One should redouble the number you will recognize meaningfully.

The words are common. They will haunt you if you don't know what they mean. They will trip you. They will get you if you don't watch out!

Because the words, then, are frequently used in modern life and were selected largely on that basis, you will find that you are familiar with some in each unit already, though you may not know the meaning or the pronunciation accurately. Watch for chances to use all of them. Apply them to experiences, situations, and persons you know. Some will fill a long-felt need. Even if you get a word correct on the pretest, that is no proof that you are really acquainted with it.

You are embarking on a *New Idea*, then — the efficient, scientific, and systematic exploration of the vocabulary of your own language. In a few minutes a day you will acquire hundreds of words which you need to acquire. Try to avoid learning any of the words by rote, however. That is the poorest as well as the hardest way. Relate them to your experiences, to life and to each other constantly. Each is highly individual, and there is no such thing as a true synonym.

Your vocabulary will grow like a snowball if you use the dictionary to supplement the units as suggested and look up new words wherever you encounter them. That is the only way to excel in understanding and using the English language. Guessing at the meaning of a new word is often misleading. Remember, there are hundreds of thousands of words in our American melting pot of languages. That is why it excels in expressiveness!

PRONUNCIATIONS

The pronunciation of each of the basic words may be found in the list at the back of the book. Only troublesome words are marked in the study guides, and diacritical marks have been avoided to a large degree in favor of a more obvious method of indicating pronunciation, even though uniformity of method had to be sacrificed thereby. Accented syllables are capitalized because this practice facilitates correct pronunciation for many pupils. Secondary accents, when they occur, have been generally ignored.

One important fact should be kept in mind, however: *Pupils depend more on hearing and imitating the teacher's pronunciation of new words than on any system of marking that could be devised.*

Key to Standard Diacritical Marks

a: āpe, senăte, bâre, făt, làugh, bär, ăffect, commȧ
e: scēne, ēlect, ĕmploy, ridēr, novĕl
i: dīme, ĭntends
o: bōld, prŏnounce, ôrb, drŏp, cŏmmand
u: ūse, popŭlar, tûrn, tŭck, censŭs
oo: bōom, lŏŏk
zh: azure

Refinements of these sounds and methods of marking consonant sounds vary from one dictionary to another.

ABBREVIATIONS

The two which have been used chiefly, with their meanings, are:

cf. — compare
i.e. — that is

Parentheses are used ordinarily to enclose words necessary to the understanding of a definition but not an essential part of the definition.

WORD WEALTH

PART ONE

Queries

Which word is easiest for girls?

Which two apply most often to auto accidents?

Which word is the most painful?

What do we eat?

What fans us (in July) while we eat?

Which words save money?

What two say yes?

Which ones cause delay?

PRETEST

Find the number of the definition that goes with each word.

VERBS

4 1. abhor
6 2. acquire
5 3. adapt
8 4. affirm
1 5. avert

10 6. coerce
12 7. concur
13 8. contort
14 9. curtail
2 10. defer
9 11. demolish
7 12. designate
11 13. divulge

1. to turn away, ward off
2. to delay, postpone
3. to happen
4. to hate or detest, loathe
5. to make suitable (by alteration)
6. to get, procure, obtain
7. to name, point out
8. to declare, assert
9. to break into pieces, destroy
10. to compel (by force)
11. to disclose, reveal
12. to agree
13. to twist out of shape
14. to reduce, lessen
15. to help or assist

NOUNS

1. decade
2. episode
3. impediment
4. interim
5. labyrinth
6. missile
7. parley
8. rapture
9. salvo

10. vanguard
11. viand
12. zephyr

1. ecstasy, keen delight
2. a quarrel or fight
3. a ten-year period
4. an article of food
5. a hindrance, obstruction
6. state of confusion
7. first line or advance guard
8. a gentle breeze
9. a conference, especially with an enemy
10. an incident
11. a simultaneous outburst
12. a projectile, object hurled
13. an interval (between happenings)
14. a maze, very complicated situation

STUDY GUIDE—VERBS

1. ABHOR . . . . **to hate or detest, loathe**

Americans abhor class distinctions.
Is spinach abhorrent (hateful) to you?
If so, do you conceal your abhorrence?

I loathe the idea of getting up early.
Leprosy is a loathsome disease.

2. ACQUIRE . . . . **to get, procure, obtain**

Where did you acquire your sun tan?
The acquisition of knowledge is worth while.

An acquisitive person has a knack for acquiring and keeping money or
property.

3. ADAPT . . . . **to make suitable (by alteration)**

Can you adapt the coupe for use as a truck?
Living in a fraternity house made him adaptable (able to con-
form readily to circumstances).
Her adaptability made her popular.

Query: Is adaptability always a virtue?

4. AFFIRM . . . . **to declare, assert**

I affirm my allegiance.
Here is my affirmation. (See a dictionary for legal meanings.)

The affirmative team argues the *yes* side of a debate.
Synonym: *asseverate.*

5. AVERT . . . . **to turn away, ward off**

He tried to avert the danger.
The danger was avertible.
What is your pet aversion (dislike)?
Are you ever averse (unwilling) to study?

Note: All forms come from a Latin verb meaning *turn from.*

6. COERCE . . . . **to compel (by force)**

Must one coerce him into submission?
Indians would not yield to coercion.

7. CONCUR . . . . **to agree**

It takes two to concur in an action or opinion.

Concurrence among the nations of Europe would make disarmament possible.

Cf. *assent* — agree, say yes: I assent to the operation.

8. CONTORT . . . . **to twist out of shape**

Pain will contort a face. Small boys produce facial contortions for fun.

9. CURTAIL . . . . **to reduce, lessen**

Father decided to curtail expenses.
Curtailment was, difficult.
Curtail always takes an object. You always curtail *something*.

10. DEFER . . . . **to delay, postpone**

Why defer the trip to the dentist?
Deferment will do no good.
Defer has a twin meaning *yield* or *give in*. See a dictionary.

11. DEMOLISH . . . . . . **to break into pieces, destroy**

Trains demolish cars when they get a chance.
The demolition (tearing down) of the old theater took a week.

12. DESIGNATE . . . . **to name, point out**

The President designated Thursday as a holiday. This designation pleased the merchants.
Do you see *design* (plan) in the word?

13. DIVULGE . . . . **to disclose, reveal**

Did he divulge the secret?
The *i* is short as in *diligent*.

STUDY GUIDE—NOUNS

1. DECADE . . . . **a ten-year period**

The airplane was invented several decades ago.
Is democracy decadent (on the decline) in the world?

Decadence (decline) and *decadent* come from Latin words meaning to fall down, whereas *decade* is derived from the Greek word for ten.

2. EPISODE . . . . **an incident**

The episode in which the spy is shot is very exciting.

3. IMPEDIMENT . . . . **a hindrance, obstruction**

Poverty is an impediment.
It did not impede Benjamin Franklin very much, however.

4. INTERIM . . . . . . **an interval (between happenings)**

Silence prevailed in the interim, but we knew that the other
side was getting ready for a surprise attack.

Interlude has a similar meaning. Look it up.

5. LABYRINTH . . . . **a maze, very complicated situation**

The factory is a labyrinth of passages.
Only the foremen understand its labyrinthine layout.

Query: Why do we speak of *threading* a labyrinth?

6. MISSILE . . . . **a projectile, object hurled**

The missiles which the natives hurled turned out to be coco-
nuts.

7. PARLEY . . . . **a conference (especially with an enemy)**

The strike parley broke up in anger.
Parliament is a place where the chief activity is talking.
A bingle, in the parlance (language) of baseball, is a base hit.

These words come from the French *parler*, to talk.

8. RAPTURE . . . . **ecstasy, keen delight**

A splendid sunset filled the artist's soul with rapture.
Baseball has its rapturous moments.
Vera talks rapturously of surfboard riding.

Transport carries one completely outside himself with intense joy.

9. SALVO . . . . **a simultaneous outburst**

The fortress was destroyed by three salvos from a cruiser.

Salvo applies to guns fired or bombs dropped simultaneously, or to explosive
sounds.

10. VANGUARD . . . . . . **first line or advance guard**

The vanguard was set in motion instantly.

This has an unusual derivation. See a dictionary.

11. VIAND . . . . **an article of food**

The table was covered with choice viands.

Her job was to prepare victuals three times a day for ten men.

Viands is usually used in the plural of food ready to eat. *Victuals* is a colloquial word.

12. ZEPHYR . . . . **a gentle breeze**

Zephyrs come in summer, tempests in winter.

It once meant the *west* wind.

FIRST SENTENCE SET

Copy the *italicized* words and opposite each write an appropriate definition.

1. The miser *abhorred* all who could not help him *acquire* wealth.
2. The manager *affirmed* his desire to *avert* a strike.
3. He will *concur* if you do not try to *coerce* him.
4. Fear *contorts* the soul and *curtails* one's pleasure.
5. He will *defer* the meeting and *adapt* his plans accordingly.
6. The foreman *designated* a low white house as the one to be *demolished*, but he would not *divulge* the owner's name.
7. His debts were an *impediment* which took a *decade* to remove.
8. During the *interim* he explored the *labyrinth* of streets near the bridge.
9. A *missile* hurled by an enemy interrupted their *parley*.
10. As the audience watched with *rapture*, a *salvo* of applause stirred the team to renewed exertions.
11. The men in the *vanguard* would not divulge what they had seen of the spy *episode*.
12. *Zephyrs* fanned us as we consumed the *viands*.

SECOND SENTENCE SET

1. Employees *abhor* a president who will not *adapt* his policies to present conditions.

2. Did he *designate* someone to attend the *parley?*
3. He swerved to *avert* a collision which would have *demolished* the car.
4. The boy's face is *contorted* because of an *impediment* in his speech.
5. The admirals *concurred* in believing that several *salvos* from the largest guns would be necessary.
6. The *episode* occurred a *decade* ago amid the *zephyrs* of a June morning.
7. During the *interim* the *vanguard* continued to march slowly.
8. One *missile* upset a table of *viands.*
9. Japan was eager to *acquire* more territory.
10. He *affirmed* his unwillingness to *coerce* anyone or *curtail* anyone's privileges.
11. With *rapture* on his face he *divulged* the news.
12. Illness made them *defer* their visit to Carlsbad Caverns, an underground *labyrinth.*

SAVED BY A THREAD

1. Look up or recall the story of Theseus and the Minotaur. A Minoan palace excavated at Cnossus on Crete appears to have been the *labyrinth* of the legend. Write a paragraph using words in this unit to answer such questions as:

   Why did Theseus want to destroy the Minotaur?
   What did Ariadne do to help Theseus?
   What did she feel afterward?
   What happened to the labyrinth?

2. Write a few sentences about two dogs, their owners, and perhaps a dogfight, with a remark or two about the bystanders. Find a natural use, if you can, for ten of the words in this manner.

Teasers

Which of the words in this unit best fill the blanks below?

Boys get punished if they __?__, if they __?__, or if they __?__ a cat.

It is fun to read about divers who __?__ sunken ships.

__?__ is a very popular quality.   So is __?__ of speech.

Nobody likes __?__, __?__, or foolish __?__s.

PRETEST

Find the number of the definition that goes with each word.

VERBS

1. discern
2. err
3. esteem
4. evict
5. filch

6. harass
7. loiter
8. manipulate
9. meditate
10. promulgate
11. relent
12. salvage

1. to save (especially goods from fire, flood, or shipwreck)
2. to expel, remove (by force)
3. to think, reflect
4. to linger or waste (time) idly
5. to see distinctly (with eye or mind)
6. to accuse of a crime
7. to publish or make known
8. to steal or pilfer
9. to make a mistake
10. to crawl slowly
11. to value highly or consider
12. to become less severe, yield
13. to operate or manage
14. to annoy or disturb

NOUNS

1. accord
2. animation
3. apprehension
4. brevity
5. cache
6. chaos
7. citadel
8. counsel
9. custodian

10. deluge
11. demeanor
12. derision
13. epoch

1. a skin disease
2. a keeper, guardian
3. shortness, conciseness
4. a fortress or refuge
5. a downpour or flood
6. an era or period of years
7. fear, anxiety
8. behavior, bearing
9. hiding place (for supplies or treasures)
10. ridicule
11. Mexican home
12. advice, admonition
13. liveliness, sprightliness
14. confusion, disorder
15. harmony, agreement

9. **CUSTODIAN** . . . . **a keeper, guardian**

The custodian of the estate did not like small boys.

An uncle asked to have the custody (guardianship) of the orphan.

The police took the prisoner into custody (imprisonment).

10. **DELUGE (DEL-ŭj)** . . . . **a downpour or flood**

Noah was out in the most famous deluge of all time.

Sister would like to be deluged (overwhelmed) with invitations to dances.

Brother's antediluvian vehicle is really but ten years old.

Antediluvian means *before The Deluge* — or just very ancient.

11. **DEMEANOR** . . . . **behavior, bearing**

His lordly demeanor impressed everyone.

Mien has the same meaning and perhaps the same origin.

12. **DERISION** . . . . **ridicule**

Inventors are often treated with derision.

It is very easy to deride (laugh at) those who are different.

Derisive (scornful) laughter greeted Oscar's attempt to sing.

Risible (laughable) and *risibilities* (inclination to laugh) come from the same Latin root as *derision*.

13. **EPOCH** . . . . **an era or period of years**

We are living in an epoch of scientific progress.

The invention of the telegraph was an epochal event.

Epochal (EP-ock-al) means *supremely important* — important enough to be the beginning or end of an epoch.

FIRST SENTENCE SET

Copy the *italicized* words and opposite each write an appropriate definition.

1. It is easy to *discern* his figure on the steps. Do you know why we *esteem* him as we do?
2. You *err* if you *evict* tenants too hastily.
3. Mother would not *relent*, and William went to bed for *filching* an apple.

STUDY GUIDE—VERBS

1. **DISCERN** . . . . **to see distinctly (with eye or mind)**

Nancy could not discern whether it was her father or not.

A light was discernible in the distance.

His powers of discernment make him a good columnist.

Cf. *perceive, descry, distinguish, discriminate.*

2. **ERR (rhymes with *her*)** . . . . **to make a mistake**

"To err is human; to forgive, divine."

Your answer is erroneous (mistaken).

Benjamin Franklin in his *Autobiography* lists several errata (errors) which he made.

Err once meant *to wander.* A knight-errant was a roving knight.

Erratic means *irregular* or *queer.*

3. **ESTEEM** . . . . **to value highly or consider**

Fathers esteem the confidence of their children. Children esteem it a privilege to confide in their fathers.

Do girls (boys) rise in your esteem (regard) as you grow older?

4. **EVICT** . . . . **to expel, remove (by force)**

Landlords evict a tenant who does not pay his rent. In such an eviction the furniture is moved into the street.

5. **FILCH** . . . . **to steal or pilfer**

The criminal started his career by learning to filch candy in a store.

It is ordinarily used of trifling thefts.

6. **HARASS** . . . . **to annoy or disturb**

Brothers and sisters like to harass each other. Such harassment is an everyday occurrence in many homes.

Accent the first syllable. Pronounce the first *a* as in *cat.*

7. **LOITER** . . . . **to linger or waste (time) idly**

Do not loiter along the way. A loiterer is not trusted.

8. **MANIPULATE** . . . . **to operate or manage**

He can manipulate a canoe skillfully.

He will some day show equal skill in the manipulation of a car.
See a dictionary for a complete explanation of *manipulate*.

9. MEDITATE . . . . to think, reflect

The speaker believes that Americans do not take enough time
to meditate.

He suggested ten minutes for meditation each morning before
breakfast.

Instead of *meditate*, might you prefer *ponder? Contemplate? Ruminate?*
Why? More later.

10. PROMULGATE (pro-MULL-gate) to publish or make known

The government promulgates the truth about harmful drugs.

The promulgation of news about the event was forbidden by
the government.

11. RELENT . . . . to become less severe, yield

The fury of the storm began to relent.

Having decided to execute his visitors, the king would not relent.

John's relentless (unrelenting) efforts to master algebra were
rewarded finally.

12. SALVAGE . . . . . . to save (especially goods from fire, flood, or shipwreck)

Attempts to salvage the cargo failed.

The salvage (saving) of the treasure ships is being attempted by
divers.

STUDY GUIDE—NOUNS

1. ACCORD . . . . harmony, agreement

Accord between France and Germany was impossible.

Police accorded (granted) him the privilege of unlimited parking.

One must live in accordance (agreement) with the laws.

See a dictionary for other meanings of *accord*. Cf. also *accordion*.

2. ANIMATION . . . . liveliness, sprightliness

Animation helps make a girl popular.

The captain's energy animates (enlivens) the wh...
Rocks and boards are inanimate (lifeless) objects.

Do you ever see animated cartoons?

3. APPREHENSION . . . . fe...

The very thought of an airplane fills grandmother's ...
apprehensions.

Sister gazed apprehensively at the spot where the m...
vanished.

Does a black cat make you apprehensive (fearful of evi...

What dangers do you apprehend?

The literal meaning of *apprehend* is *seize*. Hence, it also means *arre*...
grasp mentally:
    The police apprehended the thief.
    You apprehend my meaning correctly.

4. BREVITY . . . . shortness, concisene...

The brevity of the banker's answers made it difficult to inter...
view him.

Look up *breviary, brevet,* and *breve,* if you have time.

5. CACHE (kash) . . a hiding place (for supplies or treasures)

The boys kept their Indian weapons in a cache under the garage.

6. CHAOS . . . . confusion, disorder

The room was in chaos.

Bedlam reigns in the barn when the gang gathers.

Bedlam means *uproar* or *confusion*, whereas chaos may be noiseless. Cf.
pandemonium.
Note: *Bedlam* comes from the name of a lunatic asylum in London. Hence,
it means *madhouse*, too.

7. CITADEL . . . . a fortress or refuge

The Alcazar was a famous citadel in Spain.

8. COUNSEL . . . . advice, admonition

Your counsel seems wise.

He counsels immediate action.

Counsel also means a legal adviser or legal advice.

4. The boy was punished for *loitering* to *harass* a cat.
5. He *manipulated* the boat skillfully and managed to *salvage* his hat.
6. He *meditated* a long time before *promulgating* the story.
7. Their *animation* grows out of perfect *accord*.
8. The *brevity* of the storm made *apprehension* unnecessary.
9. Thieves left the treasure *cache* in *chaos*.
10. The *counsel* of an old veteran saved the *citadel*.
11. The *custodian* watched the *deluge*.
12. His proud *demeanor* aroused *derision*.
13. Slavery belonged to another *epoch*.

SECOND SENTENCE SET

1. They were able to *salvage* nothing from the *chaos*.
2. We could *discern* the towers of the *citadel* in the distance.
3. The *custodian erred* when he *evicted* the owner by mistake.
4. Because the boys *esteemed* their coach, there was perfect *accord* on the team.
5. The squirrel *filched* nuts and hid them in a *cache* under the eaves.
6. No amount of pleading could induce Father to *relent*. He will not let his son *harass* defenseless pets.
7. Uncle *loitered* in the park trying to *meditate*.
8. The pilot can *manipulate* a plane so well that passengers have no *apprehensions*.
9. An "extra" *promulgated* news of the *deluge*.
10. The *animation* of her *demeanor* pleased everyone.
11. The *brevity* of the *epoch* is hard to explain.
12. *Derision* greeted the old man's *counsel*.

SHIPWRECKED

Write a paragraph on this topic. If the ship is large, the cargo valuable, and your imagination adequate otherwise, you will have use for more than half the words in this unit.

An earthquake or a tornado will give you quite an adventure with this unit, if you prefer.

Quiz

Use one of the words in this unit to answer each of the questions below:

How does a deficit make one look?

Name someone who is very candid.

How does a guilty person act?

How does a sick person look?

Describe an elderly person's hair.

PRETEST

Find the number of the definition that goes with each word

ADJECTIVES

1. brusque	1. regretful, sorrowful
2. candid	2. ripe, fully developed
3. celestial	3. calm, serene
4. deficient	4. appearing true or reasonable
5. furtive	5. blunt or abrupt
6. ghastly	6. careless, reckless
7. hoary	7. powerful, mighty
8. lucid	8. sly, stealthy
9. malicious	9. heavenly, divine
10. mature	10. white or gray with age
11. motley	11. frank, truthful
12. pensive	12. uncanny, unearthly
13. placid	13. (consisting of) varied (colors or inharmonious elements)
14. plaintive	14. dreamily thoughtful, wistful
15. plausible	15. fortunate, lucky
16. potent	16. clear, transparent
17. rueful	17. lacking (in some respect), defective
18. subsequent	18. sad, mournful
19. wanton	19. spiteful, arising from ill will, ugly
20. weird	20. famous, prominent
	21. following, later (in time or order)
	22. pale or horrible

NOUNS

1. deficit	1. a wharf
2. medley	2. the remainder; a scrap or trace
3. quay	3. summit, greatest height
4. remnant	4. a shortage, especially of money
5. zenith	5. a mountain slope
	6. a mixture or jumble

STUDY GUIDE—ADJECTIVES

1. BRUSQUE . . . . blunt or abrupt
The officer was brusque with me. I answered brusquely and he
seemed nettled by my brusqueness.

2. CANDID . . . . frank, truthful
His candid manner pleased everyone.
She answered the question candidly.
Her candor (frankness) added to her charm.
The Latin roots mean white *and* whiteness.

3. CELESTIAL . . . . heavenly, divine
It sounded like the music of a celestial choir.

4. DEFICIENT . . . . lacking (in some respect), defective
Pancakes are deficient in vitamins.
A deficiency of protein kept the hens from laying.
A deficiency of iodine in drinking water was believed the cause
of goiter.
A deficit *is a lack of enough money to balance accounts.*

5. FURTIVE . . . . sly, stealthy
The thief kept darting furtive glances at the door.
That boy's furtiveness (slyness) makes me suspicious.
Other synonyms of furtive *are* thieflike *and* surreptitious.

6. GHASTLY . . . . pale or horrible
The malady made him look ghastly.
"What a ghastly crime!" the detective exclaimed.
The lady looked aghast (terrified) as she saw the corpse.
Cf. grisly, hideous, gruesome, horrible, grotesque.

7. HOARY . . . . . . white or gray with age; ancient
He stroked a long, hoary beard.
Cf. hoarfrost.

8. LUCID . . . . clear, transparent
The water was lucid (or pellucid).
The dying man during one of his lucid moments asked for his
son.

The lucidity of his explanation was amazing.

Other members of the Light family:
    lucent — shining, glowing
    lucifer — light bearer
    lucubrate — do mental work by artificial light
    lucida — brightest star of a constellation

9. MALICIOUS . . . . spiteful, arising from ill will, ugly

The neighbors keep malicious dogs.
The boy who hurt a man with a snowball intended no malice.
The malign (evil) influence of the book is well known.
The malignant demeanor of the bulldog boded us ill.

Malign and *malignant* are similar to *malicious*.
Malignity is a stronger word than *malice*. See a dictionary.

10. MATURE . . . . ripe, fully developed

The corn was mature in August.
High-school pupils are immature (not completely developed).
The proposal was premature (occurring before the proper time).
The plan reached maturity in the fall.

The Romans used the word *mature* also — only it ended in *–us* in those days.

11. MOTLEY . . . . . . (consisting of) varied (colors or inharmonious elements)

A motley flock of chickens, ducks, and geese set up a clamor in the barnyard.

12. PENSIVE . . . . dreamily thoughtful, wistful

There was a pensive look in her eyes.
Pensiveness adds a certain charm to one's appearance.

Wistfulness is a shade sadder than *pensiveness*.

13. PLACID . . . . calm, serene

The Swiss are a placid people.
"Always," he answered placidly.
High altitudes foster placidity.

Synonyms of *placid: peaceful, tranquil, quiet, unruffled.*

14. PLAINTIVE . . . . sad, mournful

The plaintive note of an owl was heard.

Do you like the plaintiveness of cowboy songs?
The plaintiff sued for $10,000 in damages.
The *plaintiff* at law is the one who *complains*.

15. PLAUSIBLE . . . . **appearing true or reasonable**

It was a plausible yarn. The author has a knack of lending plausibility to the most improbable tales.

16. POTENT . . . . **powerful, mighty**

"The potent poison quite o'ercrows my spirit."
The postmaster general was a potent influence in politics.
The potency of the drug makes it dangerous.
A tribal head is one of the lesser potentates (monarchs) of the earth.
The potential (possible) capacities of the youth have just become apparent.

17. RUEFUL . . . . **regretful, sorrowful**

A rueful expression appeared on her face.
The ruefulness of the sight awed them.
He will rue it if he goes.

18. SUBSEQUENT . . . . **following, later (in time or order)**

The subsequent incident provided a valuable clue.
The president subsequently resigned.

19. WANTON. . . . . **careless, reckless, or playful**

The soldiers showed a wanton disregard for property.
A wanton wind whisked the leaves back and forth.
He behaves with the wantonness of a child.

20. WEIRD . . . . **uncanny, unearthly**

Weird noises made the house seem haunted.
The music is weirdly beautiful. It is Oriental in its weirdness.
Note: *Weird* comes from the Anglo-Saxon word for fate or destiny.

STUDY GUIDE—NOUNS

1. DEFICIT (DEF-i-sit) . . . **a shortage, especially of money**

The treasurer reported a deficit of $25.00.
In Latin the word means, "It is lacking."

2. MEDLEY . . . . **a mixture or jumble**

The orchestra played a medley of favorite songs.
A medley of sounds could be heard in the barnyard.

3. QUAY (kee) . . . . **a wharf**

Several sailors lounged near the quay.

4. REMNANT . . . . . **the remainder; a scrap or trace**

Hash contains the remnants of a roast.
Not a remnant of its glory was left.
The word itself is a remnant.

5. ZENITH . . . . **summit, greatest height**

The star will soon be at the zenith.
The actor reached the zenith of his career.
The *zenith* is that point directly above one in the heavens.

FIRST SENTENCE SET

Copy the *italicized* words and opposite each write an appropriate definition.

1. He prefers to be *candid* even at the risk of seeming *brusque*.
2. His face became *ghastly* because he was *deficient* in courage.
3. Herbert cast *furtive* glances at the *malicious*-looking dog.
4. There is an almost *celestial* grandeur about *hoary* hair.
5. Are *mature* adults often *pensive?*
6. The old lady is very *placid* except when a *motley* gang of boys invades her yard.
7. She could think of no *plausible* reason for the *plaintive* wail, and her brother was unable to invent a *lucid* explanation.
8. He was *rueful* over the *wanton* habits he had acquired.
9. The medicine was very *potent*, as Thomas *subsequently* found out.
10. The *medley* of Chinese songs sounded very *weird*.
11. The city incurred a large *deficit* in building the *quay*.
12. Only a *remnant* is left of the fortune he possessed when his business was at its *zenith*.

SECOND SENTENCE SET

1. "Looking *rueful* will not help!" was her *brusque* response.
2. You might as well be *candid* about the *subsequent* incidents.
3. He watched the *celestial* display with *pensive* awe.
4. Your skill will be less *deficient* when you are more *mature*.
5. *Furtive* eyes watched the *weird* creature. Its *plaintive* cry startled everyone.
6. The *wanton* destruction of the property was a *ghastly* mistake.
7. The building near the *quay* is *hoary* with age.
8. In his *lucid* moments he talked about the *deficit* he had caused.
9. The *malicious* mob was a *motley* array of farmers.
10. The notion that *potent* enemies had done it seemed *plausible*.
11. A *remnant* of the crowd lingered to see what had caused such a *medley* of sounds.
12. The playing of the *placid* Swedish halfback reached its *zenith* in the third quarter.

CHOOSE YOUR TOPIC

Write a paragraph about a bank robbery, a barnyard, the members of an orchestra, a visit to the zoo, or a display of the Northern Lights. Use as many words from this unit as you can without overdoing the idea, and underline each. Draw on other units as the opportunity presents itself.

Queries

You will find the answers among the words in this unit.

How does one look when:

> He doesn't know the answer?
>
> He is very, very angry?
>
> He is extremely ill?
>
> He gets an A?
>
> He falls asleep in class?

Find the number of the definition that goes with each word.

1.	audible	1.	unceasing, uninterrupted
2.	avid	2.	joyful
3.	canine	3.	capable of being heard
4.	diminutive	4.	piercing, stinging, keen
5.	dubious	5.	discernible, observable
6.	exultant	6.	undersized, small
7.	haggard	7.	crude or simple, belonging to early ages
8.	immortal	8.	noisy
9.	incessant	9.	leaden or very pale
10.	indomitable	10.	playful, mischievous
11.	livid	11.	deathless, undying
12.	ludicrous	12.	eager, greedy
13.	luscious	13.	ill-boding, evil
14.	massive	14.	hazy, indefinite
15.	nocturnal	15.	doglike
16.	pathetic	16.	unconquerable
17.	perceptible	17.	plundering, robbing
18.	perverse	18.	necessary, essential
19.	predatory	19.	worn, gaunt, wild-looking
20.	primitive	20.	doubtful
21.	pungent	21.	fond of fighting
22.	requisite	22.	weighty or enormous
23.	sinister	23.	laughable, ridiculous, droll
24.	vague	24.	contrary, stubborn
25.	vociferous	25.	sad, pitiable
		26.	delicious
		27.	of or pertaining to night

STUDY GUIDE

1. AUDIBLE . . . . **capable of being heard**

His response took the form of a barely audible grunt.
Speak audibly when you recite. Cultivate audibility.
Cf. *audition, auditory, auditorium.*

2. AVID . . . . **eager, greedy**

She watched the boy's avid inroads on the peach.
The dog seized the bone with avidity.

3. CANINE (KAY-nine) . . . . **doglike**

The terrier bounded in with canine expressions of joy.
Canis (KAY-nis) Major is the Great Dog constellation.

4. DIMINUTIVE . . . . **undersized, small**

A diminutive quarterback barked signals.
Morning brought diminution (dim-ĭ-NEW-shun) of our hopes
of finding her.

Diminutive has the same ancestry as *diminish,* to make less. Cf. *diminuendo (dim.)* in music.

5. DUBIOUS . . . . **doubtful**

A dubious look appeared on her face.
The dubiousness of the weather discouraged us.
He is indubitably (undoubtedly) the better player.

Other doubt words: *dubiety* (dŭ-BY-ĕ-tĭ), *dubitable, indubitable, dubitation, dubitative.*

6. EXULTANT . . . . **joyful**

Victory made them exultant.
He exults in his athletic prowess.
The song expresses exultation.

7. HAGGARD . . . . **worn, gaunt, wild-looking**

Haggard and weary, he nevertheless insisted on continuing.
His haggardness alarmed everyone.

8. IMMORTAL . . . . **deathless, undying**

"A man is immortal till his work is done."
The Christian religion teaches the immortality of the soul.

A famous monument in the District of Columbia immortalizes the memory of George Washington.

Synonyms of *immortal: eternal, everlasting, imperishable.*

9. INCESSANT . . . . **unceasing, uninterrupted**

Incessant traffic flowed by all day.
She talks incessantly.

10. INDOMITABLE . . . . **unconquerable**

He began to feel indomitable as the supreme test drew near.
We are indomitably opposed to the change.

11. LIVID . . . . **leaden or very pale**

The man's face suddenly became livid.
Sometimes it means *discolored* if applied to a scar.

12. LUDICROUS . . . . . . **laughable, ridiculous, droll**

There was something ludicrous about her fury.
The ludicrousness of the cat's antics made everyone laugh.

13. LUSCIOUS . . . . **delicious**

A dish of luscious peaches stood on the table. Their lusciousness was irresistible.
Lush means *juicy, succulent,* or *rich in vegetation.*

14. MASSIVE . . . . **weighty or enormous**

Three of the massive pillars are still standing.
The massiveness of the Great Pyramid awes one.
A massive forehead is merely an impressive one.

15. NOCTURNAL . . . . . . **of or pertaining to night**

No man could go far from that ship in his nocturnal wanderings.
She played a nocturne.

A *nocturne* is a serenade, a dreamy, instrumental night song, or a painting of a night scene.

16. PATHETIC . . . . **sad, pitiable**

The man's despair over his loss was pathetic. The pathos of his situation was heightened by his courageousness.
Pathos is pronounced PAY-thŏs.

17. PERCEPTIBLE . . . . discernible, observable

The difference in color is scarcely perceptible.
Our terror did not escape his perception.

One may *perceive* through any of the senses.

18. PERVERSE . . . . contrary, stubborn

The weather made him feel perverse, and this perverseness out-
lasted the bad weather.
Bribes pervert (thwart) justice.
Perversity is a trait of spoiled children.

Cf. *refractory, froward, willful, headstrong, wayward.*

19. PREDATORY . . . . plundering, robbing

A wolf has predatory instincts.
Lions are predacious beasts.

20. PRIMITIVE . . . . crude or simple, belonging to early ages

In the museum there is a primitive Indian hatchet.
The Indians were slow in emerging from the primitiveness of
the Stone Age.

Cf. *primeval:* "This is the forest primeval."

21. PUNGENT . . . . piercing, stinging, keen

The pungent odor of ammonia filled the air.
The pungency of her comments helped to enliven the party.

Cf. *piquant* (PEE-kant).

22. REQUISITE . . . . necessary, essential

Perseverance is requisite to success in any undertaking.
In getting along with others a sense of humor is a requisite.

Degrees of need: 1. needful 2. expedient 3. necessary 4. essential
5. indispensable

23. SINISTER . . . . ill-boding, evil

The room was filled with a sinister glow.
There was something ominous in his attitude.
It proved to be a portentous (ill-omened or remarkable) day.

Synonyms of *sinister: ominous, portentous.*

24. VAGUE . . . . hazy, indefinite

Vague plans seldom materialize.

The vagueness of his answers made the police suspicious.

Cf. *nebulous, obscure, ambiguous.*

25. VOCIFEROUS . . . . **noisy**

Vociferous boys disturb the neighbors.

Their vociferousness makes them unwelcome.

Cf. *clamorous, obstreperous, blatant.*

See *vociferate, vociferant.*

FIRST SENTENCE SET

Copy the *italicized* words and opposite each write an appropriate definition.

1. The faintest call is *audible* to *avid* eaters.
2. The *diminutive* fighter was *exultant* over winning.
3. The coach looked *dubious* because the boy's *canine* devotion was hard to disappoint.
4. *Incessant* strain made him look *haggard.*
5. Napoleon was an *indomitable* general who won *immortal* fame.
6. His face went *livid* when he saw how *massive* his opponent was.
7. Larry looks *ludicrous* licking *luscious* limes.
8. *Nocturnal* noises sometimes sound *sinister.*
9. Failure is *pathetic* when *perceptible* effort has been made.
10. The tiger was *perverse* and his *predatory* instincts were strong.
11. *Primitive* ideas about farming were very *vague.*
12. Firmness is *requisite* in quieting *vociferous* children.
13. Ammonia has a *pungent* odor.

SECOND SENTENCE SET

1. *Avid* eyes watched a *luscious* apple.
2. The *nocturnal* howlings had a *canine* sound.
3. She heaved an *audible* sigh and acted *dubious.*
4. The *diminutive* coach had *indomitable* determination.
5. The struggle left him *haggard* but *exultant.*

6. The Greeks believed that the soul is *immortal*.
7. Her *vociferous* friends kept up an *incessant* chatter.
8. His face went *livid* as the *pungent* odor of smoke seeped into the room.
9. Her sense of the *ludicrous* was very *primitive*.
10. Wolves have a *sinister* reputation because of their *predatory* instincts.
11. A crack was *perceptible* in the *massive* boulder.
12. Because his plight was genuinely *pathetic*, he forgot to act *perverse*.
13. Clearness is a *requisite* quality; *vague* ideas mean failure.

ADVENTURE STORY

Write about an outdoor adventure or a sports contest, using eight or ten of the words in this unit. Watch for opportunities to employ opposites, such as *inaudible* and *imperceptible*, as well as variant forms and synonyms of the basic words presented in these units. The adventure may be real or imaginary.

Questionnaire

What should you like to do with homework?

What does one do with a liability?

Which verbs have a sinister flavor?

Which two often go to court?

Which of the nouns would do the most good in the world?

PRETEST

Find the number of the definition that goes with each word.

VERBS

1. abate
2. abet
3. abolish

4. advocate
5. cite

6. depose
7. deviate
8. entice
9. feign

10. frustrate
11. incur
12. lament

1. to gamble
2. to feel sorrow for, bewail
3. to mention or refer to (as a proof or example)
4. to allure, inveigle, beguile
5. to aid or encourage (crime or mischief, usually)
6. to thwart or defeat
7. to plead for, recommend
8. to lessen, decrease
9. to bring upon oneself (by one's actions)
10. to deprive of office
11. to tease or annoy
12. to wander from, diverge
13. to pretend
14. to do away with

NOUNS

1. abyss
2. advent

3. amity
4. anecdote
5. aquatics
6. aroma
7. fiend
8. guile
9. malady
10. novice
11. omen
12. penury
13. pestilence

1. deceit, trickery
2. a brief story (of some incident, characteristic or funny)
3. a widespread disease
4. a demon or monster
5. a deep chasm or pit
6. a remedy for poison
7. friendliness
8. a beginner
9. extreme poverty
10. water sports
11. a poison
12. a sign or foretoken
13. a coming or arrival
14. odor or fragrance
15. an illness or sickness

STUDY GUIDE—VERBS

1. ABATE . . . . **to lessen, decrease**

They waited for the epidemic to abate.
Its abatement caused all to rejoice.

2. ABET . . . **to aid or encourage (crime or mischief, usually)**

He likes to abet others in wrongdoing.
"Ma" Barker was a famous abettor of bad men.
Sanction is a synonym of *abet*, but it applies to good as well as bad.

3. ABOLISH . . . . **to do away with**

Lincoln wanted to abolish slavery.
Is the abolition of poverty possible?

4. ADVOCATE . . . . **to plead for, recommend**

Most pupils would advocate a shorter school day and abolition
of homework.
An advocate (supporter) of the President's plan spoke here
today.
An *advocate*, technically, is one who pleads your case in court or intercedes
on your behalf.

5. CITE . . . . **to mention or refer to (as a proof or example)**

He will cite chess as a game that is fascinating and educational.
The corporal was cited for bravery.
The citation (mentioning a passage) from an official guidebook
was too convincing to question.
See a dictionary for the legal meaning of *cite*.

6. DEPOSE . . . . **to deprive of office**

Why did the English people depose and behead Charles I?
In law, *depose* means *to testify under oath.*

7. DEVIATE . . . . **to wander from, diverge**

Do not deviate in a single detail from the printed instructions.
His deviation caused him to fail.
The forest is full of devious (rambling) paths.
Each synonym of *deviate* has a very special use that colors its meaning.
See a dictionary.

8. ENTICE . . . . **to allure, inveigle, beguile**

Green apples entice most boys.

She looked at him enticingly.

Yielding to the enticement of spring, they went for a walk.

Entice sometimes means *tempt:* "If sinners entice thee, consent thou not."

9. FEIGN . . . . **to pretend**

"Feign a virtue if you have it not."

Fighters feint (make a false movement) to fool their opponents.

Do not confuse *feign* with *fain*, meaning *gladly*.

10. FRUSTRATE . . . . **to thwart or defeat**

The villain always tries to frustrate the hero.

The frustration of the scheme saved many from losing hard-earned money.

Synonyms of *frustrate: circumvent, disappoint.*

11. INCUR . . . . **to bring upon oneself (by one's actions)**

How did Harvey incur his father's displeasure?

12. LAMENT . . . . **to feel sorrow for, bewail**

You did not lament the loss of your milk teeth.

Cries of lamentation filled the air.

The accident was a lamentable (regrettable) mishap.

Lament is a noun, too: No word of lament escaped his lips.

Accent *lamentable* on the first syllable.

STUDY GUIDE—NOUNS

1. ABYSS . . . . **a deep chasm or pit**

The climber slipped and fell to the bottom of an abyss.

The ignorance of some persons is abysmal (immeasurable or unfathomable).

A *fissure* is merely a narrow opening or crack.

2. ADVENT . . . . **a coming or arrival**

The advent of airplanes made it possible to cross the Atlantic in a day.

An adventitious (coming by chance or accident) mishap spoiled our chances of winning.

The Advent (capital *A*) has a religious meaning. See a dictionary.

3. AMITY . . . . **friendliness**

A spirit of amity exists between Great Britain and the United States.

The captain is very amiable (friendly, agreeable).

His amiability makes him popular.

Amicable (friendly, peaceable) relations between schools are sometimes strained by rivalry.

Wholesome competition should foster amicability.

Everyone likes a genial (kindly, cordial) person.

Affable is another word meaning *friendly*, and *affability*, *friendliness*.

4. ANECDOTE . . . . . **a brief story (of some incident, characteristic or funny)**

"His wife did not care much for anecdotes concerning pretty women."

Query: What is wrong with a man who is in his "anecdotage"? (Look up *dotage*.) What is the word for something to offset the effect of a poison?

5. AQUATICS . . . . **water sports**

What form of aquatics do you prefer?

What have you learned of aquatic (living-in-water) plants?

A *regatta* (rĕ-GATT-à) is a boat race or races.
List a few other *aqua* (water) words. See Appendix One, p. 284.

6. AROMA . . . . **odor or fragrance**

The aroma of new-mown hay is sweet.

The cabinet was filled with aromatic (spicy, pungent) herbs of various kinds.

7. FIEND . . . . **a demon or monster**

Only a fiend could commit such a crime.

The fighter attacked with fiendish (savage) energy.

Fiend also means a person very fond of a drug (an opium fiend) or a field of study (a chemistry fiend).

8. GUILE . . . . **deceit, trickery**

No evidence of guile could be found.

He looked as guileless (innocent) as a kitten.
Cf. *beguile.*

9. **MALADY** . . . . **an illness or sickness**
Doctors could not identify his malady.

10. **NOVICE** . . . . **a beginner**
For a novice, he plays good golf.
He served his novitiate under a skillful manager.
One's *novitiate* is the state or period of being a novice.

11. **OMEN**. . . **a sign or foretoken (of good or evil about to happen)**
Howling of a dog is said to be an omen of death.
See: *augury, premonition, foreboding.*

12. **PENURY** . . . . **extreme poverty**
Penury hounded Poe all his later life.
Rich men are often penurious.
Penurious (pē-NEW-rĭ-*ŭ*s) means *stingy* and *miserly.*

13. **PESTILENCE** . . . . . **a widespread disease (deadly or devastating)**
The pestilence raged for months.
His head is full of pestilent ideas.
Pestilent means *poisonous, pernicious, harmful.*

FIRST SENTENCE SET

Copy the *italicized* words and opposite each write an appropriate definition.

1. He will *advocate* a new law as soon as the trouble *abates.*
2. Sam would not *abet* her in an attempt to *abolish* traffic lights.
3. The aviator *cited* three reasons why he *deviated* from his course.
4. The attempt to *depose* the king was *frustrated.*
5. The bird *feigns* lameness to *entice* hikers away from her nest.

6. I *lament* the fact that you *incurred* his wrath.
7. The *anecdote* had to do with *aquatics*.
8. The *advent* of Aunt Jenny restored *amity*.
9. A strange *aroma* ascended from the *abyss*.
10. The *fiend* is no *novice*.
11. He believed the howling of the dog to be an *omen* that he would die of the *malady*.
12. No hint of *guile* appeared on his Chinese face.
13. A *pestilence* raged in the land and the *penury* of the inhabitants made escape impossible.

SECOND SENTENCE SET

1. He *abetted* a plot to push the knight into the *abyss*.
2. The *advent* of spring *entices* us out of doors.
3. The envoy *advocated* a plan to create *amity* between the two countries.
4. When the laughter *abated* he continued his *anecdote*.
5. The college *abolished aquatics* from its program.
6. The *aroma* of flowers is an *omen* of summer.
7. The *fiend* in the story spread a pestilence.
8. Her *guile* was *feigned*.
9. A *novice laments* his lack of skill.
10. *Penury* compelled the boy to *deviate* from this original plans.
11. It is a *malady incurred* by overeating.
12. The speaker *cited* several attempts to *depose* a king and told how each was *frustrated*.

A BETTER WORLD

Cite a few of the evils you would like to abolish, and list measures you would like to advocate to make the world better. In discussing them, find ways to use several words in the unit.

Teasers

Can you find the missing words?

Rattlesnakes __?__ the safety of the goat which we __?__ near the woods.

Mystery Story

What did they utter when they found the body?

What had killed the man?   (It was a deadly one.)

What was the ship on which the body was found?

What did they play for his funeral?

What did they put on his tombstone?

PRETEST

Find the number of the definition that goes with each word.

VERBS

1. manifest
2. menace

3. pervade
4. pulverize
5. reconcile
6. regale
7. reproach
8. resent
9. satiate
10. tether
11. wane
12. wrest

1. to grind to powder
2. to restore harmony between or to harmonize
3. to display, reveal
4. to chew thoroughly
5. to satisfy or overfill
6. to blow hard
7. to scold, rebuke, or chide
8. to diminish, decline
9. to threaten
10. to tie with a rope or chain
11. to take offense at
12. to wrench or pull away by force
13. to spread through
14. to entertain or delight

NOUNS

1. delusion
2. derelict

3. dirge
4. ejaculation
5. epitaph
6. harbinger
7. penitence

8. perplexity
9. potion
10. progeny
11. robot
12. severity
13. transgression

1. an exclamation
2. harshness; plainness (of outline)
3. a liquid dose, a drink
4. offspring
5. a prison or jail
6. a false idea
7. bewilderment, that which puzzles
8. a tombstone inscription
9. a race horse or horses
10. an abandoned ship
11. a messenger, forerunner
12. a funeral song
13. an offense, misdeed
14. a mechanical "man," automaton
15. sorrow for sin

1. MANIFEST . . . . to display, reveal

A salesman must manifest enthusiasm.

His manifest (clear, plain) interest in aquatics appealed to the coxswain.

The manifestation (disclosure) of his talents occurred slowly.

A *manifesto* is a formal declaration.

2. MENACE . . . . to threaten

Bad habits menace one's health.

Rats are a public menace.

There was a menacing look in Grit's eye.

3. PERVADE . . . . . . to spread through (every part of)

The aroma of roses pervades the room.

Sunshine permeates the atmosphere.

Synonyms: *permeate, saturate.*

4. PULVERIZE . . . . to grind to powder

Pulverize each pill and dissolve it in water.

A machine was devised for the pulverization of limestone.

Pulvis is Latin for *dust.*

5. RECONCILE . . . . . to restore harmony between or to harmonize

Our attempt to reconcile father and son failed, but we did not give up until every hope of reconciliation was exhausted.

It was quite hard for the Major to reconcile his words with his deeds.

Cf. *conciliate.* Are capital and labor irreconcilable?

6. REGALE . . . . to entertain or delight

The explorer will regale us for three hours with tales of his adventures.

Regale is used chiefly of oral entertainment.

7. REPROACH . . . . to scold, rebuke, or chide

Do not reproach him for failing if he did his best.

Reproach is hard to bear.

Why the reproachful look?
His life is irreproachable.
Cf. *reproachless* (faultless) also.

8. RESENT . . . . **to take offense at**

He resents any kind of interference.
The insult aroused resentment (anger accompanied by ill will).
Use in a sentence: *resentfully, resentfulness.*

9. SATIATE (SAY-shĭ-ate) . . . . . **to satisfy or overfill**

Here is enough food to satiate your appetites.
Satiate (SAY-shĭ-åt) with despair, he collapsed.
The man was idolized to the point of satiety (så-TIE-ĕ-tĭ).
Synonyms of *satiate: glut, surfeit, cloy.*

10. TETHER . . . . **to tie with a rope or chain**

He says to tether the cow by the fence.
The goat broke his tether.
A *tether* is usually stronger than a leash.

11. WANE . . . . **to diminish, decline**

"The long day wanes."
Summer is on the wane by the middle of August in the far
North.

12. WREST . . . . . . **to wrench or pull away by force**

Sister tried to wrest the sucker from Sonny's grasp.

STUDY GUIDE—NOUNS

1. DELUSION . . . . **a false idea**

It is a delusion to think that one can escape work.
You can't delude (deceive) all the people all the time.

2. DERELICT. . . . . . **an abandoned ship or an outcast**

The derelict stayed afloat for two years.
The hobo is a human derelict.
Dereliction of duty does damage.
Relict means *widow.* See its derivation.

3. DIRGE . . . . **a funeral song**

The natives chanted a heathen dirge.

Dirge has a curious origin and is related to *dirigible*. Investigate.

4. EJACULATION . . . . **an exclamation**

An ejaculation escaped his lips.

"Don't!" he ejaculated in terror.

The word comes from *jaculum*, a javelin.

5. EPITAPH . . . . **a tombstone inscription**

Collecting epitaphs in old cemeteries is an alluring hobby.

A *cenotaph* ("empty tomb") is a monument for someone who was buried elsewhere.

6. HARBINGER . . . . **a messenger, forerunner**

Dawn was, in this case, the harbinger of victory.

Synonym: *precursor.*

7. PENITENCE . . . . **sorrow for sin**

"I come to express my penitence," he declared.

"You look penitent," the man replied.

"I am glad you are in a penitential mood."

Query: Why is a prison sometimes called a penitentiary?

8. PERPLEXITY . . . . . **bewilderment, that which puzzles**

He was in a state of perplexity.

The problem perplexes all of us.

Its newness makes it all the more perplexing.

9. POTION . . . . **a liquid dose, a drink**

Socrates drank the deadly potion without hesitation.

10. PROGENY . . . . **offspring**

Their progeny populated a new country.

One's *progenitors* are one's forefathers.

11. ROBOT (RO-bŏt) . . . . **a mechanical "man," automaton**

Robot controls operate the plane part of the time.

The word comes from the Czech language.

12. SEVERITY . . . . . harshness; plainness (of outline)

Recruits do not always like the severity of military discipline. The striking effect of the cathedral grew out of its severity of outline.

13. TRANSGRESSION . . . . an offense, misdeed

At camp, transgressions seldom occur.
If you transgress (break, violate) the law, you must pay the penalty.

FIRST SENTENCE SET

Copy the *italicized* words and opposite each write an appropriate definition.

1. One must *manifest* courage when danger *menaces*.
2. *Pulverize* moth balls and their aroma will *pervade* the house.
3. No one will *reproach* you if you fail to *reconcile* them.
4. He *regaled* the *satiated* banqueters with hunting tales.
5. The broncho *resented* every effort to *tether* her.
6. As his vigor *waned*, there were frequent attempts to *wrest* from him the control of the company.
7. The idea that black cats are *harbingers* of bad luck is a *delusion*.
8. An *ejaculation* escaped his lips as he sighted the *derelict*.
9. The music sounded like a *dirge*, but it was intended to express a spirit of *penitence*.
10. She gazed in *perplexity* at the moss-covered *epitaph*.
11. The *potion* reduced his performance to that of a *robot*.
12. Their *progeny* suffered from both the *severity* of the climate and the effects of their father's *transgression*.

SECOND SENTENCE SET

1. *Delusions* of grandeur *pervade* his insane mind.
2. *Derelicts menace* the safety of ships.
3. The *dirge manifests* genuine sorrow.
4. With an *ejaculation* he *wrested* the line from my grasp.

5. The *epitaph reproaches* all who mourn too much.
6. March winds *waned,* and soft sunlight became a *harbinger* of spring.
7. In their *penitence* they were *reconciled.*
8. *Pulverize* the pill and add it to the *potion.*
9. The rabbit searched in obvious *perplexity* for her *progeny.*
10. The scientist *regaled* them with anecdotes about *robot* mechanisms.
11. *Tether* the cow where she will be able to *satiate* her appetite.
12. He *resents* the *severity* of the punishment for his *transgression.*

BELIEVE IT OR NOT

Compose the imaginary biography of a goat or some other animal, tame or wild. It is possible in doing this to use most of the base words in the unit somehow or other, if one is sufficiently ingenious. Give your account an appropriate title. A criminal may be the subject if you prefer.

Simile Seeking

Who can best complete the similes below?   Try the animal kingdom.

1. As agile as __?__.

   2. As docile as __?__.

      3. As hostile as __?__.

         4. As vindictive as __?__.

            5. As wary as __?__.

PRETEST

Find the number of the definition that goes with each word.

1. agile
2. copious
3. docile
4. eminent
5. frugal
6. homely
7. hostile
8. humid
9. immaculate
10. jubilant
11. laudable

12. lenient
13. luminous
14. lurid
15. nomadic
16. obnoxious
17. perpetual
18. regal
19. roguish
20. taut
21. vehement
22. vindictive
23. vulnerable

24. wary
25. zealous

1. thrifty, sparing
2. pale yellow, grimly horrible
3. unfriendly, warlike
4. damp, moist
5. very joyful, exultant
6. gentle, teachable
7. stretched tight
8. easy to copy or read
9. never-ceasing, endless
10. nimble, quick-moving
11. eager, enthusiastic (especially in promoting a cause)
12. royal, splendid
13. capable of being injured
14. always in motion
15. famous, prominent, illustrious
16. cautious (in facing danger)
17. plain, plain-featured
18. mild, merciful
19. abundant, plentiful
20. spotlessly pure or clean
21. inclined to hold a grudge
22. praiseworthy, commendable
23. wandering, having no fixed home
24. glowing, radiant
25. very violent or fiery
26. hateful, odious
27. mischievous or waggish

STUDY GUIDE

1. AGILE . . . . nimble, quick-moving

Monkeys are very agile.
Acrobats have great agility.
Wild animals are very lithe.
He has the litheness of a bobcat.
She is a lithesome (lissome) maid.

Lithe means *limber* or *supple;* also (gracefully) *nimble.*

2. COPIOUS . . . . abundant, plentiful

Copious showers made the cisterns overflow.
The copiousness of the supply invited waste.

Derivation: What does *cornucopia* mean?
Synonyms of *copious: plenteous, profuse, bountiful, ample.*

3. DOCILE . . . . . . gentle, teachable, easy to manage

Cows and sheep are very docile.
He was appointed because of his docility.

Synonyms of *docile: tractable, submissive.*

4. EMINENT . . . . famous, prominent, illustrious

Dr. Straus, eminent Austrian surgeon, is in this country.
The eminence of the author insured the success of his book.
From an eminence (elevation or hill) Napoleon watched the
    battle.

Query: What is the *right of eminent domain?*

5. FRUGAL . . . . thrifty, sparing

Their frugal habits enabled them to save a thousand dollars a
    year.
Is frugality one of your virtues?

Prodigal (lavish) and *prodigality* mean the opposite.

6. HOMELY . . . . plain, plain-featured

It is not always a handicap for a girl to be homely. Homeliness
    is a minor disadvantage.

Food, as well as faces, may be homely.

7. HOSTILE (HOS-till) . . . . unfriendly, warlike

The hostile glances of the braves showed their enmity.
The hostility of the natives made it unsafe to land.

8. **HUMID** (HUE-mid) . . . . **damp, moist**
   Humid air seems warmer than dry air.
   The tropical humidity of the atmosphere was oppressive.
   Query: What is a humidifier? Does your home have one?

9. **IMMACULATE** . . . . . . **spotlessly pure or clean**
   The linen was immaculate.
   Her immaculateness of character was inspiring.

10. **JUBILANT** . . . . **very joyful, exultant**
    The whole school was jubilant over the victory.
    In little groups we jubilated for hours.
    See *jubilee* in a dictionary.

11. **LAUDABLE** . . . . . . **praiseworthy, commendable**
    It was a laudable effort you made.
    Laud those who gave their lives in a noble cause.
    Cf. *laudation, laudatory, laudably,* etc.

12. **LENIENT** (LEAN-ĭ-ĕnt) . . . . **mild, merciful**
    The warden is very lenient with some convicts. He encourages such leniency (lenience) where justifiable.
    Lenity is almost the same as *leniency.*

13. **LUMINOUS** . . . . **glowing, radiant**
    The skies are luminous at night.
    The luminousness (luminosity) of the moon seems greatest in the fall.
    Jupiter is the brightest luminary among the planets.
    See: *lumen, luminescence, luminiferous,* and *illuminate.*
    Review *lucid* and the Light family in Unit 3.

14. **LURID** . . . . **pale yellow, grimly horrible**
    A halo of lurid light hovered over the blast furnace.
    The paper carried a lurid account and lurid pictures of the airplane disaster.
    Lurid always keeps ugly, evil company.

15. **NOMADIC** . . . . . **wandering, having no fixed home**
    Hobos live a nomadic life.
    They are nomads forever.

16. OBNOXIOUS . . . . **hateful, odious**

Radio advertising is sometimes obnoxious.
What is the reason for its obnoxiousness?
But *noxious* means *harmful:* Carbon monoxide is a noxious gas.

17. PERPETUAL . . . . **never-ceasing, endless**

Mexico is in a state of perpetual unrest.
This monument will perpetuate (preserve) his memory.
We hold the land in perpetuity (pûr-pĕ-TŪ-ĭ-tĭ).
Relatives of *perpetual: incessant, interminable, everlasting, eternal.*

18. REGAL . . . . **royal, splendid, fit for a king**

They entertain guests with regal lavishness.

19. ROGUISH . . **mischievous or waggish, sometimes dishonest**

His roguish pranks pleased all of his friends.
His roguery (roguishness) was always harmless.
Have you seen pictures of rogues in post offices?

20. TAUT . . . . **stretched tight**

The tent ropes were taut.
Their tautness was due to the wind.
One's nerves can be taut, too.

21. VEHEMENT . . . . **very violent or fiery**

A vehement storm broke loose.
In its vehemence it uprooted trees. ·

22. VINDICTIVE . . **inclined to hold a grudge, i.e., vengeful**

The Indians were very vindictive.
Vindictiveness is not a Christian trait.

23. VULNERABLE . . . **capable of being injured, assailable**

Achilles was vulnerable only in his heel.
His vulnerability in this one spot cost him his life.
A cat seems invulnerable.

24. WARY . . . . **cautious (in facing danger)**

Wary persons live long.
The aviator's wariness saved his life.

The Scots are often twitted because they are chary.

Chary means *frugal* or *cautious in spending.*

25. ZEALOUS . . eager, enthusiastic (especially in promoting a cause)

He is a zealous reformer.

Florence Nightingale was a zealot in the true sense of the word.

FIRST SENTENCE SET

Copy the *italicized* words and opposite each write an appropriate definition.

1. The pianist had *agile* fingers and *copious* hair.
2. The *eminent* boxer is a very *docile* man at home.
3. Her habits were *frugal* and her features *homely*.
4. An *immaculate* housekeeper is *hostile* to dirt and *zealous* in the use of soap.
5. Her eyes were *humid* and *luminous* as she spoke.
6. Her son's *laudable* achievements made her *jubilant*.
7. A *nomadic* hunter was the victim of a *lurid* disaster.
8. It was impossible to be *lenient* toward so *obnoxious* a misdeed.
9. She carried herself with *regal* dignity and her eyes expressed *perpetual* wonder.
10. With *roguish* glee he pulled the hair *taut*.
11. The man was as *vindictive* as he was *vehement*.
12. Rabbits are *wary* because they are *vulnerable*.

SECOND SENTENCE SET

1. His *agile* body could perform *laudable* feats in a football game.
2. *Copious* use of soap is the secret of being *immaculate*.
3. It was easy to be *lenient* with such a *docile* creature.
4. Years of *zealous* research made him an *eminent* inventor.
5. *Frugal* folks are *wary* of battles.
6. The *nomadic* sign painter is a very *homely* man.
7. The *hostile* Indian turned out to be very *vindictive*.

8. Foliage flourishes with *regal* luxuriance in the *humid* climate of the equator.
9. *Jubilant*, he expected *perpetual* success.
10. His *luminous* face gleamed as the rope became *taut*.
11. *Lurid* accounts of accidents were *obnoxious* to him.
12. He grew *vehement* at the *roguish* reminder that he himself was *vulnerable*.

RATHER PERSONAL

Think of a classmate, acquaintance, or celebrity to whom one or more of the adjectives in this unit may be applied.

Imagine a situation that could involve a few of the other adjectives, such as a display of fireworks or an airplane accident, and write a brief account of it.

List an *antonym* or opposite quality for each of the adjectives in the list. Verify your choices by reference to the dictionary. Illustrate and apply them to actual or imaginary persons if time permits.

Can You Put Two and Two Together?

The answer is the most appropriate word from the list in this unit.

1. Warm weather plus soft varnish: __?__

2. Penrod prank plus Father: __?__

3. Bad man minus G-men: __?__

4. One barn plus one careless tramp: __?__

5. One victory plus nothing: __?__

VERBS

1. adhere	1. to imply or hint
2. adorn	2. to display or disclose
3. alter	3. to increase or grow larger
4. assail	4. to scatter or separate
5. augment	5. to cling, stick fast
6. chastise	6. to strive to equal (or excel)
7. disperse	7. to move through the water
8. elude	8. to change or modify
9. emulate	9. to escape or evade
10. enhance	10. to decorate or beautify
11. evince	11. to heighten or increase
12. extricate	12. to hurry
13. intimate	13. to punish
	14. to disentangle
	15. to attack

NOUNS

1. antagonist	1. a guess or probable inference
2. apathy	2. rudeness, discourtesy
3. aperture	3. excited joy or pride
4. avarice	4. scornful disregard or challenge
5. churl	5. an opening
6. conflagration	6. skill (with the hands), cleverness
7. conjecture	7. soft music
8. defiance	8. greed for wealth, cupidity
9. dexterity	9. an extensive fire (or other destructive outburst)
10. discretion	10. indifference
11. elation	11. effort (vigorous)
12. exertion	12. once: a common man of low rank; now: a surly, ill-bred fellow
	13. an opponent, foe, or rival
	14. prudence, wise judgment

1. ADHERE . . . . **to cling, stick fast**

Paint will not adhere to a polished surface.

"But Prince John adhered to his own opinion . . ."

"He returns to punish every adherent of his brother Prince John."

Adhesion of two internal organs caused Napoleon much pain and illness.

The adhesive properties of glue are excellent.

2. ADORN . . . . **to decorate or beautify**

Tapestries adorn the walls.

Excessive personal adornment is in bad taste.

3. ALTER . . . . **to change or modify**

"A cry of 'Shame! shame!' . . . induced Prince John to alter his ungenerous purpose."

Will the alteration of this suit take long?

His purpose was not alterable.

Cf. *unalterable.*

4. ASSAIL . . . . **to attack**

This article assails the chief of police.

She sat fortifying her mind "against those treacherous feelings which assailed her from within."

The injured man could not identify his assailant.

The assault (attack) on the city failed.

5. AUGMENT . . . . **to increase or grow larger**

How much will the extra work augment his income?

"As the fire augmented, symptoms of it became soon apparent in the chamber where Ivanhoe was watched and tended by the Jewess Rebecca."

The governor recommended augmentation of the National Guard.

6. CHASTISE . . . . **to punish**

"We are . . . rather to lament than chastise his backsliding."

He deserved the chastisement that he received.

(Pronounce CHAS-tiz-ment.)

Castigate and *chasten* also mean *to punish.* Watch for them in your reading.

7. DISPERSE . . . . **to scatter or separate**

The crowd did not disperse at once.

The Templar "pushed across the drawbridge, dispersing the archers who would have intercepted them."

"The Prince resumed his retreat from the lists, and the dispersion of the multitude became general."

8. ELUDE . . . . **to escape or evade**

He tried in vain to elude his pursuers.

"These knights, therefore, their aim being thus eluded, rushed from opposite sides . . ."

That elusive (hard-to-catch or -hold) halfback slipped through the entire opposing team.

9. EMULATE . . . . . . **to strive to equal (or excel)**

He is a man to emulate.

"The pomp and state of a court was emulated."

Stevenson learned to write by emulation of famous authors.

10. ENHANCE . . . . **to heighten or increase**

Trees enhance the value of the property.

"The impatience of Cedric had been enhanced by his confinement."

She acquired a certain gracefulness which lent enhancement to her charms.

11. EVINCE . . . . **to display or disclose**

Poker faces never evince surprise.

"The antagonist of Grantmesnil . . . evinced awkwardness and want of management of the weapon and of the horse."

12. EXTRICATE . . . . **to disentangle**

"To extricate himself from the stirrups and fallen steed was to the Templar scarce the work of a moment."

Extrication of the ball from the heap of players took several seconds.

An *inextricable* mystery is one which can scarcely be disentangled.

---

13. INTIMATE . . . . **to imply or hint**

Did you intimate that you would go?

Rowena "drew with dignity the veil around her face as an intimation that the determined freedom of his glance was disagreeable."

STUDY GUIDE—NOUNS

1. ANTAGONIST . . . . . **an opponent, foe, or rival**

"One of their antagonists was overthrown."

His conceited manner antagonizes (renders hostile) those who might be his friends.

She has an antagonistic (hostile) attitude toward her parents.

2. APATHY . . . . **indifference**

The apathy of Cedric's companion "served to defend him against everything save the inconvenience of the present moment."

The tramp's apathetic eyes were half closed with weariness.

Kin of *apathy: listlessness, unconcern, torpor, lethargy, stupor.*

3. APERTURE . . . . **an opening**

"These apertures [loop-holes] admitted, even at midday, only a dim and uncertain light."

4. AVARICE . . . . **greed for wealth, cupidity**

"'Do not thou interrupt me with thine ill-timed avarice,' said the outlaw."

He grew more and more avaricious as the years went on.

Greed adjectives: *stingy, covetous, miserly, niggardly, parsimonious.*

5. CHURL . . . . . **once: a common man of low rank**
now: a surly, ill-bred fellow

"'What money hast thou, churl?' said one of the thieves."

He was so churlish (ill-bred) no one could work with him.

6. CONFLAGRATION . . **an extensive fire (or some other destructive outburst)**

"The maniac figure of the Saxon Ulrica was . . . tossing her arms abroad with wild exultation, as if she reigned empress of the conflagration which she had raised."

7. CONJECTURE . . . . . . a guess or probable inference

"On his retiring to his tent, many who had lingered in the lists, to look upon and form conjectures concerning him, also dispersed."

"From his dress and arms, Wamba would have conjectured him to be one of those outlaws who had just assailed his master."

8. DEFIANCE . . . . . . scornful disregard or challenge

That gesture of defiance enraged him.

"The music also of the challengers breathed from time to time wild outbursts expressive of triumph or defiance."

"It is our order which thou hast defied."

There was a defiant look in the batter's eyes.

9. DEXTERITY . . . . . . skill (with the hands), cleverness

A surgeon must possess extraordinary dexterity.

"The champions a second time . . . closed in the center of the lists, with the same speed, the same dexterity, the same violence, but not the same equal fortune as before."

"See how dexterously they avail themselves of every cover which a tree or bush affords."

The adjective is *dexterous*.
Dexterousness is its noun form.

10. DISCRETION . . . . prudence, wise judgment

"'Truly, I fear they will lose in valor what they may gain in discretion.'"

He was discreet enough to wait until his father was in a more amiable mood.

Pronounce *–cre–* of *discretion* as in *credit*.

11. ELATION . . . . excited joy or pride

Elation over his success in the contest made him jubilant. His parents were elated, too.

The Normans "still felt the elation of triumph."

12. EXERTION . . . . effort (vigorous)

"Athelstane had a disposition too inert and unambitious to make the exertions which Cedric seemed to expect from him."

Doctors exert themselves to save a life.

Tries: 1. *attempt* 2. *effort* 3. *endeavor* 4. *exertion*

FIRST SENTENCE SET

Copy the *italicized* words and opposite each write an appropriate definition.

1. Gum seldom *adorns* anything to which it *adheres*.
2. The team will *alter* its offensive and *assail* its opponents through the line.
3. Father threatened to *chastise* the boy if his playmates did not *disperse* promptly.
4. The expected opportunity to *augment* his income *eluded* his grasp.
5. The youth *evinced* no surprise when advised to *emulate* his father.
6. A knowledge of boxing will *enhance* one's ability to *extricate* himself from trouble.
7. His *antagonist intimated* that he was a coward.
8. The man's *apathy* was exceeded only by his *avarice*.
9. The *churl* peeped through an *aperture* in the wall. (This was in 1262.)
10. The *conjecture* was greeted with *defiance*.
11. The archer had *discretion* enough not to boast of his *dexterity* or show *elation* when he won.
12. All *exertions* to check the *conflagration* were useless.

SECOND SENTENCE SET

1. Their *elation* is *augmented* by the knowledge that they *adhered* strictly to the rules.
2. Smiles *adorn* a face better than frowns, she *intimated*.
3. A mere *conjecture* does not *alter* my attitude.
4. His *antagonist assailed* him from the side.
5. A *churl* watched the *conflagration* with *apathy*. (Time: the present.)
6. William was *chastised* for enlarging the *aperture* in the porch screen.
7. The players *extricated* themselves from the heap and *dispersed*.

8. You will *enhance* your skill if you *emulate* a master workman's *dexterity*.
9. He had the *discretion* to realize that he could not *elude* the police much longer.
10. His *avarice* increased along with his *defiance* of society.
11. The fat man *evinced* no enthusiasm for such *exertions*.

CONFLAGRATION

Use ten or more words from this unit in a paragraph about a fire, a wreck, or a football game. Underline the words. Avoid a stilted style.

Write three or four sentences about a party, if time permits. This will provide an opportunity to use such words as *adorn*, *enhance*, *discretion*, *intimate*, and *emulate*. Your party may include a conflagration if there are any redheads or red hot tempers present.

We Go to War

__?__ music is played as we leave home.

Bad roads __?__ our progress to the front.

When an attack comes, we __?__ it.

A sentry who is __?__ gets shot at sunrise.

The enemy proved __?__.

Our position was __?__.

In the end, however, we were able to __?__ our foe.

PRETEST

Find the number of the definition that goes with each word.

VERBS

1. liberate
2. recede

3. relinquish
4. remonstrate
5. repel
6. requite
7. retard
8. surmount
9. terminate
10. traverse
11. vanquish
12. vaunt

1. to conquer
2. to drive back, to cause dislike in
3. to fear
4. to brag of or boast
5. to withdraw or retreat
6. to repay or reward
7. to finish or end
8. to give up or abandon
9. to overcome or crown
10. to protest or expostulate
11. to quench or put out
12. to walk or move across
13. to delay or hinder
14. to release, set free

ADJECTIVES

1. inquisitive
2. intricate
3. martial
4. melancholy

5. mute
6. negligent
7. obstinate
8. officious
9. precarious
10. sage
11. sundry
12. valiant
13. wily

1. careless, heedless
2. sly, cunning, crafty
3. half-dressed
4. meddling, too forward in offering assistance
5. sick or ill
6. insecure, uncertain
7. silent, speechless
8. curious, prying
9. warlike, brave
10. various
11. brave, heroic
12. stubborn
13. complicated
14. wise or solemn
15. sad, dejected

STUDY GUIDE—VERBS

1. LIBERATE . . . . **to release, set free**

"To liberate a suitor preferred by the Lady Rowena was a pitch far above . . . De Bracy's generosity."

"The inventive genius of Wamba had procured liberation for himself and his companion in adversity."

Free-words (Lat. *liber* = *free*): *liberalize, liberal, liberality, liberty, libertine, liberator.*

2. RECEDE . . . . **to withdraw or retreat**

"De Bracy and I will instantly go among these shuffling cowards and convince them that they have gone too far to recede."

The recession of the enemy was slow.

Please remain seated until after the recessional (organ music played during withdrawal of a procession).

Query in biology: What is a *recessive* trait?

3. RELINQUISH . . . . **to give up or abandon**

Why relinquish your claim to the property?

Athelstane snatched "a mace from the pavement, on which it lay beside one whose dying grasp had just relinquished it."

Germany demanded the relinquishment of Alsace-Lorraine by France in 1870.

4. REMONSTRATE . . . . . . **to protest or expostulate**

She tried to remonstrate with him, but it was useless.

"The Saxon, indeed, had remonstrated strongly with his friend upon the injudicious choice."

"Unheeding this remonstrance, . . . Brian de Bois-Gilbert kept his eyes riveted on the Saxon beauty."

5. REPEL . . . . . . **to drive back, to cause dislike in**

The Chinese fought hard to repel the invader.

"Even he was repelled by the stern command."

A frown is very repellent.

A toad stirs in her a feeling of repugnance (or repulsion or revulsion).

Such actions are repugnant to his principles, and anyone who practices them becomes repulsive.

Repulse is almost a twin of *repel.*

6. REQUITE . . . . **to repay or reward**

"'The God of Israel requite you,' said the Jew, greatly relieved."
Old age brought requital for the wrongs of earlier years.

Making amends: *reparation, restitution, indemnification, redress, rectification.*

7. RETARD . . . . **to delay or hinder**

"But think not, and speak not, now, of aught that may retard
  thy recovery."
Retardation of the crops that year was due to a late spring.

8. SURMOUNT . . . . **to overcome or crown**

"Not even the prospect of reward . . . could surmount this apprehension."
Insurmountable difficulties loomed up.

Surmount means, literally, *to climb over.*

9. TERMINATE . . . . **to finish or end**

"Few augured the possibility that the encounter could terminate
  well for the Disinherited Knight."
Committees will remain a few moments at the termination of
  the meeting.
After what seemed an interminable delay, she was ready.

Query: What is the *terminus* of a railroad or bus line?

10. TRAVERSE . . . . **to walk or move across**

Experienced woodsmen traverse the forest without a compass.
"The scoutmaster arrived after a brief delay, during which John
  traversed the apartment with unequal and disordered steps."

Accent the *first* syllable.

11. VANQUISH . . . . **to conquer**

The Syrians were able to vanquish their foes.
The Normans "were jealous of permitting to the vanquished
  Saxons the possession or the use of swords and spears."

Cf. *subdue, defeat, subjugate, quell.*

12. VAUNT . . . . **to brag of or boast**

"'I conjure thee . . . by the knighthood thou dost vaunt . . .
  are these things true?'"

He makes it his vaunt that no one can throw him.
Slaying the mouse was another instance of Father's unvaunted heroism.

STUDY GUIDE—ADJECTIVES

1. INQUISITIVE . . . . **curious, prying**

Small boys are very inquisitive.
"But their officious inquisitiveness was not gratified."
Query: What is a coroner's inquisition?

2. INTRICATE . . . . **complicated**

"'The way is somewhat intricate, though perfectly well known to me.'"
The intricacy of the corridors was too much for visitors.
Accent the first syllable of both *intricate* and *intricacy*.

3. MARTIAL . . . . **warlike, brave**

"All that was beautiful and graceful in the martial array had disappeared."
The old lady couldn't remember whether it was a field marshal or a court-martial that her nephew got.
Martial law is military rule and courts-martial take the place of regular courts.

4. MELANCHOLY . . . . **sad, dejected**

His melancholy smile showed how hopeless he felt.
He would go off by himself whenever a fit of melancholy seized him.

5. MUTE . . . . **silent, speechless**

The maidens "remained mute as statues."
We visited a home for deaf mutes.

6. NEGLIGENT . . . . **careless, heedless**

The driver was punished for being criminally negligent.
The Templar and De Bracy expected the besiegers "to avail themselves of every negligence which might take place in the defense elsewhere."
Neglectful is an own cousin of *negligent*.
Negligible details are small enough to disregard or treat carelessly.

---

7. OBSTINATE . . . . stubborn

The mule is notoriously obstinate.

"The followers of Front-de-Bœuf and his allies showed an obstinacy in defence proportioned to the fury of the attack."

Sleeves and gloves are now made from "less obdurate materials" than linked mail.

Obdurate has a meaning similar to that of *obstinate*. (Accent first syllable.)

8. OFFICIOUS . . meddling, too forward in offering assistance

"But their officious inquisitiveness was not gratified."

His sister's officiousness irritated him.

Synonyms of *officious: meddlesome, intrusive, obtrusive.*

9. PRECARIOUS . . . . insecure, uncertain

"The situation of the inferior gentry was unusually precarious."

The precariousness of Bob's position on the roof alarmed Mother.

10. SAGE . . . . wise or solemn

"'A marvelously sage plan,' said Fitzurse."

The sageness of his advice gradually became plain.

Watch for *sagacious* and other words which mean *wise.*

11. SUNDRY . . . . various

"The path, which hangs over the river, has lately given way in sundry places."

Drugstores and ten-cent stores are well stocked with sundries (various minor articles too numerous and different to list).

12. VALIANT . . . . brave, heroic

It was a valiant army.

"Rowena selected Ivanhoe with judgment which was admired as much as his valor."

"'I shall be at York at the head of my daring and valorous fellows.'" (DeBracy)

Cf. *valid — sound, well grounded*
validate — confirm or *make sound*
They come from the same ancestors as *valiant.*

13. WILY . . . . sly, cunning, crafty

Fitzurse was a wily Norman.

The wiliness of the Indian made him a source of continual danger.

FIRST SENTENCE SET

Copy the *italicized* words and opposite each write an appropriate definition.

1. Police *liberated* the suspect and *relinquished* their charges.
2. The clouds *recede;* the sun seems to *repel* them.
3. I *remonstrate* because you *requite* me badly for the service I did you.
4. Nothing could *retard* them in their desire to *surmount* every obstacle.
5. The chase did not *terminate* until he had *traversed* the entire country.
6. They did not *vaunt* their ability to *vanquish* the other team.
7. The lad was too *inquisitive* about the *intricate* interior of his father's watch.
8. *Martial* music will dispel a *melancholy* mood.
9. He was *mute* when charged with being *negligent*.
10. The man was *officious* and *obstinate*.
11. It was the *sage* advice of a *valiant* man that a *precarious* situation or a *wily* enemy should make one very cautious.
12. The *sundry* details of a large task are often irritating.

SECOND SENTENCE SET

1. He was *inquisitive* about the situation but not *officious*.
2. *Intricate* plans were made to *liberate* the captive.
3. The turkey gobbler struts with *martial* mien and *vaunts* his superiority before the whole barnyard.
4. We *remonstrated* with her for being so *melancholy*.
5. *Mute*, he watched the plane *recede* in the distance.
6. The man's *obstinate* air *repels* everyone.
7. Our old rivals failed to *vanquish* us because they were *negligent* about training rules.
8. Red's *valiant* plunge through left guard made victory less *precarious*.

9. The coach's *sage* advice enabled us to *surmount* our handicap in weight.
10. Their *wily* passing attack *retarded* our chances of winning for a while.
11. As the game was about to *terminate*, a halfback *traversed* the entire field for the winning touchdown.
12. The halfback was *requited* by being elected captain at a victory banquet.
13. This made it necessary for him to *relinquish* a number of *sundry* responsibilities which he had accepted.

REDSKIN RELUCTANCE

Indians will make a good creative topic for this unit. Naturally they were unwilling to relinquish territory to the white man, and a battle is to be expected. A powwow is preferable, however, and will serve to illustrate just as many of the words — more, in fact, because the chiefs can always *talk* about fighting. Besides, a parley is likely to be a fight, using words instead of guns and tomahawks.

If you want to play fair, remember that the Indians kept treaties better than white men did.

Frequent Phrases

__?__ indigestion   A __?__ from justice

__?__ prices   A prince traveling __?__

__?__ danger   The __?__ of disaster

__?__ trust in someone   A dark (or ugly) __?__

__?__ machine (or bomb)   "I have a __?__ with death."

PRETEST

Find the number of the definition that goes with each word.

ADJECTIVES

1. acute
2. adjacent
3. corpulent
4. devious
5. ensuing
6. errant
7. exorbitant
8. impending
9. implicit
10. inert
11. inferior
12. infernal

1. of poorer quality
2. following
3. unquestioning or implied
4. excessive
5. bright, shining
6. neighboring
7. hellish, fiendish
8. fat
9. roving, wandering
10. keen, sharp, severe
11. very inactive
12. rambling, roundabout
13. nervous, inclined to worry
14. threatening, imminent

NOUNS

1. fugitive
2. incognito
3. indignation
4. insolence
5. obeisance
6. recompense
7. rendezvous
8. repose
9. retinue
10. succor
11. tyranny
12. verge
13. visage

1. edge or border
2. rest, quiet, peace, composure
3. a reward or compensation
4. slowness, tardiness
5. aid, help
6. one who flees; a runaway or deserter
7. face (countenance) or aspect
8. insulting behavior, impudence
9. a disguise; in disguise
10. cruel, unjust government; cruelty
11. an appointed meeting (place)
12. a train of attendants
13. anger, wrath (justifiable)
14. sincere affection
15. a bow or curtsy

STUDY GUIDE—ADJECTIVES

1. ACUTE . . . . **keen, sharp, severe**

Cedric "was not naturally acute of perception."
The acuteness of the pain doubled him up in agony.

2. ADJACENT . . . . **neighboring**

The adjacent forest abounded with outlaws.
The adjacency of a playground makes the location a noisy one.
Similar words: *adjoining, contiguous, abutting.*

3. CORPULENT . . . . **fat**

The corpulent gentleman was more good-natured than athletic.
Corpulence is an asset in some ways but a handicap in others.
Fat persons are also: *portly, obese, burly, pursy, adipose.*
Look them up if possible.

4. DEVIOUS . . . . **rambling, roundabout**

"Yet his purpose was baffled by the devious paths through
  which he rode."
The deviousness of her habits troubled everyone.
Devious may also mean *sinful* or *wrong.*

5. ENSUING . . . . **following**

Ivanhoe might "with safety travel to York . . . on the ensuing
  day."
"During this combat and the brief conversation which ensued,
  Cedric . . . had pushed across the bridge."

6. ERRANT . . . . **roving, wandering**

Gurth was worried at the thought of the "errant knights and
  errant squires, errant monks and errant minstrels, errant jug-
  glers and errant jesters" who might rob him.
Review *err* (Unit 2).

7. EXORBITANT . . . . **excessive**

"Said Isaac, 'I cannot make the choice, because I have not the
  means of satisfying your exorbitant demand.'"
She protested against the exorbitance of the price.

8. IMPENDING . . . . **threatening, imminent**

"The apprehension of impending evil was inspired by a large, lean, black dog."

The presence of troops proves that some danger impends.

9. IMPLICIT . . . . **unquestioning or implied**

"They promised implicit obedience and departed with alacrity on their differing errands."

The implicitness (absoluteness) of his faith in the coach was justified.

10. INERT . . . . **very inactive**

Athelstane had an inert disposition.

His inertness was a Saxon trait.

A state of inertia (sluggishness, lack of activity) prevailed.

Variations of *inactive*: *idle, passive, indolent, supine, slothful, lethargic, torpid, phlegmatic, apathetic.*

11. INFERIOR . . . . **of poorer quality**

To the Prior, Rebecca was "far inferior to the lovely Saxon, Rowena."

The inferiority of the cloth could not be detected at night.

An inferiority complex is a feeling that you are inferior to others.

Ersatz material is a substitute, usually inferior.

12. INFERNAL . . . . **hellish, fiendish**

"'Would I were out of the shade of these infernal bushes!'" (Gurth)

Note: An *inferno* is a hell or a scene so horrible as to resemble hell, e.g.: Soon the house was a blazing inferno.

Similar to *infernal*: *diabolical, devilish, satanic, demoniac.*

STUDY GUIDE—NOUNS

1. FUGITIVE . . . . . **one who flees, a runaway or deserter**

"Oswald deemed it his duty to secure Gurth, as a fugitive of whose fate his master was to judge."

The fugitive bank robber shot himself in despair.

Cf. *refugee.*

2. INCOGNITO (ĭn-COG-nĭ-toe) . . . . **a disguise; in disguise**

The Disinherited Knight's squire "seemed to affect the incognito as much as his master."

The aviator traveled incognito to escape reporters.

3. INDIGNATION . . . . **anger, wrath (justifiable)**

"The Prince rolled his eyes in indignation."

"The indignant swineherd resumed his sullen silence."

4. INSOLENCE . . . . . **insulting behavior, impudence**

"'Woe betide him unless his skill should prove some apology for his insolence!'"

"'I have a debt to pay to that insolent peasant who yesterday insulted our person.'"

Similar to *insolence: rudeness, sauciness, abusiveness.*

5. OBEISANCE (ŏ-BAY-sance) . . . . . **a bow or curtsy**

The Palmer, "after a low obeisance, tasted a few drops."

6. RECOMPENSE . . . . **reward or compensation**

"'An evil recompense,' said Rebecca, 'for the surrender of the rights which are dearest to humanity.'"

Locksley directed Cedric to recompense his followers with half the spoil.

7. RENDEZVOUS . . . . . **an appointed meeting (place)**

Gurth believed "both that the gang was strong in numbers and that they kept regular guards around their place of rendezvous."

8. REPOSE . . . . . . **rest, quiet, peace, composure**

"The looks of Wamba . . . indicated . . . a sort of vacant curiosity, and fidgety impatience of any posture of repose."

The inferior gentry "might indeed purchase temporary repose."

"The travellers paused . . . to repose their horses."

The place has a reposeful atmosphere.

9. RETINUE . . . . **train of attendants**

"A grand flourish of trumpets announced Prince John and his retinue."

The Prior and his small retinue requested lodging for the night.

10. SUCCOR . . . . aid, help

"'Yet, father, let me entreat you by the vow you have taken on you,' replied the suppliant, 'not to leave the oppressed and endangered without counsel and succor.'"

Wamba "made a brave though ineffectual attempt to succor his master."

11. TYRANNY . . . . . . cruel, unjust government; cruelty

"A circumstance . . . tended to enhance the tyranny of the nobility and the sufferings of the inferior classes."

"'Tell your tyrannical master, I do only beseech him to dismiss the Lady Rowena in honor and safety.'"

A dictator is apt to be a tyrant.
Tyrannize means *to rule sternly or oppressively.*

12. VERGE . . . . edge or border

"On the very verge of the thicket two men spoke to his conductors."

Such an act verges on (approaches closely) kidnaping.
Verge the verb is a different word entirely. See a dictionary.

13. VISAGE . . . . face (countenance) or aspect

"The scars with which his visage was seamed added to the ferocity of his countenance."

The boy envisaged (pictured) himself as a second Babe Ruth.

FIRST SENTENCE SET

Copy the *italicized* words and opposite each write an appropriate definition.

1. *Acute* famine stalked the *adjacent* towns.
2. The *corpulent* one charges *exorbitant* prices.
3. Several *devious* trails were explored during the *ensuing* week.
4. *Errant* minstrels warned the king that an invasion was *impending.*
5. Mentally *inert* herself, she had *implicit* confidence in her husband's judgment.

6. *Inferior* coal is an *infernal* nuisance.
7. The *fugitive* was traveling *incognito*.
8. The man's *insolence* aroused her *indignation*, and his sinister *visage* alarmed her.
9. The knight accepted his *recompense* with a deep *obeisance*.
10. The *rendezvous* in the woods provided a place of *repose*.
11. The priestly *retinue* was very impressive.
12. The king's *tyranny* brought the country to the *verge* of revolution, and his subjects sought *succor* abroad.

SECOND SENTENCE SET

1. The *fugitive* hid in an *adjacent* building.
2. The prince set out in the *incognito* of an *errant* priest.
3. The man's *indignation* was fierce when *succor* did not come.
4. I recalled her *insolence* on the *ensuing* day.
5. His *recompense* came in the form of perfect *repose*.
6. A *devious* path led to the *rendezvous*.
7. No one in the bride's *retinue* was *corpulent*.
8. *Exorbitant* prices were one result of the monarch's *tyranny*.
9. He remained *inert* in the face of *impending* disaster.
10. *Implicit* faith in false ideas brought him to the *verge* of ruin.
11. *Inferior* food caused *acute* abdominal pains.
12. The *infernal visage* of an Iroquois Indian adorned the wall.
13. With an *obeisance* he excused himself.

TERMINAL TASKS

Make a list of adverbs formed from the words presented in Part One. There will be 100 or more if you have the patience, the persistence, and the skill. Use every tenth one in a sentence or write a paragraph on moods at home, at school, at the zoo, or in the barnyard. Perhaps you can compose a jingle of some kind from the adverbs you have listed.

FINAL TESTS

Copy the *italicized* words and opposite each write an appropriate definition.

UNIT 1

1. Each *zephyr* released a little *salvo* of maple seedlings.
. 2. It will be necessary to *defer* the *parley*.
3. He had a weakness for choice *viands*. This was a distinct *impediment*.
4. Three *decades* ago parents often *coerced* their children into obedience.
5. He hoped to *acquire* health and *avert* disease.
6. Mike gave the coach a moment of *rapture* because he *adapted* his defense to the situation remarkably well.
7. A shower of *missiles demolished* the toy house.
8. He refused to *divulge* his part in the *episode*.
9. The general *designated* a drummer to march with the *vanguard*.
10. The treasurer *affirmed* his desire to *curtail* expenses.

UNIT 2

1. They were in complete *accord* on a plan to *salvage* valuables from the sunken liner.
2. The *custodian's animation* attracted attention.
3. *Apprehensions* of misfortune *harassed* her night and day.
4. The *brevity* of the speech made the audience *relent*.
5. A sudden *deluge* produced *chaos* at the picnic.
6. The inhabitants finally *evicted* the invaders from their *citadel*.
7. He did not *err* because he followed wise *counsel*.

8. It is hard to *discern* the beginning of an *epoch* of prosperity.
9. His quiet *demeanor* hinted that he liked to *meditate*.
10. *Derision* met every attempt to *promulgate* the truth.

UNIT 3

1. The hobo's voice was *plaintive* and his manner *furtive*.
2. The *placid* lake looked *weird* in the moonlight.
3. A *pensive* look appeared in her eyes as the *medley* of tunes was played.
4. A *motley* crowd of football fans in *wanton* glee uprooted the goal posts.
5. He is *mature* enough to know that he should avoid making *potent* enemies.
6. A *malicious* grin appeared on the thief's *ghastly* face.
7. "I am *deficient* in patience," was the *candid* answer.
8. As he walked along the *quay* he tried to think up a *plausible* excuse.
9. The singer with the *celestial* voice is at her *zenith*.
10. Sale of the *remnants* reduced the *deficit* slightly.

UNIT 4

1. Was it a face *haggard* from hardships or *livid* with rage?
2. *Vociferous nocturnal* behavior of cats tempts one to use gunpowder.
3. That fighter is *massive* but not *indomitable*.
4. Her *exultant* antics were *ludicrous* to watch.
5. *Incessant* whining is a *sinister* trait.
6. The *diminutive* jockey displayed *canine* devotion.
7. Brute strength was a *requisite* quality among *primitive* men.
8. The sight of *luscious* fruit stirred Joe's *predatory* instincts.
9. Does an *avid* appetite make your eating *audible?*
10. *Vague* outlines of trees were *perceptible* in the distance.

UNIT 5

1. Doctors took steps to *abolish* the *pestilence*.
2. The *aroma* of fresh cookies *entices* the boys into the kitchen.
3. He *advocates incurring* debt, if necessary.
4. When the tempest *abates*, you will see how far you *deviated* from your course.
5. *Cite*, if you can, three reasons why you *abetted* her.
6. The *malady* was only *feigned*.
7. The attack of the *novice* was easy to *frustrate*.
8. He *laments* the fact that *penury* should hinder him.
9. The dove is an *omen* of peace and *amity*.
10. The *advent* of the *fiend* spread terror everywhere.

UNIT 6

1. The father bird *manifests* great interest in his *progeny*.
2. *Delusions* about fasting *menace* her health.
3. The music of a *dirge pervaded* the church.
4. The *epitaph* urged all to *reconcile* themselves to God.
5. *Regale* our ears with the story of the haunted *derelict*.
6. She *reproached* him for his lack of *penitence*.
7. Why should one *resent* honest *perplexity?*
8. Such a *potion* alone is powerful enough to counteract the *severity* of the disease.
9. As his ambition *waned*, he forgot the *transgression*.
10. Can *robots wrest* the control of the world from us?

UNIT 7

1. The *luminous* face of the clock seemed *hostile* as it announced the hour.
2. In the *lurid* light he appeared doubly *vindictive*.
3. The *agile* Arabs are a *nomadic* race.
4. War, with its *copious* bloodshed, becomes more and more *obnoxious*.
5. He lives in *perpetual* distress because he is *homely*.

6. The *eminent* singer carries herself with *regal* grace.
7. Though *roguish* among friends, he is solemn and *wary* in the presence of strangers.
8. The coach was *vehement* at first but *lenient* in the end.
9. Her *immaculate* appearance is truly *laudable*.
10. Her *docile* yet *zealous* nature made her very popular.

UNIT 8

1. With shouts of *defiance* the knights *assailed* the castle.
2. Because of their *dexterity* nothing could *elude* them.
3. With admirable *discretion* the defenders *dispersed*.
4. Some of their *antagonists* were unable to *extricate* themselves from their armor.
5. The shields of those who *adhered* to the lord of the castle were *adorned* with crescents.
6. The defenders tried to *emulate* the *exertions* of their leader.
7. The arrival of another band of knights *augmented* the *elation* of the attackers.
8. Their motions *intimated* that they wanted to *alter* the plan of attack.
9. It would *enhance* their chance of winning if they could toss a firebrand through an *aperture* in the wall.
10. This was done. It started a *conflagration* which drove the *churls* outside and brought victory.

UNIT 9

1. The prince was *liberated* on the condition that he would *relinquish* his title.
2. Still in *martial* array, the unit *receded*.
3. Do you blame her for *remonstrating* with neighbors who are too *officious?*
4. The army *vaunts* its ability to *repel* invaders.
5. *Requiting* good for evil *retards* enmity.
6. Scientists are *inquisitive* enough to *surmount* the difficulties that beset their search for new knowledge.

7. The hunt for the *wily* culprit *terminated* in a barn.
8. What is the best way to *vanquish* a *melancholy* state of mind?
9. It is hard to tell whether he is *valiant* or merely *obstinate*.
10. The clerk was too *negligent* to handle the *intricate* details of his office properly.

UNIT 10

1. Her *indignation* was *acute*.
2. The *adjacent* farms are *inferior*.
3. *Corpulent fugitives* seldom get far.
4. A *devious* road leads along the *verge* of an abyss.
5. The *insolence* of a farmer irritated a famous banker who was traveling *incognito*.
6. During the *ensuing* weeks, his *visage* grew more sinister.
7. A period of *exorbitant* prices was *impending*.
8. His faith in the old man grew less *implicit* when *succor* did not arrive.
9. Night brought *repose* except for *infernal* beasts that populated his dreams.
10. His body lay *inert* at the *rendezvous*.

THE HERO OF PART ONE

Try writing two or three "chapters" in the life of the Hero of Part One. Give him a name, and use such headings as the following:

What He Does

He holds his parents in high esteem. He manipulates a canoe skillfully. He meditates a few minutes every day. He advocates shorter school hours.

Personal Qualities

He is an agile athlete, an avid reader, and a frugal spender, but he has disturbing nomadic and nocturnal tendencies. He is not predatory, malicious, or vindictive, however, and his efforts to overcome his faults are very laudable.

DIVISION TEST

Find the number of the definition that goes with each word:

A.

1. episode
2. interim
3. parley
4. salvo
5. zephyr
6. apprehension
7. chaos
8. counsel
9. deluge
10. epoch

1. a conference (especially with an enemy)
2. advice, admonition
3. a gentle breeze
4. an era or period of years
5. a kind of fairy
6. an interval (between happenings)
7. a downpour or flood
8. fear, anxiety
9. a committee
10. confusion, disorder
11. a simultaneous outburst
12. an incident

B.

1. medley
2. zenith
3. advent
4. aquatics
5. fiend
6. novice
7. penury
8. derelict
9. epitaph
10. penitence

1. water sports
2. an odd occurrence
3. extreme poverty
4. a mixture or jumble
5. a beginner
6. a tombstone inscription
7. summit, greatest height
8. sorrow for sin
9. a coming or arrival
10. an abandoned ship or an outcast
11. imprisonment
12. a demon or monster

C.

1. progeny
2. severity
3. apathy
4. churl
5. conjecture

6. discretion
7. exertion
8. incognito
9. obeisance
10. rendezvous

1. indifference
2. prudence, wise judgment
3. a disguise; in disguise
4. a brilliant child
5. once: a common man of low rank
   now: a surly, ill-bred fellow
6. an appointed meeting (place)
7. effort (vigorous)
8. a bow or curtsy
9. a guess or probable inference
10. offspring
11. a type of electric generator
12. harshness; plainness of outline

D.

1. acquire
2. adapt
3. coerce
4. contort
5. designate
6. err
7. filch
8. harass
9. meditate
10. salvage

1. to twist out of shape
2. to think, reflect
3. to pretend
4. to steal or pilfer
5. to get, procure, obtain
6. to annoy or disturb
7. to save
8. to compel (by force)
9. to make a mistake
10. to make suitable (by alteration)
11. to make hay
12. to name, point out

E.

1. abet
2. cite
3. deviate

4. frustrate
5. lament
6. menace

7. reconcile
8. reproach
9. tether
10. wrest

1. to thwart or defeat
2. to restore harmony between
3. to aid or encourage (crime or mischief usually)
4. to scold, rebuke, or chide
5. to threaten
6. to wrench or pull away by force
7. to build
8. to feel sorrow for, bewail
9. to speak rudely
10. to wander from, diverge
11. to tie with a rope or chain
12. to mention or refer to (as a proof or example)

F.

1. adorn
2. augment
3. disperse

4. enhance
5. extricate
6. recede
7. repel
8. retard
9. traverse
10. vaunt

1. to heighten or increase
2. to go first
3. to drive back, to cause dislike in
4. to move gracefully
5. to scatter or separate
6. to brag of or boast
7. to disentangle
8. to delay or hinder
9. to decorate or beautify
10. to walk or move across
11. to withdraw or retreat
12. to increase or grow larger

1. candid
2. furtive
3. hoary
4. mature
5. pensive
6. plausible
7. rueful
8. weird
9. avid
10. dubious

1. ripe, fully developed
2. uncanny, unearthly
3. appearing true or reasonable
4. dirty, discolored
5. white or gray with age
6. frank, truthful
7. doubtful
8. eager, greedy
9. regretful, sorrowful
10. comical, funny
11. sly, stealthy
12. dreamily thoughtful; wistful

H.

1. haggard
2. indomitable
3. ludicrous
4. nocturnal
5. perceptible
6. primitive
7. requisite
8. vociferous
9. copious
10. frugal

1. discernible
2. mysterious
3. necessary, essential
4. abundant, plentiful
5. worn, gaunt, wild-looking
6. sad, sorrowful, gloomy
7. laughable, ridiculous, droll
8. unconquerable
9. thrifty, sparing
10. noisy
11. of or pertaining to night
12. crude or simple, belonging to early ages

1. hostile	1. mild, merciful
2. jubilant	2. inclined to hold a grudge
3. lenient	3. never-ceasing, endless
4. nomadic	4. eager, enthusiastic (especially in promoting a cause)
5. perpetual	5. moody, ill-humored
6. taut	6. complicated
7. vindictive	7. unfriendly, warlike
8. zealous	8. very religious
9. intricate	9. stretched tight
10. mute	10. very joyful, exultant
	11. silent, speechless
	12. wandering, having no fixed home

J.

1. obstinate	1. following
2. sage	2. very inactive
3. valiant	3. nimble, quick-moving
4. adjacent	4. hellish, fiendish
5. ensuing	5. highly spiced
6. exorbitant	6. wise or solemn
7. inert	7. ugly, unattractive
8. infernal	8. neighboring
9. agile	9. hateful, odious
10. obnoxious	10. stubborn
	11. excessive
	12. brave, heroic

SUPPLEMENTARY TEST

This test is based on words introduced in the illustrative sentences and small type notes.

Find the number of the definition that goes with each word:

A.

1. parlance
2. bedlam
3. custody
4. mien
5. risibility

6. plaintiff
7. potentate
8. nocturne
9. fissure
10. affability

1. guardianship, imprisonment
2. a narrow opening or crack
3. in law, the one who complains
4. drowsiness, lethargy
5. a dreamy, instrumental night song
6. language, way of speaking
7. friendliness
8. an inclination to laugh
9. behavior, bearing, appearance
10. habit of complaining
11. a monarch
12. uproar, confusion

B.

1. novitiate
2. premonition

3. manifesto
4. cenotaph
5. progenitor
6. cornucopia

7. jubilee
8. recessional
9. inertia
10. inferno

1. a formal declaration
2. music played during the withdrawal of a procession
3. an inscription on a tombstone
4. a horn of plenty
5. a period of being a beginner
6. a tomb-monument for one buried elsewhere
7. sluggishness, lack of activity
8. a forefather, ancestor
9. hell, scene of horror
10. an occasion of rejoicing
11. a forewarning, foreboding
12. delight in newness

1. assent
2. apprehend
3. ruminate
4. digress
5. lucubrate
6. circumvent
7. chide
8. castigate
9. envisage
10. permeate

1. to muse or reflect
2. to worry over wrongs
3. to scold or reprove
4. to do mental work by arti>
5. to agree, say yes   [ficial light
6. to punish or criticize severely
7. to spread through
8. to last indefinitely
9. to wander from the subject
10. to outwit, thwart, go around
11. to have a mental picture of
12. to arrest; to grasp mentally

D.

1. loathsome
2. decadent
3. inanimate
4. antediluvian
5. erratic
6. lucent
7. premature
8. wistful
9. indubitable
10. eternal

1. helpless, hopeless
2. detestable, disgusting
3. everlasting, never-ceasing
4. without life, lifeless
5. huge, enormous
6. occurring too soon
7. before the Flood, very ancient
8. on the decline
9. shining, glowing
10. unquestionable
11. irregular, queer
12. wishful, sadly thoughtful

E.

1. refractory
2. obstreperous
3. adventitious
4. amicable
5. penurious
6. lithe
7. noxious
8. recessive
9. repugnant
10. obese

1. coming by chance or accident
2. secret, sly, stealthy
3. receding, inclined to go back
4. sparing in the use of money
5. very fat or fleshy
6. harmful, injurious to health
7. friendly
8. highly distasteful
9. noisy, turbulent, unruly
10. made or done quietly
11. limber, supple, nimble
12. unyielding, disobedient

CAN YOU PRONOUNCE THEM?

Being able to pronounce words correctly is as important today as knowing what they mean. Below are some of the most treacherous words from Part One. The location of each by page number is given in order that you may look back in case there is any doubt.

divulge	5	regatta	34
err	11	penurious	35
harass	11	satiate (verb)	40
promulgate	12	satiety	40
cache	13	hostile	46
deluge	14	humid	47
deficit	20	chastisement	54
quay	21	discretion	56
diminution	25	traverse	62
pathos	26	intricacy	63
piquant	27	obdurate	64
lamentable	33	incognito	71
		obeisance	71

The pronunciation of all basic words is given in the list at the back of the book.

WORD WEALTH

PART TWO

We Go Into Business

1. Our plant is new now, but it will gradually __?__ in value.

2. As orders come in we shall __?__ production.

3. Sometimes a customer will __?__ an order.

4. Our salesmen must pursue prospects with great __?__.

5. A strike would place us in a real __?__.

6. The president would be filled with __?__.

PRETEST

Find the number of the definition that goes with each word.

VERBS

1. accelerate		1.	to enlarge or swell; to explain fully and copiously
2. allege		2.	to pacify, reconcile
3. annihilate		3.	to dislike or feel disgust
4. appall		4.	to declare, assert
5. badger		5.	to destroy utterly
6. bequeath		6.	to decrease (in value)
7. conciliate		7.	to tease, annoy
8. constitute		8.	to make a distinction or observe differences
9. countermand		9.	to say, state, or assert
10. culminate		10.	to increase the speed
11. depreciate		11.	to revoke, cancel
12. dilate		12.	to horrify, dismay
13. discriminate		13.	to come to a climax
		14.	to form or comprise
		15.	to give by will

NOUNS

1. admonition		1.	a predicament, plight
2. alacrity		2.	an ally or accomplice
3. carcass		3.	horror, dismay, panic
4. chagrin		4.	an old soldier
5. coincidence		5.	a descriptive title
6. confederate		6.	warning, advice
7. consternation		7.	a device or scheme
8. contrivance		8.	a shoulder ornament
9. decorum		9.	an occurrence which matches some other remarkably
10. dilemma		10.	eager readiness, briskness
11. effrontery		11.	shame and vexation
12. epithet		12.	fitting conduct
		13.	boldness, impudence
		14.	a dead body

1. ACCELERATE . . . . . . **to increase the speed of**

Unfilled orders caused the company to accelerate production. This acceleration provided two hundred new jobs.

Now you know why the foot accelerator is thus named.

2. ALLEGE . . . . **to declare, assert**

The defense alleges that the prisoner is insane.

N. B. This is the way newspapers escape responsibility for unproved statements.

All of these allegations are false.

3. ANNIHILATE . . . . **to destroy utterly**

Strictly speaking, it is impossible to annihilate even a sheet of paper.

Rain obliterated every clue.

Madame Defarge wanted to exterminate an entire family and bring about its annihilation.

A terrible trio: *obliterate, exterminate, annihilate*.

4. APPALL . . . . **to horrify, dismay**

It appalls one even to think of such cruelty as Madame intended. The cruelty she had once endured was equally appalling.

5. BADGER . . . . **to tease, annoy**

It is cruel to badger a defenseless pet.

6. BEQUEATH . . . . **to give by will**

His father will bequeath the estate to a brother. This bequest will be worth $150,000 after taxes have been paid.

7. CONCILIATE . . . **to pacify, reconcile, make peace with**

He decided to conciliate his enemy if conciliation was possible and the enemy was in a conciliatory mood.

Three more ways to restore harmony: *placate, appease, propitiate* (and their families).

8. CONSTITUTE . . . . **to form or comprise**

The judge had trouble deciding whether refusal to sign a contract in itself constitutes a violation of the labor laws.

The Senator received telegrams from many of his constituents (voters). His constituency as a whole sanctioned his act.

Constituent is also an adjective: A mild acid is one of the constituent parts of honey.

9. COUNTERMAND . . . . to revoke, cancel

Countermand the order before it is too late.

Accent the first syllable.

10. CULMINATE . . to come to a climax, reach the highest point

The affair is bound to culminate soon.

What will the culmination of his career in baseball be?

The highest point is the summit, acme, crown or zenith. See a dictionary and review I, 3.

11. DEPRECIATE . . . . to decrease (in value)

The value of time depreciates as one grows weary.

The depreciation in the value of the lands was slight.

Why depreciate honest effort, even if it was futile? Depreciation does no good.

Depreciate also means *to speak slightingly of* (disparage).

12. DILATE . . . to enlarge or swell; to explain fully and copiously

The pupils of the eyes dilate in the dark.

The professor dilated at length upon the influence of environment.

13. DISCRIMINATE . . . to make a distinction or observe differences

Some people discriminate against persons of a different race.

Can you discriminate between these two shades of blue?

Her excellent discrimination makes her a good buyer.

STUDY GUIDE—NOUNS

1. ADMONITION . . . . warning, advice

John ignored his father's admonition to be careful, even though his father admonished him twice.

With an admonitory gesture, he motioned us away from the edge.

2. ALACRITY . . . . **eager readiness, briskness**

James works and plays with equal alacrity.

3. CARCASS . . . . **a dead body**

Vultures promptly descended on the carcass of the cow and picked it clean.

It is used of human corpses only in contempt.

4. CHAGRIN . . . . **shame and vexation**

Imagine his chagrin when the machine failed to work.

The athlete was chagrined (mortified) to learn that he could not compete at all.

Mortify means *to humiliate or humble painfully.*

5. COINCIDENCE . . **an occurrence which matches remarkably and unexpectedly some other event or circumstance**

What a coincidence that I should meet my next-door neighbor in San Francisco!

It was a coincidence that the father should find his long-lost son in the orphan asylum where he came in search of a job.

Our interests coincide (match) perfectly.

Use only the first five words in the sentence sets.

6. CONFEDERATE . . . . **an ally or accomplice**

The thief's confederates snatched their leader from prison.

Ten men formed a confederacy (alliance).

Jefferson Davis was president of the Confederate States of America. This confederation lasted several years.

7. CONSTERNATION . . . . . . **horror, dismay, panic**

Sister fled in consternation when Brother dangled a live snake in the air.

8. CONTRIVANCE . . . . **a device or scheme**

The first telegraph was an awkward contrivance.

Contrive to find out, if you can, who planned the prank. The contriver should be thrown into the lake.

9. **DECORUM** . . . **fitting conduct (dress and language)**

Prime ministers are models of decorum.

With a decorous (DEK-ō-rŭs) gesture, he waved me aside.

10. **DILEMMA** . . . . **a predicament, plight**

Oscar found himself in a dilemma when some boys stole his clothes while he was swimming in the river.

A *quandary* is a dilemma — more puzzling but less embarrassing.

11. **EFFRONTERY** . . . . **boldness, impudence**

The captain was put out of the game because he had the effrontery to insult the referee.

It takes audacity to fly across the ocean.

Literally, *effrontery* means *without forehead.*
Synonyms: *audacity, temerity.*

12. **EPITHET** . . . . . . **a descriptive title or appellation**

"Carrot-Top" is an odd epithet.

Mr. Cruncher's appellation was "Jerry."

FIRST SENTENCE SET

Copy the *italicized* words and opposite each write an appropriate definition.

1. The foreman *alleges* that he was ordered to *accelerate* production.

2. She was *appalled* that he should wish to *annihilate* all the cats in town.

3. Uncle *bequeathed* $10,000 to the nephew he liked to *badger* with the *epithet* "Spark Plug."

4. These two facts *constitute* our only hope of *conciliating* the manager.

5. He *countermanded* the order when the market value began to *depreciate.*

6. He *dilated* on the idea that the situation would *culminate* in war.

7. Can you *discriminate* between an *admonition* and a rebuke?

8. With *alacrity* she hurried away from the *carcass.*
9. The *coincidence* of meeting his uncle there increased his *chagrin.*
10. He gazed with *consternation* at his dead *confederate.*
11. He had the *effrontery* to place the explosive *contrivance* under his uncle's plate.
12. The *dilemma* did not ruffle his *decorum* in the least.

SECOND SENTENCE SET

1. The *admonition constituted* a threat.
2. With *alacrity* he *countermanded* the instructions he had given.
3. Fire will *annihilate* the *carcasses* of the sheep.
4. The tragedy *appalled* his *confederate.*
5. *Chagrin* nearly kept him from trying to *conciliate* his foes.
6. It is *alleged* that his being in the next room was a *coincidence.*
7. *Consternation accelerated* his flight.
8. The beanshooter is a *contrivance* which Mr. Maxim used to *badger* a policeman.
9. The property he *bequeathed* to me is beginning to *depreciate.*
10. The *dilemma* compelled us to *discriminate* against one group of friends or the other.
11. His lack of *decorum* showed in his tendency to *dilate* upon the faults of his friends.
12. The boy's *effrontery culminated* in applying the *epithet* "Horsefeathers" to his dignified aunt.

ONCE UPON A TIME

Recall a contrivance, a dilemma, or a coincidence you have experienced or read about. Describe it, using several words from this unit, either basic or supplementary.

We Get Sick

1. It was foolish to __?__ our health that way.

2. Mother did not __?__ the seriousness of wearing wet clothing.

3. We have great confidence in the doctor's __?__.

4. He likes us to display real __?__.

5. "You must not expect to __?__ too fast," he warned as he left.

PRETEST

Find the number of the definition that goes with each word.

VERBS

1. divert
2. exaggerate
3. improvise
4. incriminate
5. infringe

6. insinuate
7. jeopardize
8. obsess
9. perpetrate
10. procrastinate
11. recuperate
12. resuscitate
13. retaliate

1. to violate or encroach upon
2. to revive or bring back to life
3. to turn aside or to amuse
4. to perform or commit
5. to compose offhand or to arrange a makeshift
6. to return a favor
7. to delay, postpone
8. to endanger
9. to involve, implicate
10. to make everlasting
11. to regain former strength
12. to give like for like, esp. evil
13. to beset or haunt
14. to overstate, magnify
15. to imply or hint something; to worm a path into

NOUNS

1. ferocity
2. fortitude
3. lethargy
4. pandemonium
5. prerogative
6. propensity
7. restitution
8. sagacity
9. seclusion
10. sequence

11. stratum
12. tenacity

1. separation; solitude
2. a tendency to hold fast
3. restoration, making amends
4. a layer
5. courage (passive); endurance
6. a series or order of succession
7. just punishment
8. fierceness, savageness
9. a right or privilege
10. unhealthy drowsiness; state of inaction
11. act of shutting out
12. shrewd judgment, practical wisdom
13. a bent, natural tendency
14. wild uproar; disorder

STUDY GUIDE—VERBS

1. DIVERT . . . . **to turn aside or to amuse**

The purpose of a trick play is to divert attention from the actual ball carrier.

Books divert one's attention from worries and cares.

Chess is a diversion (pastime) few enjoy.

Everyone should cultivate a diversity (variety, unlikeness) of interests.

Are your pleasures diverse (varied)?

A farmer should diversify (vary) his crops, a banker his bond holdings.

2. EXAGGERATE . . . . **to overstate, magnify**

Newspapers exaggerate the number killed.

Such exaggeration grows out of haste and excitement.

Nobody believes a habitual exaggerator.

3. IMPROVISE . . **to compose offhand or arrange a makeshift**

Minstrels could improvise poetry as they sang.

"Scotty," by putting his coat on inside out, improvised a Chinese costume.

The pianist played an improvisation.

4. INCRIMINATE . . . **to involve or implicate in a crime**

The yellow gloves provided enough evidence to incriminate the suspect.

Incrimination is the noun form.

5. INFRINGE . . . . **to violate or encroach upon**

Keeping chickens in a city infringes upon the rights of neighbors.

Infringements of the law will be promptly punished.

Query: What are patent infringements?

6. INSINUATE . . . **to hint or imply something; to worm a path into**

She insinuated that her brother was not a good basketball player. The insinuation nettled him considerably.

Gradually George insinuated himself into his employer's confidence.

Innuendo is a high-priced word for a low-down insinuation.

---

7. JEOPARDIZE . . . . **to endanger**

Fast driving jeopardizes many lives.
Such jeopardy is usually unnecessary.

8. OBSESS . . . . **to beset or haunt**

A desire to write obsesses him.
Cleanliness is almost an obsession (mania) with her.
To be *obsessed* is to be ruled by one idea.

9. PERPETRATE . . . . **to perform or commit**

It took two to perpetrate such a crime.
One perpetrator was soon caught.
The perpetration of such a fraud is a prison offense.

10. PROCRASTINATE . . **to delay, postpone (from day to day)**

Is it ever wise to procrastinate?
Procrastination soon becomes a habit.
Are you a procrastinator?
See *defer* (I, 1).

11. RECUPERATE . . . . **to regain former strength**

A storage battery will recuperate slightly after a heavy drain.
Recuperation (recovery) is slow after a long illness.
Youth has great recuperative power.
Pronounce the *u* of *recuperate* as in *use*.

12. RESUSCITATE . . . . . **to revive or bring back to life**

Every Scout learns to resuscitate a victim of drowning. Flut-
tering eyelids are one sign that that resuscitation is progress-
ing.
Dying societies and institutions can be resuscitated, too.

13. RETALIATE . . . **to give like for like (especially evil)**

A vindictive person watches for a chance to retaliate. The
Christian code outlaws retaliation (revenge).
Retaliative steps were taken.
Cf. *reprisal*.

1. FEROCITY . . . . fierceness, savageness

The ferocity of the police dog caused consternation in the neighborhood. Yet he looked more ferocious than he really was.

Cf. *truculence, truculent* (TRUK-ŭ-lent).

2. FORTITUDE . . . . . . courage (passive); endurance

The President showed great fortitude.

Pronounce the *u* as in *use*.

3. LETHARGY . . . unhealthy drowsiness; state of inaction

Disaster will overtake him unless he awakens from his lethargy. Hot weather makes us lethargic.

Study: *torpor, torpid, stupor, dormant.* Review *inert* (I, 10).

4. PANDEMONIUM . . . wild uproar; a place of disorder

Pandemonium broke loose as the winning touchdown crossed the goal line.

Review *chaos* and *bedlam* in I, 2.

5. PREROGATIVE . . . . a right or privilege

Riding for half fare on the railroads is one of a minister's prerogatives.

See a dictionary for a more complete definition.

6. PROPENSITY . . . . a bent, natural tendency

Rockefeller had a propensity for earning money rapidly.

7. RESTITUTION . . . . . . restoration, making amends

Restitution is a proof of penitence.

Pronounce the *u* as in *use*.

8. SAGACITY . . . . shrewd judgment, practical wisdom

Indian chiefs were noted for their sagacity.

The junk dealer was very sagacious (să-GAY-shŭs).

Emerson was called "the sage [profoundly wise man] of Concord."

Franklin's *Autobiography* is full of sage advice.

Types of brain skill: *penetration, judiciousness, acumen, perspicacity, astuteness, acuteness.*

9. SECLUSION . . . **separation from the society of others; solitude**

The widow lives in quiet seclusion. It was the death of her husband which caused her to seclude herself.

Pronounce the *u* as in *use*.
Retirement and *privacy* are partial synonyms of *seclusion*.
See *sequester*.

10. SEQUENCE . . . . . **a series or order of succession**

A sequence of minor mishaps made him lose the race.
Events followed in their usual sequence.
The sequel to the victory was a celebration.
If you liked this book you will enjoy the sequel.

A *sequel* is something which follows (and continues or completes).

11. STRATUM (STRAY-tum) . . **a layer (of material of any kind)**

A geology class studies rock strata. (*Strata* is plural.)
He came from the lowest stratum of society.
In a gorge or glen one may see stratified rock.

Note: *stratify* has a short *a*.

12. TENACITY . . . . **a tendency to hold fast**

Bulldogs are famous for their tenacity.
In other words, they are very tenacious.
Two blocks of wood become very tenacious when glue is applied.

A *tenacious* memory is a retentive one — it hangs on well to facts.

FIRST SENTENCE SET

Copy the *italicized* words and opposite each write an appropriate definition.

1. One detective will *divert* his attention while the other searches for evidence that will *incriminate* him.
2. The veteran *exaggerates* the extent to which he *jeopardized* his life in the war.
3. Did you *insinuate* that I am not clever enough to *improvise* a bridge across the rivulet?
4. The idea that someone would *infringe* his patent *obsessed* the inventor continually.

5. They *perpetrated* a fake drowning to see whether the life-guard knew how to *resuscitate* a person.
6. He *procrastinated* because he was reluctant to *retaliate*.
7. Her *fortitude* never wavered, though it took weeks to *recuperate* after the crisis had passed.
8. The *ferocity* of the dog shook him out of his *lethargy*.
9. She sought *seclusion* after the *pandemonium* of the city.
10. Each *stratum* adhered with unusual *tenacity*.
11. It is the law's *prerogative* to require *restitution*.
12. A *sequence* of hard cases revealed the judge's *sagacity*.
13. The boy's *propensity* for music pleased his father.

SECOND SENTENCE SET

1. It was natural for him to *exaggerate* the *ferocity* of the beast and the *fortitude* he had displayed.
2. Such *lethargy* and the tendency to *procrastinate* which goes with it *jeopardizes* his future.
3. *Pandemonium* broke loose in the stadium when Michigan *retaliated* with a touchdown on the next kick-off.
4. Doctors quickly *resuscitated* the unconscious captain, but it took a month for him to *recuperate* from his injuries.
5. Choosing the team is a coach's *prerogative*, and its success depends largely upon his *sagacity*.
6. The *tenacity* of the team led to a *sequence* of victories.
7. The boy's *propensity* for mischief frequently *diverted* his father's attention and made him long for *seclusion*.
8. He *insinuates* that ours is a lower *stratum* of society.
9. We made *restitution* for damage done by the Hallowe'en prank which we had *perpetrated*.
10. He *infringed* the patent; the evidence *incriminates* him.
11. A longing to *improvise* music *obsessed* him all day.

VARIETY

Write pungently about an illness, an accident, a game, a prank, or an insult, using several words from this unit.

Our Moods

1. At a party we grow __?__.

2. We are always apt to be too __?__, our parents say.

3. In the spring, girls are likely to act very __?__.

4. When we get old, we shall enjoy (we hope) great __?__.

   Perhaps younger persons will not care to hear our __?__.

5. May we always be __?__ toward our foes!

P. S. Are you sure that you have the *best* one for each blank?

Reconsider the matter after you have studied the unit.

PRETEST

Find the number of the definition that goes with each word.

ADJECTIVES

1. accessible
2. capricious
3. conducive
4. facetious
5. facile

6. hilarious
7. impetuous
8. impromptu
9. infinitesimal

10. insidious
11. magnanimous
12. mellifluous
13. meticulous

1. rash, hasty, headlong
2. very painstaking
3. merry, mirthful
4. noble, great-souled
5. done on the spur of the moment; unprepared
6. large, roomy
7. immeasurably small
8. easily done, skillful
9. approachable; easy to reach or influence
10. affording passage to electricity
11. leading or tending (to)
12. treacherous, deceitful
13. humorous or jocular
14. honeyed
15. subject to whims, changeable

NOUNS

1. magnitude
2. opulence
3. posterity

4. precedent
5. precision
6. proximity
7. rancor
8. reminiscence
9. reprisal
10. shambles
11. stigma
12. tranquillity

1. scene of devastation
2. a view from the rear
3. a former instance (serving as a model or pattern)
4. calmness, serenity
5. an obstruction in the eye
6. a recollection
7. largeness, bigness
8. future generations
9. a mark of disgrace
10. intense spitefulness or enmity
11. exactness
12. great riches, wealth
13. act of retaliation (or revenge)
14. immediate nearness

STUDY GUIDE—ADJECTIVES

1. ACCESSIBLE . . **approachable; easy to reach or influence**

The president is a very accessible man.
The accessibility of the site is a very important consideration.

2. CAPRICIOUS (ka-PRISH-ŭs). . **subject to whims, changeable**

The girl is said to be very capricious.
An actress has many caprices (ka-PREES-es — whims, notions).

3. CONDUCIVE . . . . **leading or tending (to)**

Laziness is not conducive to success.
Mountain air is famous for its conduciveness to health.

4. FACETIOUS . . . . **humorous or jocular**

Do you enjoy facetious remarks?
Were you ever rebuked for ill-timed facetiousness?
Other *funny* words: *witty, waggish, sportive, droll.*

5. FACILE . . . . **easily done, skillful**

With facile motions he tied the most complicated knot of all.
He speaks French with great facility (ease or skill).
Electrical equipment facilitates (makes less difficult) housework.

6. HILARIOUS (pronounce *hi* as in *him*) . . . **merry, mirthful**

The party was a hilarious affair.
Hilarity (noisy merriment) ran riot.
See *maffick, to celebrate hilariously.*

7. IMPETUOUS . . . . **rash, hasty, headlong**

Shelley was an impetuous youth.
His impetuosity disappeared somewhat in Italy.
The arrival of the train made a precipitate departure necessary.
Impetuous is a stronger word than *impulsive.*
Cf. *precipitate,* which means *overhasty, headlong.*

8. IMPROMPTU . . . . **done on the spur of the moment; unprepared**

The mayor made an impromptu speech. He spoke impromptu.
It is used most often as an adverb.

---

9. INFINITESIMAL . . . . immeasurably small

The width of a cell is infinitesimal.

Literally, it means too small to be measured.

10. INSIDIOUS . . treacherous, deceitful; also, sly and crafty

Scarlet fever is an insidious disease.

Its insidiousness makes it especially dangerous.

Cf. wily (I, 9), subtle, furtive (I, 3).

11. MAGNANIMOUS . . . . . . noble, great-souled

He would accept no reward for his magnanimous deed because he considered magnanimity its own reward.

The Magna family (magna = great): magnate, magnify, magniloquent, magnitude.

12. MELLIFLUOUS (mel-LIF-lŏo-ŭs) . . . . honeyed

Her mellifluous tones soothed the baby.

Ralph sings mellifluously.

I like the mellifluence of a Negro quartet.

Mellifluent means smooth and sweet. Melliferous means honey-bearing.

13. METICULOUS . . very painstaking (about minute details)

He adjusted the net with meticulous care.

Employers do not always appreciate meticulousness.

STUDY GUIDE—NOUNS

1. MAGNITUDE . . . . largeness, bigness

The magnitude of the offense appalled us.

Page the Magna family again (No. 11 above).

2. OPULENCE (OP-you-lence) . . . . great riches, wealth

The opulence of Croesus pales beside that of the Nizam of Hyderabad, one of the most opulent men who ever lived.

Op- pronounced as in hop. Opulent also means luxuriant, plentiful, abundant.

3. POSTERITY . . . . . . future generations (collectively)

Posterity will honor the memory of Lindbergh's flight.

A posterior (rear) view of the animal showed that its tail was missing.

Posteriority is the state of being later or behind.

---

4. PRECEDENT . . a former instance (serving as a model or pattern for action)

The British Constitution is an accumulation of precedents.

There was an unprecedented (unparalleled) demand for earmuffs that winter.

The girl precedes the boy down the aisle if there are ushers.

Do you see the verb *precede* (to go or occur before) in the word *precedent?*

5. PRECISION . . . . exactness

His mind operates with the precision and evenness of a fine watch.

She is very precise in her speech.

The tie was precisely what he wanted.

6. PROXIMITY . . . . immediate nearness

The proximity of a water supply made our insurance rate lower.

Their propinquity in blood relationship made marriage impossible.

Propinquity (prŏ-PĬNG-kwĭ-tĭ) is almost an exact synonym of *proximity.*

7. RANCOR . . . . . . intense spitefulness or enmity

The man's soul was on fire with rancor because he had lost the contract. Ten years later a rancorous feeling still persisted.

Butter gets rancid (sour) in hot weather.

Cf. *malignity, malice, animus, resentment.* See I, 3. Noun forms of *rancid: rancidity, rancidness.*

8. REMINISCENCE . . . . a recollection

Reminiscences of school days will always be pleasant.

It is fun to reminisce because the unpleasant is soon forgotten.

Old persons particularly enjoy reminiscent moods.

9. REPRISAL . . . . . an act of retaliation (or revenge)

Ten of the prisoners were shot in reprisal.

See *retaliate* in Unit 2, *vindictive* in I, 7.

10. SHAMBLES . . . . a scene of devastation

The living room was a shambles after the party.

Literally, a *shambles* is a slaughterhouse or *abattoir* (ăb-ă-TWÄR).

11. STIGMA . . . . . . a mark of disgrace or dishonor

There is no stigma attached to failure if one did his best. Cowardliness stigmatizes a person, however.

12. TRANQUILLITY . . . . calmness, serenity

The tranquillity of evening rested us.
Our thoughts became as tranquil as the lake.
Other forms: *tranquilize, tranquilly, tranquilness.*

FIRST SENTENCE SET

Copy the *italicized* words and opposite each write an appropriate definition.

1. Uncle is most *accessible* when he is feeling *facetious.*
2. *Capricious* behavior is not *conducive* to friendship.
3. The girls grew *hilarious* and one recited an *impromptu* farewell to the clock.
4. With *meticulous* care she warned us not to be *impetuous.*
5. An *infinitesimal* spark proved highly *insidious.*
6. His *mellifluous* tones suggest that he is truly *magnanimous.*
7. With *facile* motions he gauged the *magnitude* of the star.
8. *Posterity* will long remember the *opulence* of the Rockefellers.
9. The bitterness of his *rancor* was without *precedent.*
10. The *proximity* of the coach accounted for the *precision* with which the plays were executed.
11. The *stigma* of his treachery does not disturb the *tranquillity* of his *reminiscences.*
12. A campaign of *reprisal* made the village a *shambles.*

SECOND SENTENCE SET

1. Are minor executives less *accessible* and less *magnanimous* than major ones?
2. Does *opulence* have an *insidious* influence on those who possess it?
3. Brother adjusted his tie with *meticulous precision.*

4. A *capricious* person often has *impetuous* moments.
5. Confidence is *conducive* to success in *impromptu* speaking.
6. With *facile* grace and a *mellifluous* laugh the fencer parried each thrust.
7. The crowd grew *hilarious* as the speaker continued his *reminiscences*.
8. There is no *precedent* for dealing with a crisis of such world-wide *magnitude*.
9. *Posterity* will remember that Madrid was a *shambles* for weeks.
10. A *stigma* upon them for harboring such *rancor* and perpetrating such *reprisals!*
11. The *proximity* of the lake makes its *tranquillity* contagious.
12. The effect of her *facetious* remarks was *infinitesimal*.

MEMORIES

Reminisce in such a way as to need ten or more of the words in this unit. Perhaps a family gathering will provide a scene of sufficient magnitude for your purposes. The interview with Dad when you tried to obtain funds for questionable purposes has real possibilities, too.

We Go to Prison

We showed our __?__ toward the __?__ who had seized
the government by burning an __?__ of him. Such an _?_
could scarcely be perpetrated with __?__ in a country where
the laws are so __?__.

PRETEST

Find the number of the definition that goes with each word.

NOUNS

1. affinity
2. affront
3. animosity

4. condolence
5. denizen
6. despot
7. docket
8. effigy
9. hybrid
10. illusion
11. impunity
12. irony
13. levity

1. something deceptive or unreal; a deception
2. a ruler with absolute power
3. freedom from punishment or loss
4. frivolity, light-heartedness
5. hatred, hostility
6. a railroad station
7. (mild) sarcasm
8. attraction, kinship
9. an inhabitant or citizen
10. a cross (between two varieties)
11. effectiveness
12. a list of cases for trial
13. a deliberate insult
14. an image (often stuffed)
15. (expression of) sympathy

ADJECTIVES

1. loquacious
2. morbid
3. munificent

4. precocious
5. prosaic
6. simultaneous
7. stringent
8. subtle
9. supercilious
10. venomous
11. virile
12. wizened

1. dull, commonplace
2. forceful or manly
3. happening or existing at the same time
4. harsh, shrill
5. artful, penetrating
6. liberal, generous
7. disdainful, contemptuous
8. very silly or foolish
9. shriveled, withered
10. talkative
11. poisonous or malicious
12. strict, rigid, severe
13. forward in development
14. unwholesome, diseased

STUDY GUIDE—NOUNS

1. AFFINITY . . . . attraction, kinship

Mercury has an especial affinity for gold.

The affinity between them is based on their fondness for books.

2. AFFRONT . . . . a deliberate insult

It was an affront not to say yes.

He will not affront even an enemy if he can avoid it.

3. ANIMOSITY . . . . hatred, hostility

A certain animosity exists between the two boys.

She acted without animus.

Animus means *moving spirit* or *hostile intention.* Cf. *rancor* in Unit 3.

4. CONDOLENCE (kon-DOE-lence) . . . (expression of) sympathy

He wrote a note of condolence.

Does condolence help?

The two sons condoled with each other.

Condole usually is followed by *with.* Synonyms of *condolence: commiseration, compassion.*

5. DENIZEN . . . . an inhabitant or citizen

Frogs are denizens of swamp land.

Lions are denizens of the jungle.

6. DESPOT . . . . a ruler with absolute power (i.e., a tyrant)

Hitler became a despot.

Caesar ruled with despotic power.

The despotism of Alexander the Great did not last.

Query: What does despotism have to do with modern industry? See *tyranny* (I, 10).

7. DOCKET . . . . a list of cases for trial

The police-court docket was full that morning.

Is the shipment properly docketed?

Sometimes *docket* means *a waybill.*

8. EFFIGY . . . . . . an image (often stuffed) or portrait

The mob burned an effigy of the despot.

Effigies adorned the mantel.

See an encyclopedia for the origin of the custom of burning effigies.

9. HYBRID . . . . a cross (between two varieties)

That man is neither a Democrat nor a Republican — he is a hybrid.

The car is a hybrid (crossbred) variety. The body is of one make, the chassis of another.

Biologists are quite exact about the scientific meaning of *hybrid*.

10. ILLUSION . . something deceptive or unreal; a deception

The pools of water which seemed to cover the pavement were an illusion. This illusion is one form of mirage.

Some kinds of pain and sickness are very illusory (imaginary, unreal).

An *hallucination* is one form of *illusion*, especially in insane persons who imagine they see demons or ghosts.

11. IMPUNITY . . . . . freedom from punishment or loss

One cannot steal with impunity. A despot can murder with impunity, though.

Pronounce *u* as in *use*.
Do you see the PUNISH in *impunity?*
Query: What are *punitive* measures?

12. IRONY . . . . (mild) sarcasm

The irony of his remarks amused many.

The irony (grim humor) of the situation was that a rich man who owns three cars won an automobile in the lottery.

"Now isn't that something!" was his ironical comment.

13. LEVITY . . . . frivolity, light-heartedness

A spirit of levity pervaded the carnival.

Levity is not appropriate during the service.

See a dictionary for other meanings.

STUDY GUIDE—ADJECTIVES

1. LOQUACIOUS (lŏ-KWAY-shŭs) . . . . . . talkative

Girls are very loquacious.

Their loquacity is proverbial. (Pronounce lŏ-QUĂS-ĭ-tĭ)

Synonyms of *loquacious: garrulous, verbose, prolix.*

---

2. **MORBID** . . . . **unwholesome, diseased**

Some think murder mystery stories are morbid.
Poe liked morbidity (unwholesome gloom).

3. **MUNIFICENT** . . . . **liberal, generous**

Rockefeller was called the most munificent giver of all time.

4. **PRECOCIOUS** . . . . **forward in (mental) development**

Sally was a precocious child. Her mother loved to parade
Sally's precocity (precociousness).
Cf. *premature.*

5. **PROSAIC** . . . . **dull, commonplace**

Some pupils find school quite prosaic.
Prose is more commonplace than poetry.
A prosy account is especially uninteresting.
Life itself is quite prosaic — sometimes.

6. **SIMULTANEOUS** . . **happening or existing at the same time**

The simultaneous movement of the pipes showed that all were
startled.
The two planes attacked simultaneously.
Cf. *synchronous.*

7. **STRINGENT** . . . . **strict, rigid, severe**

Foreign trade is subject to stringent rules.
A pupil mentioned the stringency of Draco's laws.
Query: What is an astringent?

8. **SUBTLE** (suttle) . . . . **artful, penetrating**

The salesman's methods of persuasion were very subtle.
The Indian's subtlety was uncanny.
A subtle mind enjoys puzzles.
The teacher is fond of subtle humor.
Subtle has varied uses. See a dictionary for other meanings as in *subtle* poisons
(quietly insidious).

9. **SUPERCILIOUS** . . . . . . **disdainful, contemptuous**

Pomeranian pups have a supercilious air.
Is such superciliousness justified?
With raised eyebrows, it means literally.

---

10. VENOMOUS . . . . **poisonous or malicious**

She has a venomous tongue.
The speech was full of venom.

11. VIRILE . . . . **forceful or manly**

That was a virile address.
The speaker's virility is stimulating.
Vir in Latin means *man.*

12. WIZENED . . . . **shriveled, withered**

The wizened face of an old lady appeared at the window.

FIRST SENTENCE SET

Copy the *italicized* words and opposite each write an appropriate definition.

1. The note of *condolence* revived a sense of *affinity* that they had always felt.
2. The *affront* stirred her *animosity* to the boiling point.
3. The *despot's* enemies must necessarily be *denizens* of darkness.
4. The case of the thief who stole the *effigy* was first on the *docket*.
5. You cannot with *impunity* sell *hybrids* for thoroughbreds.
6. With *virile irony* he condemned the *illusion* of prosperity.
7. Are *loquacious* persons fond of *levity?*
8. *Morbid* thoughts seldom troubled the *precocious* child.
9. His *munificent* acts kept his life from becoming *prosaic.*
10. Several cities took *simultaneous* action to make their traffic laws more *stringent.*
11. She had a *subtle* charm in spite of her *supercilious* manner.
12. The *wizened* snake has a *venomous* sting.

SECOND SENTENCE SET

1. Is pain a *morbid illusion?*
2. His *irony* is keen and *subtle.*

3. A *despot's* subjects cannot criticize him with *impunity*.
4. In a spirit of *levity* they burned an *effigy* of the governor.
5. The *hybrid* peas are *wizened* and small.
6. The *loquacious* clerk made several *prosaic* remarks as he examined the *docket*.
7. A *denizen* of the underworld wrote a *venomous* speech.
8. There was a *virile* quality about his *condolence* that steadied her.
9. The feeling of *animosity* toward his *precocious* brother gradually vanished.
10. The two *affronts* were almost *simultaneous*.
11. He felt an especial *affinity* for persons in *stringent* circumstances.
12. She was very *munificent* but with a certain *supercilious* air that was irritating.

AS OTHERS SEE US

"Pupils I Have Known" is one of the creative topics suggested by this unit. It should call forth most of the adjectives and more than half of the nouns, but let there be no trace of animosity or superciliousness in your sentences.

Another topic is "Speed Laws." It should elicit (II, 6) some of the words not needed in discussing pupils.

Simile Search

1. As austere as __?__.

2. As disconsolate as __?__.

3. As droll as __?__.

4. As formidable as __?__.

5. As transient as __?__.

6. As trivial as __?__.

Why not decorate the winner with a medal for a Distinguished Feat of the Imagination?

Find the number of the definition that goes with each word.

ADJECTIVES I

1. austere
2. competent
3. defunct
4. despicable
5. disconsolate
6. droll
7. formidable
8. gossamer
9. imperative
10. inflexible
11. languid
12. mercenary
13. oblique

1. drooping, spiritless, listless
2. slanting, indirect
3. fond of sports
4. gauzy, filmy
5. dead, extinct
6. stern, severe
7. sad, dejected
8. very mysterious
9. capable, qualified
10. urgent, commanding
11. comical, queer, amusing
12. contemptible, vile
13. actuated chiefly by desire for money (or reward)
14. incapable of yielding or bending
15. hard to overcome; menacing

ADJECTIVES II

1. omniscient
2. plebeian
3. precipitous

4. pugnacious
5. punctilious
6. querulous
7. spontaneous
8. stentorian
9. transient

10. trite
11. trivial
12. water-logged

1. all-knowing
2. fretful, complaining
3. water-soaked (until it will no longer float)
4. fleeting, short-lived
5. high in scholarship
6. exact in conduct; particular
7. common, ordinary
8. trifling, ordinary
9. arising from within; natural; self-generated
10. odd, peculiar
11. very steep
12. extremely loud
13. stale, worn out
14. quarrelsome, inclined to fight

STUDY GUIDE—ADJECTIVES I

1. AUSTERE . . . . **stern, severe**

The Puritans were very austere. Their austerity was a result of their religious ideas.

Synonyms of *austere: strict, rigid, rigorous, harsh.*

2. COMPETENT . . . . **capable, qualified**

A competent secretary is needed.
Her competence will be determined by means of an interview.
The previous secretary was incompetent.

3. DEFUNCT . . . . **dead, extinct**

The assets of the defunct corporation were liquidated.
Defunct is not often used of a person.

4. DESPICABLE (accent the first syllable) . . **contemptible, vile**

Treachery is despicable.
The despicableness of the deed infuriated them.
The original word means *to look down.* Cf. *despise.*

5. DISCONSOLATE . . . . **sad, dejected**

Defeat made him disconsolate.
Such disconsolateness was unsportsmanlike, we thought, as we tried to console (comfort) him.
Gradually he found solace (consolation) in his books.

Note: *Solace* is pronounced SOL-ĭs.
Synonyms of *disconsolate: cheerless, melancholy* (I, 9), *forlorn, inconsolable, sorrowful.*

6. DROLL . . . . **comical, queer, amusing**

We watched the pet duck's droll antics.
His drollery (jesting) is irresistible.
The Fun team includes: *diverting, facetious, witty, ludicrous, jocose, risible.*

7. FORMIDABLE . . . . . **hard to overcome; menacing**

We had a formidable team that year.
Solid geometry is a formidable subject.
The formidableness of Latin discourages some.
Accent the first syllable of *formidable.*

8. GOSSAMER . . . . gauzy, filmy

A gossamer cloud slipped past the moon.
The sword was so sharp that it would cut through a gossamer
veil in mid-air.

Gossamer as a noun means a fine spider's web or a gauze for veils.

9. IMPERATIVE . . . . urgent, commanding

The imperative need for rain was evident everywhere.
The imperativeness of the man's manner demanded instant attention.

Cf. *peremptory, dictatorial.*

10. INFLEXIBLE . . . . incapable of yielding or bending

The rules at camp are inflexible.
Father was inflexibly (unalterably) opposed.
Porcelain has the inflexibility of cast iron.
Glass is surprisingly flexible.

Some of the Stiff team: *rigid, unalterable, obstinate* (I, 9), *obdurate, implacable* (*pla* = PLAY), *inexorable* (accent *ex*).

11. LANGUID . . . . drooping, spiritless, listless

Hot July days make one languid.
A feeling of delicious languor steals over one.
The flowers languished for lack of water.
Her lassitude was compelling, but the work had to be done.

Cf. *languish, to droop* or *pine away; lassitude, weariness.*

12. MERCENARY . . . actuated chiefly by desire for money
(or reward)

Great souls are seldom mercenary.
Mercenaries are soldiers hired by a foreign government.
Silas sought only pecuniary (financial) gain.
What is the government's monetary policy?
The fiscal (financial) year closes soon.

Pertaining to money: *pecuniary, financial, monetary, fiscal.*

13. OBLIQUE (*o–* as in *Bob*) . . . . . slanting, indirect

The spy made an oblique approach to the fortress.
A crook's methods are oblique.

STUDY GUIDE—ADJECTIVES II

1. OMNISCIENT . . . . **all-knowing**

The police seemed omniscient and omnipresent to the fleeing culprit.

We are taught that God is omnipresent.

Boys have omnivorous appetites.

Churches teach the omniscience, omnipotence, and omnipresence of God.

The Omni-family is a good one to know:
omnipotent — all-powerful
omnipresent — present everywhere (at the same time)
omnivorous — eating everything, voracious

2. PLEBEIAN . . . . . **common, ordinary (or even vulgar)**

Are his tastes in music quite plebeian?

Everything about the man seemed very plebeian.

A "plebe" at West Point or Annapolis is a freshman.
Derivation: The *plebs* was the Roman populace.

3. PRECIPITOUS . . . . **very steep**

Straight down a precipitous mountainside the car plunged.

It was very precipitate of him to ask for a date before he had been introduced.

Precipitant action only made the strike worse.

The blow precipitated him into the ropes.

Precipitate (prĕ-SIP-ĭ-tăt) and *precipitant*, adjectives, in literature mean *sudden, rash, overhasty.*
Precipitate (prĕ-SIP-ĭ-tāte), verb, means *to hurl headlong* or *bring to a crisis.*

4. PUGNACIOUS . . . . . . **quarrelsome, inclined to fight**

The bulldog acted pugnacious.

It seemed wiser not to arouse his pugnacity (pugnaciousness).

Fond of fight: *pugilistic, bellicose, belligerent, contentious.*

5. PUNCTILIOUS . . . . . . **exact in conduct; particular**

Mrs. Post is very punctilious in observing the niceties of etiquette.

The ceremony was conducted with the utmost punctilio (punctiliousness).

Punctual (prompt) persons are proud of their punctuality.

Punctilio is exactness in conduct or forms.

6. QUERULOUS (KWĔR-ŏŏ-lŭs*) . . . fretful, complaining

Querulous persons are hard to please.

Querulousness soon becomes a habit.

*First *e* pronounced as in *edge*.

Relatives of *querulous: petulant, peevish, captious*.

7. SPONTANEOUS . arising from within; natural; self-generated

There was a spontaneous outburst of enthusiasm.

She possessed a spontaneousness (spontaneity) which was be-witching.

Query: Can you explain spontaneous combustion?

8. STENTORIAN . . . . extremely loud

The man's voice called forth, fraternal, stentorian.

A stentorian yell pierced the air.

Stentor was a Greek herald (*Iliad*) with a loud voice.

9. TRANSIENT . . . . fleeting, short-lived

Transient beams of sunlight filtered through.

The transience of joy is matched by the transience of sorrow.

Life itself is very transitory.

Most newspaper writing is highly ephemeral.

Her favor is as evanescent as a morning-glory.

Cf. *ephemeral* (lasting but a day), *transitory* (of brief duration), *evanescent* (fading quickly).

10. TRITE . . . . stale, worn out

Name three trite expressions.

Why do you suspect them of triteness?

"Nuts to you!" is a vapid, banal, stereotyped, hackneyed cliché.

Synonyms of *trite: banal, stereotyped, vapid, hackneyed. Cliché* is a noun.

11. TRIVIAL . . . . trifling, ordinary

He wastes too much time on trivial details.

Sometimes trivialities are more important than they seem.

The word means, in Latin, a place where three roads meet. Do you see the connection?

12. WATER–LOGGED . . water-soaked (until it will no longer float)

The pontoons of the clipper ship became water-logged and it sank before aid could reach it.

FIRST SENTENCE SET

Copy the *italicized* words and opposite each write an appropriate definition.

1. She is *austere* and distant but very *competent*.
2. The *despicable* president of the *defunct* corporation was finally imprisoned.
3. Her *droll* way of pretending to be *disconsolate* made us laugh.
4. Their team is as *formidable* as a *gossamer* web.
5. It is *imperative* that the police be *inflexible* in prosecuting reckless drivers.
6. He directed an *oblique* look out of his *languid* eyes.
7. The father always acted *pugnacious* when accused of *mercenary* motives or *plebeian* tastes.
8. The teacher was *punctilious* and seemingly *omniscient*.
9. Father in *stentorian* tones ordered little Charles to keep away from the edge of the *precipitous* embankment.
10. She showered *spontaneous* smiles on the *querulous* invalid.
11. It is almost *trite* to say that happiness is very *transient*.
12. To him the loss of the *water-logged* boat was a *trivial* misfortune.

SECOND SENTENCE SET

1. Father seemed *omniscient* and his penalties for misbehavior were *inflexible*.
2. The *oblique* rays of the setting sun seemed to form a *gossamer* veil.
3. To him the scheme was *despicable* because it was *mercenary*.

4. Her *languid* manner does not alter the fact that she is very *competent*.
5. It is *imperative* that gestures seem *spontaneous* when you are speaking.
6. The *formidable* algebra problem about a *water-logged* derelict was finally solved.
7. Baby rabbits have a strangely *droll* yet *pugnacious* appearance.
8. The boy looked *disconsolate* as his toy slid down the *precipitous* bank out of reach.
9. He had only a *transient* interest in the *defunct* society.
10. Such an expression is very *trite* and *plebeian*.
11. He is an *austere* man with a *stentorian* voice who is very *punctilious* in all his dealings.
12. A sick person is apt to be *querulous* about the most *trivial* matters.

WORDS, WORDS, WORDS

Contrive a conversation using words in this unit. It may concern itself with trite phrases, mercenary motives, formidable tasks, imperative needs, droll antics, or some other topic that appeals. Include words from other units as opportunity permits.

Think of an antonym for each of the words if time permits. Use the dictionary for verification.

One Word

1. What does Mother do when you are reluctant?

2. What does one do when he finds he is wrong?

3. What is the verb for high-hats?

4. What does the minister do?

5. What might the jury do?

6. What did the criminal have?

7. What caused him to commit the crime?

8. What did he feel afterward?

9. What did he accuse the judge of showing?

PRETEST

Find the number of the definition that goes with each word.

VERBS

1. ascertain
2. cajole
3. concede
4. condescend
5. deprecate
6. disrupt
7. dissipate
8. elicit
9. emaciate
10. embezzle

11. exasperate

12. exhort
13. exonerate

1. to squander or scatter
2. to irritate thoroughly, enrage
3. to disapprove of
4. to urge, advise earnestly
5. to find out
6. to drink or sip
7. to cause to become very lean
8. to lose strength
9. to break apart, rend
10. to coax, wheedle, or deceive by flattery
11. to come down (to another's level), stoop
12. to free from blame
13. to draw out
14. to yield or grant
15. to take by fraud

NOUNS

1. alibi

2. alien
3. anguish
4. apparition
5. bias
6. casualty
7. catalepsy
8. clairvoyant
9. contour

10. cupidity
11. duplicity
12. façade

1. an abnormal desire to get wealth
2. prejudice or inclination
3. a medium
4. double-dealing, deception
5. a foreigner or stranger
6. the chief front of a building
7. love, affection
8. a fit (in which muscles stiffen)
9. the claim of having been elsewhere
10. a dangerous criminal
11. a ghost
12. an outline or profile
13. a mishap, accident
14. intense suffering

STUDY GUIDE—VERBS

1. ASCERTAIN . . . . **to find out**

He went upstairs to ascertain the reason for the mysterious noise.
Reconnaissance is a term for military ascertainment, esp. by planes.

2. CAJOLE (kä-JOLE) . **to coax, wheedle, or deceive by flattery**

Dunstan planned to cajole Silas into lending him money. He "felt as if there must be a little frightening added to the cajolery . . ."

3. CONCEDE . . . . **to yield or grant**

"Concede nothing!" shouted the orator.
I concede your claim to the purse.
Labor leaders won several concessions from employers.
Concede may mean *to surrender:* He conceded the chess game.

4. CONDESCEND . . **to come down (to another's level), stoop**

She would not condescend (deign) to notice him.
"The squire condescended to preside in the parlor of the Rainbow rather than under the shadow of his own dark wainscot."
The policeman's air of condescension irritated the youth.

5. DEPRECATE . . . . **to disapprove of**

Do you deprecate what you do not understand?
"The evil principle deprecated in that religion [trusting to chance] is the orderly sequence by which the seed brings forth a crop after its kind."
Literally, *deprecate* means *to pray down* something.

6. DISRUPT . . . . **to break apart, rend**

A fire across the street might disrupt the meeting.
Rivalry in baseball resulted in the disruption of their friendship.

7. DISSIPATE . . . . . . **to squander, scatter, or dispel**

Some dissipate too much energy in unimportant activities.
Mr. Crackenthorp brought a present "well calculated to dissipate unfounded prejudices against the clerical character."
The sun soon dissipated the mist.

8. ELICIT . . . . **to draw out**

Police sometimes elicit a confession by means of "the third degree."

Had the peddler worn earrings? A great deal depended on the eliciting of this fact.

Cf. *educe, evoke, extort.*

9. EMACIATE (ė-MAY-shĭ-āte). . **to cause to become very lean**

Fasting emaciates one very quickly.

Molly was described as "a young woman, but emaciated, with long black hair."

Emaciation is no sign of piety.

10. EMBEZZLE . . . . **to take by fraud (especially for one's own use)**

"And how long have you been so thick with Dunsey that you must collogue with him to embezzle my money?"

The trooper drama was about an embezzler.

The bank clerk's embezzlement involved $30,000.

11. EXASPERATE . . . . . **to irritate thoroughly, enrage**

Did Dunsey exasperate his father?

"Nancy was so exasperatingly quiet and firm."

Godfrey's exasperation over the loss of Wildfire scarcely exceeded Dunstan's.

Synonyms of *exasperate: tease, vex, inflame, incense.*

12. EXHORT . . . . **to urge, advise earnestly**

I exhort you to try again.

"On this, William exhorted his friend to confess, and not to hide his sin any longer."

The exhortations of Mr. Crackenthorp had little effect on Silas.

13. EXONERATE (ĕg-ZON-ĕr-āte, *o* as in *on*) . . . . **to free from blame, exculpate**

Investigation by police served to exonerate (exculpate) "Gimpy," accused of murder. His exoneration (exculpation) resulted from the testimony of friends.

See a dictionary for derivations.

STUDY GUIDE—NOUNS

1. ALIBI . . . . the claim of having been elsewhere when a crime was committed

The police checked each suspect's alibi with great care.

Godfrey's "imagination constantly created an alibi for Dunstan."

In common speech *alibi* means *an excuse.*

2. ALIEN . . . . a foreigner or stranger

Linen weavers "were to the last regarded as aliens by their rustic neighbors."

Bad manners will alienate (make strangers of) even one's closest friends.

Citizens of this country have certain inalienable rights. Name a few.

3. ANGUISH . . . . intense suffering

"He must have made the effort at a moment when all his energies were turned into the anguish of disappointed faith."

4. APPARITION. . . . . a ghost

"Every man present . . . had an impression that he saw, not Silas Marner in the flesh, but an apparition."

Synonyms of *apparition: phantom, specter.*

See a dictionary for other meanings of *apparition.*

5. BIAS . . . . a prejudice or inclination

I shall examine all the samples without bias.

The judge was accused of being biased in the matter.

Bias also means *a slanting or diagonal line.*

6. CASUALTY . . . . a mishap, accident

It was a casualty which could have been prevented.

Eighteen casualties were reported in the area.

The plural means losses from death and other causes.

7. CATALEPSY . . . . . a fit (in which muscles stiffen and a person appears dead)

Victims of catalepsy must guard against being buried alive.

"It was at this point in their history that Silas's cataleptic fit occurred during the prayer meeting."

8. CLAIRVOYANT . . a medium; one who has unusual insight
or discernment

The actress decided to consult a clairvoyant.

Mr. Snell talked "like a docile clairvoyant, who would really not make a mistake if he could help it."

Scientific experiments in clairvoyance are in progress.

Clairvoyance is the ability to discern what is beyond the normal range of the senses or merely what is going on in the mind of another.

9. CONTOUR . . . an outline or profile (of something like a body, coast, or mountain range)

The contour of the mountains is very uneven.

Accent the first syllable.

10. CUPIDITY . . . . . an abnormal desire to get wealth

Silas's cupidity, after he went to Raveloe, was due to the lack of any other interest.

Synonyms of *cupidity: greed, covetousness, avarice.*

11. DUPLICITY . . . . double-dealing, deception

The man's duplicity made him the arch-traitor of the Revolutionary War.

Godfrey was not "sufficiently aware that no sort of duplicity can long flourish without the help of vocal falsehoods."

Query: Whose duplicity was more extensive, Dunstan's or Godfrey's?

12. FAÇADE (få-SAD, second *a* as in *far*) . . the chief front of a building

Have you seen the facade of the Supreme Court building?

"It *was* an apparition from that hidden life which lies . . . behind the goodly ornamented façade that meets the sunlight and gaze of respectable admirers."

Point out the façade of your school building or of some large public building.

FIRST SENTENCE SET

Copy the *italicized* words and opposite each write an appropriate definition.

1. He tried to *ascertain* why his competitor *conceded* the right to use the special process.

2. *Cajole* her a little and she will *condescend* to smile at you.
3. I *deprecate* any attempt to *disrupt* their friendship.
4. He tried to *elicit* facts that would *dissipate* suspicion.
5. Worrying about attempts to *embezzle* company funds *emaciates* the treasurer.
6. Mother *exhorts* him daily not to *exasperate* the neighbors.
7. The *alibi* should *exonerate* you.
8. The *alien* was in *anguish* over his loss.
9. A *bias* against believers in *apparitions* influenced him.
10. *Catalepsy* can cause *casualties* in modern traffic.
11. The *clairvoyant* traced the *contour* of a large building and sketched in its *façade*.
12. *Cupidity* tempts some misers to *duplicity*.

SECOND SENTENCE SET

1. The lawyer *conceded* the genuineness of the *alibi*.
2. We *ascertained* that the man was an *alien*.
3. Attempts to *embezzle* funds brought him only *anguish*.
4. Who *deprecated* belief in *apparitions?*
5. Perhaps you can *cajole* him into forgetting his *biases*.
6. Seven *casualties* in one day *exasperated* company officials.
7. The judge *exhorted* the jury to *exonerate* the man.
8. The *clairvoyant* suffered from *catalepsy*.
9. How could one *condescend* to such *duplicity?*
10. I could not *elicit* from him his reasons for wishing to *disrupt* the society.
11. He *dissipates* energy drawing *contour* maps of the Aegean Sea and *façades* of Greek temples.
12. *Cupidity* somehow accounted for his *emaciated* features.

SINISTER SAGA

Write about a fortune teller. Have her arrested if you like. Fortune telling is illegal in some states. Besides, her duplicity may have led her to embezzle.

Which Word Describes These Best?

1. Sounds from a baby?

2. Flashes of lightning?

3. A minister or priest?

4. A bashful boy?

5. Bad habits?

PRETEST

Find the number of the definition that goes with each word.

VERBS

1. galvanize
2. gratify
3. iterate
4. nurture
5. prevaricate
6. renounce
7. revoke
8. scrutinize
9. transfigure
10. vacillate
11. vindicate

12. vitiate

1. to vary from the truth
2. to justify or defend
3. to stimulate or excite
4. to learn to read and write
5. to debase or render worthless
6. to give up, abandon
7. to help or assist
8. to please or afford pleasure to
9. to nourish, foster, or rear
10. to inspect closely
11. to transform, exalt into something glorious
12. to call back (a power or privilege); cancel or repeal
13. to repeat
14. to waver or be changeable

ADJECTIVES

1. inarticulate
2. intermittent
3. juvenile
4. monotonous
5. niggardly
6. pallid
7. pious
8. protuberant
9. provident
10. reticent
11. skeptical
12. surreptitious
13. vicious

1. stingy, miserly
2. doubtful, unbelieving
3. bulging, swelling out
4. speechless, unintelligible
5. trusting in God
6. secret, stealthy, sly
7. inclined to be silent, reserved
8. repeating
9. harmful, evil
10. tedious, wearisome
11. pale or wan
12. occurring at intervals
13. forward-looking, thrifty, possessing foresight
14. godly, religious
15. youthful, for children, childish

1. GALVANIZE . . . . to stimulate or excite

The news will galvanize him into immediate action.

A galvanic (electric) thrill went through the stands as the full-back crossed the goal line.

Galvanism is a phase of science which has to do with electric currents, especially those produced by chemical action.

Electrify is a synonym of *galvanize.* See a dictionary for scientific meanings and relations.

2. GRATIFY . . . . to please or afford pleasure to

This victory will gratify the coach.

"The more opportunities remained for him [Godfrey] to snatch the strange gratification of seeing Nancy."

The response to the appeal was gratifying.

3. ITERATE . . . . to repeat; utter a second time

The lawyer iterates and reiterates his demands.

Such iteration often gains its end.

4. NURTURE . . . . to nourish, foster, or rear

He nurtures the plan eagerly and expectantly.

"The little child knows nothing of parental love, but only knows one face and one lap toward which it stretches its arms for refuge and nurture."

George Eliot speaks of pale-faced weavers as having "unnurtured souls."

5. PREVARICATE. . . . . . to vary from the truth, quibble

One who prevaricates must have a good memory.

"Godfrey . . . had entangled himself still further in prevarication and deceit."

Cf. *equivocate, evade.*

6. RENOUNCE . . . . . . to give up, abandon, repudiate

The prince will renounce his claim to the throne.

Godfrey "had not moral courage enough to contemplate that active renunciation of Nancy was possible for him."

Synonyms of *renounce: disavow, abjure, recant, retract, disclaim.*

7. REVOKE . . . . . to call back (a power or privilege); cancel or repeal

The council voted to revoke the charter.

The revocation of the law hurt business.

Godfrey believed "he must irrevocably lose *her* as well as the inheritance."

A parliamentary and legal family: *abrogate, cancel, annul, recall, nullify, rescind.*

8. SCRUTINIZE . . . . to inspect closely

Nancy's spirit of rectitude "had made it a habit with her to scrutinize her past feelings and actions with self-questioning solicitude."

James escaped his mother's scrutiny that morning.

9. TRANSFIGURE . . . to transform, exalt (into something glorious)

Reforestation will transfigure those barren hills.

Why did the presence of Eppie transfigure Silas Marner? This transfiguration was a gradual process.

" 'Twas a land transfigured, 'twas a new creation,

Oh, a singing wind swept the Negro nation."

10. VACILLATE . . . . . . to waver or be changeable

A strong man is not apt to vacillate.

Godfrey "fell back on suspense and vacillation with a sense of repose."

11. VINDICATE . . . . . to justify or defend successfully

Later events failed to vindicate the Treaty of Versailles.

"Wisdom is vindicated of her children."

"The vindication of the loved object is the best balm affection can find for its wounds."

Cf. *exculpate, exonerate* (Unit 6).

12. VITIATE . . . . . . to debase or render worthless

The fact that he was insane vitiates the contract.

Bad company results in vitiation of character.

Cf. *invalidate, contaminate.*

STUDY GUIDE—ADJECTIVES

1. INARTICULATE . . . . . . **speechless, unintelligible**

"The little one . . . squatted down on the sack . . . gurgling and making many inarticulate communications to the cheerful fire."

See *articulate*.

2. INTERMITTENT . . . . **occurring at intervals; periodic**

Intermittent flashes of lightning illuminated the landscape.
The intermittence of the showers made us reluctant to start.

Intermission comes from the same root.

3. JUVENILE . . . . **youthful, for children, childish**

Bob Cass was praised "in a tone that implied . . . the very highest stamp of juvenile merit."
Jumping up and down with anger is very puerile.

Pronounce *i* of *juvenile* and *puerile* as in *ill*. *Puerile* means *childish* in an uncomplimentary sense.

4. MONOTONOUS. . **tedious, wearisome (because unvaried)**

The monotonous noise of the train began to seem distant.
"The livelong day he [Silas] sat at his loom, his ear filled with its monotony."
Some pupils talk always in a monotone.

Literally, *monotonous* means *one-toned*.

5. NIGGARDLY . . . . **stingy, miserly**

Silas ceased to be niggardly with his money after Eppie came.
A niggard is not always liked.
Many jokes have been written about the niggardliness of the Scotch.

Other "close" words: *avaricious, parsimonious*.

6. PALLID . . . . **pale or wan**

"He was then simply a pallid young man."
Pallidness (pallor) may indicate ill health.

Synonyms of *pallid*: *ghastly* (I, 3), *ashen, bloodless*.

7. PIOUS . . . . **godly, religious**

There was a pious look on his face.

William Dane "was regarded as a shining instance of youthful piety."

Sometimes piousness is only pretended, as in "pious frauds."

8. PROTUBERANT . . . . bulging, swelling out

"For how was it possible to believe that those large, brown, protuberant eyes in Silas Marner's pale face really saw nothing very distinctly that was not close to them . . . ?"

A mole is a small protuberance somewhere on the body.

Pronounce *u* as in *use.*

9. PROVIDENT. . forward-looking, thrifty, possessing foresight

Marner was a "highly welcome settler . . . even to the more provident cottagers."

She was thankful for God's providential care.

Providence is a term for God.

10. RETICENT . . . . inclined to be silent, reserved

War veterans are usually reticent about discussing their experiences at the front.

The reticence of the boy made him seem uninteresting at first.

Synonyms of *reticent: taciturn, uncommunicative.*

11. SKEPTICAL . . . . doubtful, unbelieving

The farrier was skeptical about ghosts. The sudden appearance of Marner almost destroyed his skepticism.

A *skeptic* is a doubter.

12. SURREPTITIOUS . . . . secret, stealthy, sly

Bobby and Herbert made a surreptitious expedition into the pantry.

The note was circulated surreptitiously.

Note: *Clandestine* is a synonym. *Furtive* (I, 3) and *wily* (I, 9) are also Sly-words. Review them and watch their use in books and stories. Note differences in meaning.

13. VICIOUS . . . . harmful, evil

A bull becomes vicious when he sees red.

A lecturer described the viciousness of the block-booking system.

Vicious also means *tricky* and *unruly.*

FIRST SENTENCE SET

Copy the *italicized* words and opposite each write an appropriate definition.

1. *Gratified*, Father was *galvanized* into action.
2. *Iteration nurtures* memory.
3. Will he *renounce* his tendency to *prevaricate?*
4. The officer *scrutinized* the license which had been *revoked*.
5. He *vindicated* his claim that shrubs *transfigure* a lawn.
6. Will a tendency to *vacillate* really *vitiate* character?
7. *Inarticulate* at first, she soon recovered enough to talk in *intermittent* bursts about the *surreptitious* expedition.
8. *Juvenile* books are not always *monotonous* to adults.
9. Are *pious* persons apt to be *niggardly?*
10. Silas had a *pallid* face and *protuberant* eyes.
11. She is *provident* at home and *reticent* socially.
12. I was *skeptical* about harboring a *vicious* dog.

SECOND SENTENCE SET

1. The baby *iterated* her *inarticulate* protest.
2. His *intermittent* flights of oratory *galvanized* the audience.
3. Her *juvenile* tendency to *prevaricate* was soon curbed.
4. In *monotonous* tones he *renounced* all previous claims.
5. The project was *vitiated* by *niggardly* planning.
6. The child's *pallid* face was *transfigured* by the sunshine.
7. His *pious* habits *gratify* his father.
8. We *scrutinized* the *protuberant* headlights on the car.
9. She *nurtures* her children with *provident* affection.
10. The manager *revoked* the pass because he knew of her *surreptitious* plots and was *skeptical*.
11. A tendency to *vacillate* is a *vicious* trait.
12. He was *reticent* about discussing the plan to *vindicate* him.

ONE SUMMER

Prevaricate paragraphicallly about a summer vacation — afoot, on a bicycle, in a car, at a lake, or by the sea.

Find

1. A common cause for failure

2. A zerolike word

3. A description of the search for a lost airliner

4. A quality of George Washington

5. A stock-market word

6. A word that describes Shakespeare as a man

PRETEST

Find the number of the definition that goes with each word.

ADJECTIVES

1. ardent
2. benign
3. civil
4. cogent
5. complacent
6. culpable
7. eccentric
8. fallible
9. futile
10. inane
11. incipient
12. incredible

1. queer, odd, or peculiar
2. empty, senseless
3. self-satisfied
4. (formally) polite
5. liable to error
6. nimble, light-footed
7. eager, zealous, enthusiastic
8. unbelievable
9. beginning (to be or appear)
10. blameworthy
11. convincing, forceful
12. kindly, gentle
13. having teeth like a gear
14. useless, vain

NOUNS

1. fallacy
2. fluctuation
3. indolence
4. inference

5. irresolution
6. metamorphosis
7. presentiment
8. prostration

9. pseudonym
10. retribution

11. subterfuge
12. utility
13. veracity

1. punishment or requital
2. a conclusion
3. truthfulness
4. rise and fall, a rolling to and fro
5. a fictitious name
6. laziness or love of ease
7. usefulness
8. false reasoning or mistaken idea
9. a medical instrument
10. a transformation or change of form
11. the act of giving a gift
12. indecision, vacillation
13. a foreboding
14. a trick or artifice
15. exhaustion or a falling down in worship

STUDY GUIDE—ADJECTIVES

1. ARDENT . . . . **eager, zealous, enthusiastic**

"He was believed to be a young man of exemplary life and ardent faith."

The boy is admired because of his ardor.

Literally, *ardent* means *burning*. See its derivation.

2. BENIGN . . . . **kindly, gentle**

The benign influence of the minister touched the entire village.

"The rude mind with difficulty associates the ideas of power and benignity."

Benignant suggests condescension more than *benign* does.

3. CIVIL . . . . **(formally) polite**

Shakespeare was very modest and civil.

She treated her friends with the utmost civility.

See a dictionary for other meanings: *civil service, civil war, civil year*, etc.

4. COGENT (CŌ-jĕnt). . . . . . . **convincing, forceful**

His reasons were very cogent.

Their cogency impressed his audience.

5. COMPLACENT . . . . **self-satisfied**

The Squire "looked across the table at Nancy with complacent gravity."

Complacency is sometimes a man's worst enemy.

6. CULPABLE . . . . **blameworthy**

"If there is an angel who records the sorrows of men as well as their sins, he knows how many and deep are the sorrows that spring from false ideas for which no man is culpable."

The man's culpability was taken for granted by the police.

Cf. *culprit, an offender.*

7. ECCENTRIC . . . . **queer, odd, or peculiar**

Linen weavers "usually contracted the eccentric habits which belong to a state of loneliness."

One of her eccentricities was a fondness for June bugs.

Literally, *eccentric* means *off center*. Related words: *erratic* (irregular), *singular*.

Query: What is an eccentric in machinery?

8. FALLIBLE . . . . **liable to error**

All human beings are fallible.
The fallibility of scientific theories was discussed.
Opposite: *infallible, infallibility.*

9. FUTILE . . . . **useless, vain**

All efforts to find the missing plane proved futile.
The drama showed the futility of trying to live without working.

10. INANE . . . . **empty, senseless**

She made several inane remarks.
The conversation died of inanition.
"Do we not while away moments of inanity . . . by repeating some trivial movement or sound?"

Inane rhymes with *wane,* but *a* in *inanition* and *inanity* is pronounced as in *tan.*

11. INCIPIENT . . . . **beginning (to be or appear)**

Examination by a doctor showed incipient tuberculosis. Because of its incipiency it was quickly curable.

12. INCREDIBLE . . . . **unbelievable**

The word "fit" was used in Raveloe "to explain things otherwise incredible."
The incredibility of the story made many doubt the teller's truthfulness.
The magical powers of radium pass the bounds of credibility.

STUDY GUIDE—NOUNS

1. FALLACY . . . . . **false reasoning or a mistaken idea**

Suspicion of the peddler was based on the fallacy that all foreigners are dishonest.
The boy's reasoning was fallacious. (*la* = LAY)

Is this fallacious? All Fords are made by Henry Ford. This car was made by Henry Ford. Therefore, it is a Ford.

2. FLUCTUATION . . . **rise and fall, a rolling to and fro**

Silas noticed "that Sarah's manner towards him began to exhibit a strange fluctuation."
The price of eggs fluctuates considerably.

---

3. **INDOLENCE** . . . . laziness or love of ease

The man's indolence kept him from succeeding at anything.
She was very indolent.

4. **INFERENCE** . . . . a conclusion

"A dull mind, once arriving at an inference that flatters a desire, is rarely able to retain the impression that the notion
from which the inference started was purely problematic."
From your answer, I infer that you understand the topic well.

5. **IRRESOLUTION** . . . . indecision, vacillation

Godfrey's irresolution was his outstanding trait.
His father was by no means irresolute.

6. **METAMORPHOSIS** . . a transformation or change of form

"Marner's inward life had been a history and a metamor-
phosis."
The stamens metamorphose into petals.
Query: What does *metamorphosis* have to do with butterflies and moths?

7. **PRESENTIMENT** . . . . a foreboding

"His legs were weary, but his mind was at ease, free from the
presentiment of change."

8. **PROSTRATION** . . exhaustion or a falling down in worship

"Yes, there was a sort of refuge which always comes with the
prostration of thought under an overpowering passion."
He was lying prostrate on the ground.
You should prostrate yourself as the king enters.
You have heard of nervous prostration and heat prostration, no doubt. See
other meanings.

9. **PSEUDONYM** . . . . a fictitious name

"George Eliot" was the pseudonym of Mary Ann Evans.
Astrology is called a pseudo-science (false, pretended).
Cf. *alias, an assumed name* (that a criminal uses).

10. **RETRIBUTION** . . . . punishment or requital

Retribution overtook Dunstan unexpectedly.
There was retributory justice in Eppie's refusal.

11. SUBTERFUGE (SUB-tĕr-fewj) . . . . . a trick or artifice

Godfrey was frequently obliged to use subterfuges with his father.

She used pretended illness as a subterfuge.

Synonyms: *maneuver, stratagem, ruse, finesse, feint* (I, 5).

12. UTILITY . . . . usefulness

Dunstan's delight in lying was "grandly independent of utility."

He spoke often of the utility of newspaper experience.

One packing company utilizes every part of a pig but the squeal.

The utilitarian (practical) values of an education are numerous.

13. VERACITY . . . . truthfulness

Everyone has confidence in his own veracity.

Poe's stories often sound like veracious (*ra* = RAY) accounts of actual events.

FIRST SENTENCE SET

Copy the *italicized* words and opposite each write an appropriate definition.

1. He is always *benign* and *civil*.
2. With *ardent* gestures and *cogent* arguments he slowly won them over.
3. If he were *culpable*, could he act so *complacent?*
4. He is an *eccentric* old man, more *fallible* in judgment than most humans.
5. Such actions are *inane* and *futile*.
6. It is *incredible* that the *incipient* stages of the disease could appear so soon.
7. It is a *fallacy* to believe that the *fluctuation* of the tides is due to the tipping of the earth.
8. The only possible *inference* is that your neglect is due to *indolence*.
9. He had no *presentiment* that such a *metamorphosis* would take place in his life.
10. Spells of *irresolution* nearly give him nervous *prostration*.

11. Under the *pseudonym* of I. M. Porter he describes the *subterfuges* by which he sought to escape *retribution*.
12. He is willing to stake his reputation for *veracity* on the *utility* of the new substance.

SECOND SENTENCE SET

1. His arguments seemed *cogent* though based on the *fallacy* that airpower alone could win the war.
2. With *ardent* eyes we watched the *fluctuations* of battle.
3. *Indolence* makes a man *complacent*.
4. His *inferences* regarding the enemy seemed *incredible*.
5. *Irresolution* kept *incipient* plans from being carried out.
6. With *benign* satisfaction, the commanding officer described the *metamorphosis* our outfit had undergone.
7. An *eccentric* old Frenchman had a *presentment* that *retribution* was near for the Nazis.
8. It was strange to see the *prostration* of the natives before a man as *fallible* as they.
9. The *pseudonym* was a *subterfuge* to mislead the enemy.
10. It was *futile* to discuss the *utility* of a nonexistent weapon.
11. In spite of his seeming *veracity*, he proved *culpable*.
12. Remain *civil* no matter how *inane* his remarks may be.

WORD WIZARDRY

With an eye on the study guide and with motives of utility, write cogently and ardently about eccentric persons (how do they act?) popular fallacies (name some), or human fallibility (the pupil is always wrong?).

Compile an Adverbial Auxiliary with a membership from this unit of 15–18. Be sure spellings are correct.

How many words ending in *nym* can you list with *pseudonym?* Don't overlook *acronym* — a word like WAC formed from the tips or initial letters of a group of words.

He Went to Court

Note: This is a criminal case, unfortunately.

1. What brought him there? An __?__ by the grand jury.

2. What did he hope the jury would do? __?__ him.

3. What did he discover about the law? It is __?__.

4. What happened to the stolen goods? __?__ by the police.

5. What did his witnesses try to do? __?__ his alibi.

6. What kind of criminal did the judge say he was? __?__.

Find the number of the definition that goes with each word.

VERBS

1. abridge
2. acquiesce
3. acquit
4. aggravate
5. corroborate
6. garnish
7. inundate
8. propitiate
9. protract

1. to make heavier or worse
2. to appease or conciliate
3. to adorn or decorate
4. to steal or pilfer
5. to condense, shorten
6. to prolong or lengthen
7. to change the date of
8. to agree (by not objecting)
9. to flood or flow over
10. to verify or confirm
11. to set free, declare not guilty

NOUNS

1. altercation
2. confiscation
3. execration
4. hazard
5. indictment
6. jargon
7. resurrection
8. sanction

1. a risk or danger
2. an accusation
3. soulful devotion
4. a rising again
5. approval, act of authorizing
6. seizure of property
7. confusing chatter, lingo
8. a rebellion or uprising
9. a dispute, heated debate
10. a curse (act of cursing)

ADJECTIVES

1. culinary
2. diffident
3. incorrigible
4. inexorable
5. inscrutable
6. inveterate
7. obsequious
8. prodigious

1. bad beyond correction
2. (too) submissive; servile
3. pertaining to cooking
4. having had experience in war
5. immense, enormous
6. shy, timid, modest
7. mysterious, incomprehensible
8. difficult to operate
9. deep-seated, habitual
10. unyielding, unrelenting

STUDY GUIDE—VERBS

1. ABRIDGE . . . . **to condense, shorten**

Because the time was short, the speaker was obliged to abridge his remarks.

The magazine prints abridgments of current books.

Query: What is an unabridged dictionary?

Varieties of summary: *epitome, compendium, abstract, digest, synopsis,* and *syllabus.* Watch for them in your reading.

2. ACQUIESCE . . . . . . **to agree (by not objecting)**

I am sure that he will acquiesce in whatever plan I make.

He "gave no other answer than a gruff sound of acquiescence."

Other yes verbs: *assent* (I, 1), *accede, concur* (I, 1).

See *quiescent* (calm), *tranquil, inactive.*

3. ACQUIT . . . . **to set free, declare not guilty**

Jerry Cruncher watched the jury acquit Charles Darnay when he was on trial for treason. Lucy desired his acquittal.

Cf. *vindicate* (Unit 7), *exonerate, exculpate* (Unit 6). Observe differences.

4. AGGRAVATE . . . . . . **to make heavier or worse**

Violence always aggravates a strike situation.

"The energy which had at once supported him under his old sufferings and aggravated their sharpness had been gradually restored to him."

Monseigneur was blind to aggravation of the distress in Saint Antoine.

5. CORROBORATE . . . . **to verify or confirm**

The police could not corroborate the alibi.

"Mr. Cruncher had no particular meaning in these sulky corroborations."

Who can furnish corroborative evidence?

6. GARNISH . . . . **to adorn or decorate**

Garnish the potatoes with parsley.

"In the meantime, his son, whose head was garnished with tenderer spikes . . . kept the required watch upon his mother."

Noun forms: *garnishment, garniture.*

7. **INUNDATE** . . . . **to flood or flow over**

The Nile inundates its banks every year.

The French Revolution inundated Paris with bloodshed. It was an inundation which swept away guilty and guiltless without discrimination.

8. **PROPITIATE** . . . . **to appease or conciliate**

The life of Charles Darnay was not enough to propitiate Madame Defarge.

Sidney Carton's act of propitiation was well carried out.

January was a propitious (favorable) month for a strike.

Synonyms of *propitiate: pacify, mollify, atone, expiate.*

9. **PROTRACT** . . . . . . **to prolong or lengthen in time**

Do not protract the meeting unnecessarily.

Dr. Manette's term of imprisonment was protracted indefinitely. This protraction nearly destroyed his mind.

STUDY GUIDE—NOUNS

1. **ALTERCATION** . . . . . . **dispute, heated debate**

"The altercation was conducted in a low tone of voice . . ."

The first syllable is pronounced like *all.*

2. **CONFISCATION** . . . **seizure of property (as a forfeit)**

Many of the nobles, "anticipating plunder or confiscation, had made provident remittances at Tellson's."

The government will confiscate the property.

Query: What do teachers like to confiscate?

3. **EXECRATION** . . . . **a curse (act of cursing)**

"Shrieks, volleys, execrations, bravery without stint" accompanied the storming of the Bastille.

The food was execrable.

Other forms of curse: *imprecation, anathema, malediction.*

4. **HAZARD** . . . . **a risk or danger**

Mr. Lorry was quite safe from the hazards of the Revolution.

Charles Darnay's undertaking in behalf of Gabelle was very hazardous.

He would not hazard an estimate on the outcome.

5. **INDICTMENT** . . **an accusation (especially by a grand jury)**

His indictment by the grand jury amounted almost to a conviction. He was indicted on three charges.

6. **JARGON** . . . . **confusing chatter, lingo**

Girls seldom understand baseball jargon.
The indictment was full of legal jargon.

7. **RESURRECTION** . . **a rising again (especially from the dead)**

A resurrection takes place each spring in the woods and fields.
Sydney kept repeating the words: "I am the Resurrection and the Life, saith the Lord."

8. **SANCTION** . . . . . . **approval, act of authorizing**

Dr. Manette was imprisoned with the sanction of a corrupt government.
The Church of England would not sanction divorce.
See legal meaning of *sanction*.

STUDY GUIDE—ADJECTIVES

1. **CULINARY** (KUE-lǐ-nĕ-rǐ) . . . . **pertaining to cooking**

Miss Pross searched for "impoverished French, who . . . would impart culinary mysteries to her."
The hotel advertises that its cuisine is the very finest.
Cf. *cuisine* (kwĕ-ZEEN), *kitchen* or *style of cooking*.

2. **DIFFIDENT** . . . . **shy, timid, modest**

Scothe is very diffident in the presence of company.
The diffidence of youth slowly vanished as he grew older.
Shades of shy: *coy, bashful, taciturn, inhibited, retiring, reticent* (Unit 7).

3. **INCORRIGIBLE** . . . . . . **bad beyond correction**

The prisoner was considered incorrigible and was so treated.
He soon gave evidence of his incorrigibility by trying to escape.
The newcomer proved to be an incorrigible liar.
Incorrigible refers to incurable *faults* or *evils*.

4. **INEXORABLE** . . . . **unyielding, unrelenting**

Madame Defarge's vengeance was inexorable. The Vengeance

also inexorably opposed pleas for mercy. This inexorableness matched that of the erstwhile nobles who were being swept away.

The Stiff family again: *inflexible, rigid, unalterable, obstinate, obdurate, implacable.*

5. INSCRUTABLE . . . . . mysterious, incomprehensible or past finding out

"In any of the burial-places of this city through which I pass is there a sleeper more inscrutable than its busy inhabitants are?"
Houdini had all the inscrutability (inscrutableness) of genius.

6. INVETERATE . . . . deep-seated, habitual

Americans are inveterate coffee drinkers.
It was the inveteracy of Dr. Manette's prison habits which made them reassert themselves when he was overwrought.

Query: Can you find a connection between *inveterate* and *veteran?*

7. OBSEQUIOUS (ob-SEE-kwĭ-ŭs) . . (too) submissive; servile

Barsad became very obsequious when Sydney threatened to play his trump card. This obsequiousness depended, however, on Carton's pledge.

Uxorious means being that way toward one's wife.

8. PRODIGIOUS . . . . immense, enormous

George made a prodigious effort to learn golf, but it was useless.
The article was about a child prodigy who could speak six languages.

A *prodigy* is an especially gifted child or some other marvel.

FIRST SENTENCE SET

Copy the *italicized* words and opposite each write an appropriate definition.

1. The foreman will *abridge* his account of the reasons which led the jury to *acquit* the prisoner.
2. The boy's unwillingness to *acquiesce* only *aggravated* the situation.

3. Several witnesses *corroborated* reports of the man's bravery when the river *inundated* the city.
4. A flower *garnished* his buttonhole when he went to *propitiate* the manager.
5. Why *protract* the *altercation?*
6. *Execrations* did not prevent the *confiscation* of his car.
7. The *indictments* create *prodigious hazards.*
8. The engineer, with much technical *jargon*, gave his *sanction* to the project.
9. She seemed *diffident* about discussing the *resurrection.*
10. In *culinary* performances she was *incorrigible.*
11. His decisions were *inexorable*, his reasons *inscrutable.*
12. Ordinarily *obsequious*, he displayed *inveterate* opposition to his niece's marriage.

SECOND SENTENCE SET

1. Have I the *sanction* of the president to *abridge* the report?
2. *Acquiesce* in any fair plan that will *propitiate* labor.
3. The penalty is *inexorable* if the jury does not *acquit* you.
4. He is too *obsequious* to *aggravate* her displeasure.
5. Can anyone *corroborate* the story of the *prodigious* fish?
6. Yellow stains *garnish* the fingernails of *inveterate* smokers.
7. The air was suddenly *inundated* with *execrations.*
8. A *protracted* discussion of the *resurrection* ensued.
9. The *indictment* described the *altercation* in legal *jargon.*
10. *Confiscation* is one of the *hazards* of civil war.
11. Praise of her *culinary* skill made her all the more *diffident.*
12. The reasons for his *incorrigible* dislike were *inscrutable.*

BOOKWARD EXCURSION

Use a dozen or more of the words somehow in connection with a book or books the class has read. You may apply them to characters, situations, style, or the author(s). Any correct form of a word is acceptable.

The French Revolution

1. Many a noble had to abandon his desire for __?__.

2. The __?__ was terrible.

3. The __?__ of the authorities in preventing escapes

   was __?__.

4. La Guillotine brought __?__ to its victims.

5. Some of the Revolutionists were __?__ __?__s, worse than

   the nobles they executed.

PRETEST

Find the number of the definition that goes with each word.

NOUNS

1. abeyance
2. carnage

3. detriment
4. fidelity
5. heresy
6. interment

7. longevity

8. mirage
9. miscreant
10. oblivion
11. respite
12. vigilance

1. faithfulness
2. an optical illusion or deception out of doors
3. watchfulness, caution
4. a movement in music
5. burial
6. a holding or keeping inactive for a time; suspension
7. harm, damage, that which injures or reduces in value
8. false teaching
9. great length of life
10. a wrongdoer, villain
11. that which hinders
12. state of forgetfulness
13. butchery, slaughter
14. (a period of) rest or relief

ADJECTIVES

1. atrocious
2. belligerent
3. diabolic(al)
4. implacable
5. ingenious
6. intrepid
7. laconic
8. lucrative
9. morose
10. ostensible
11. pernicious
12. sanguine
13. ubiquitous

1. warlike, quarrelsome
2. devilish, very wicked
3. clever, skillfully done
4. profitable, gainful
5. apparent, seeming
6. hopeful, confident
7. difficult to locate
8. horrible, outrageous
9. daring, fearless
10. relentless
11. concise, terse, pithy
12. sullen, crabbed, sour
13. striking in appearance
14. highly injurious
15. being everywhere at once

STUDY GUIDE—NOUNS

1. ABEYANCE (a-BAY-ance) . . a holding or keeping inactive for a time; suspension

The normal processes of law are in abeyance while martial law exists.

2. CARNAGE . . . . butchery, slaughter

"The crowd had taken him through the scene of carnage to the prison of La Force."

From the Latin root *carn*-(flesh) come *carnal, carnality, carnation* (a color), *carnival* and *carnivorous*. See especially the origin of *carnival*.

3. DETRIMENT . . . . harm, damage, that which injures or reduces in value

Serious detriment to his reputation as a doctor resulted.
His deafness is a serious detriment.
The letter contained nothing detrimental.

4. FIDELITY . . . . faithfulness

His only crime "was fidelity to himself and his family."

Long *i* is preferred, but short *i* as in *fib* is correct.
Query: What does "Adeste, Fideles" mean?

5. HERESY . . . . false teaching

The church seldom punishes heresy today.
The court was shocked by "that tremendous heresy about George Washington."
Heretical beliefs flourish everywhere.

Heretics were once burned at the stake for their heretical teachings.

6. INTERMENT . . . . burial

The interment of Roger Cly had a peculiar interest for Jerry Cruncher.

It may be traced back to Latin *in* plus *terra* (earth).

7. LONGEVITY (lŏn-JEV-ĭ-tĭ) . . . . great length of life

Elephants are noted for their longevity.
Longevity is sometimes a family trait.

---

8. MIRAGE (mě-RAZH) . . . an optical illusion or deception out of doors

What seem like pools of water on the pavement ahead are a mirage.

See sentence under *sanguine*.

A pronounced as in *far*.

9. MISCREANT . . . . a wrongdoer, villain

The miscreant was severely punished.

Foulon's miscreant (villainous) deeds cost him his life.

Rogue's gallery: *evildoer, rascal, ruffian, caitiff, scoundrel.*

10. OBLIVION . . . state of forgetfulness or of being forgotten

Sleep provides temporary oblivion.

The government issued "blank forms for the consignment of anyone to the oblivion of prison for any length of time." (*Lettres de cachet*)

His obliviousness to the pangs of hunger was due to intense concentration.

First *o* of *oblivion* pronounced as in *compare*.

11. RESPITE . . . . (a period of) rest or relief

He had not a moment of respite all day long.

In the music she found temporary respite from her grief.

It has a legal meaning which is similar.

12. VIGILANCE . . . . watchfulness, caution

The vigilance of the sentry saved us.

Dr. Manette's "vigilance and skill in conducting ingenious experiments brought a moderate number of patients."

A vigilant but futile search was conducted.

STUDY GUIDE—ADJECTIVES

1. ATROCIOUS . . . . horrible, outrageous

An atrocious murderer was executed.

Atrocity stories are a familiar phase of warfare.

Synonyms of *atrocious: flagrant, monstrous, heinous, outrageous, nefarious, villainous.*

2. BELLIGERENT . . . . warlike, quarrelsome

"Some area-railings had been torn up, to arm the more belligerent spirits."

The belligerents (noun) are those participating in a fight or war.

His bellicose attitude stirred unexpected antagonism.

Synonyms of *belligerent*: *bellicose*, *pugnacious*.

3. DIABOLIC(AL) . . . . devilish, very wicked

It was a diabolical trick to perpetrate on a person.

The heathen religion is a form of diabolism (worship of devils).

Le Diable is the Devil in French.

4. IMPLACABLE (ĭm-PLAY-kȧ-ble) . . relentless, irreconcilable

Madame Defarge was implacable. The implacableness of her desire for vengeance is terrible to read about.

The manufacturer was implacably opposed to labor unions.

See *inexorable* and the Stiff family in Unit 9.

5. INGENIOUS . clever, skillfully done, having inventive ability

The solution to the puzzle is very ingenious.

He is a very ingenious youth. The ingenuity with which he fixes household appliances is remarkable.

6. INTREPID . . . . daring, fearless

The pilot showed himself an intrepid aviator.

The intrepidity of scientists like Pasteur has made possible the conquest of many diseases.

7. LACONIC (lȧ-CON-ĭc) . . . . . . concise, terse, pithy

"A light frown and a laconic 'Yes,' were the answers."

Note: This word commemorates the Spartans or Laconians, who were trained from childhood to say everything in the briefest and most pointed manner.

8. LUCRATIVE . . . . profitable, gainful

Mr. Stryver was already "fast shouldering his way to a large and lucrative practice."

Query: Do you know what "filthy lucre" is?

9. MOROSE . . . . sullen, crabbed, sour

Misfortune made her morose.

His moroseness was due to ill health.

10. OSTENSIBLE . . . . **apparent, seeming**

"He was brushed and washed at the usual hour, and set off with his son to pursue his ostensible calling."

The G-man was ostensibly a hobo.

11. PERNICIOUS . . . . **highly injurious, wicked**

Opium is a pernicious drug.

"The prisoner had already engaged in these pernicious missions."

12. SANGUINE (SANG-gwinn) . . . . . **hopeful, confident**

A sanguine nature seldom experiences despair.

"Then, that glorious vision of doing good, which is so often the sanguine mirage of so many good minds, arose before him."

Hope words: *optimistic, buoyant.* Cf. *ardent* (Unit 8).

13. UBIQUITOUS (you-BIK-wĭ-tŭs) . . . **being (or seeming to be) everywhere at once**

"It was an inconsistent and ubiquitous fiend, too."

The ubiquitousness of the police made escape impossible.

Cf. *omnipresent* (Unit 5).

FIRST SENTENCE SET

Copy the *italicized* words and opposite each write an appropriate definition.

1. Looters find *carnage lucrative.*
2. The right of free speech cannot be kept in *abeyance* without serious *detriment* to society.
3. He was never very *sanguine* about the man's *fidelity.*
4. *Heresy* of any kind is *pernicious.*
5. Sadly they watched the *interment* of their *intrepid* leader.
6. "I covet *longevity,*" was her *laconic* comment.
7. It was an *ingenious* explanation of *mirages.*
8. The *atrocious* and *diabolical* crime was the result of a *belligerent* attitude toward society.
9. "The Vengeance" was *implacable* and *morose.*
10. Fear of thieves was the *ostensible* reason for his *vigilance.*

11. The *ubiquitous miscreant* was seen several times in one night in different parts of the city.
12. A few moments of *oblivion* provided the *respite* which she needed.

SECOND SENTENCE SET

1, 2. The *miscreant's* part in the *carnage* was both *ingenious* and *diabolical*.
3. His *fidelity* to scientific truth and his exposure of *heresy* led to a *lucrative* career as a writer.
4. A *mirage* on the desert made him think that *respite* was near.
5. An *implacable* enemy sought for him *oblivion* complete and permanent.
6. Only by exercising *vigilance* can one escape the *pernicious* effects of such a system.
7. She became *belligerent* when told that her singing was *atrocious*.
8. The *intrepid* explorer was famous for his *laconic* remarks.
9. His hope for *longevity* is not too *sanguine*.
10. Their *ostensible* reasons for wishing immediate *interment* aroused suspicion.
11. A *morose* attitude causes physical *detriment*.
12. *Ubiquitous* soldiers kept the operation of civil law in *abeyance* for weeks.

THE LAST ENEMY

Death — in the air, on the desert, at the stake, in a war, a revolution, or an earthquake — is a logical topic for paragraph perpetration because many of the words in this unit are connected with it in one way or another.

The Inquisition, if you care to look it up, has a definite attraction for several of the words and will provide a use for most of the others.

FINAL TESTS

Copy the *italicized* words and opposite each write an appropriate definition.

UNIT 1

1. Queer *coincidences constitute* fascinating material for a scrapbook.
2. He *alleges* that the *contrivance* is harmless.
3. In his *admonition* the doctor ordered her to *discriminate* between the richness of her food and mere bulk.
4. Her eyes seemed to *dilate* with *consternation* at the news.
5. The *alacrity* with which he worked earned him the *epithet* "Flash."
6. The search for the *carcass culminated* in a deep ravine.
7. With *chagrin* he watched his holdings *depreciate*.
8. His *confederate bequeathed* the fortune to a beggar.
9. His disregard for *decorum appalled* his friends.
10. The *dilemma* grew out of his failure to *conciliate* the one man who could help.

UNIT 2

1. The *ferocity* of your dog *jeopardizes* the safety of our children.
2. The professor clung with great *tenacity* to his theory about the rock *strata*.
3. Do girls who ask for "dates" *infringe* upon a boy's *prerogatives?*
4. He dared not *insinuate* that you lack *fortitude*.
5. *Lethargy* leads one to *exaggerate* the effort required.
6. A desire to make *restitution* for the harm he had done *obsessed* him.

7. The *pandemonium* of the stock exchange did not upset his *sagacity.*
8. She will *recuperate* fast in *seclusion.*
9. Any attempt to *retaliate* will *incriminate* you also.
10. If we *procrastinate* longer, all efforts to *resuscitate* the company will be useless.

UNIT 3

1. In spite of its *proximity* to the city, it is not *accessible* by automobile.
2. Lincoln was too *magnanimous* to cherish *rancor* toward his enemies.
3. Iodine in *infinitesimal* quantities is believed to be *conducive* to health.
4. Fortune is *capricious* in distributing *opulence.*
5. *Facetious* quips rolled off a *facile* tongue.
6. There is a *stigma* attached to anything *insidious.*
7. *Posterity* will never consider him too *meticulous* in money matters.
8. He later regretted the *impetuous* words of his *impromptu* outburst.
9. Such *tranquillity* is without *precedent* in that rebellious country.
10. In his *reminiscences* he was inclined to exaggerate the *magnitude* of the offense.

UNIT 4

1. With *supercilious* glee they burned an *effigy* of the king.
2. The two *despots* made a *simultaneous* effort to seize the land.
3. Camels may with *impunity* be called *denizens* of the desert.
4. The *condolence* of friends helped her to avoid growing *morbid* in her sorrow.
5. The *animosity* that you think he feels is an *illusion.*
6. His praise contained a *subtle affront.*
7. Its *irony* was *venomous.*

8. The spaniel displayed a *precocious affinity* for water.
9. *Levity* lightens *prosaic* tasks.
10. His giving is *munificent*, but it is subject to *stringent* rules.

UNIT 5

1. Why the *languid* sigh and *disconsolate* air?
2. The excuse was neither *trivial* nor *trite*.
3. *Transient* tufts of cloud formed a *droll*, distorted face in the sky.
4. Her *spontaneous* good humor makes others like her and her *punctilious* habits make them trust her.
5. A half-*querulous*, half-*pugnacious* look gathered in his eyes.
6. The *precipitous* slope of the mountain provided a *formidable* obstacle.
7. The *plebeian* delights of rural life are by no means *despicable*.
8. She is so *competent* that she seems *omniscient*.
9. He appeared *austere* in the *oblique* light of the old-fashioned lamp.
10. The editors of the *defunct* magazine were too *mercenary*.

UNIT 6

1. The *clairvoyant* believes in *apparitions*.
2. The *alien* sketched the *contour* of a mountain range in Europe.
3. Do you *deprecate cupidity?*
4. We *exhorted* him to avoid *duplicity*.
5. Do you *concede* the beauty of this style of *façade?*
6. Circumstances will *exonerate* him in spite of anyone's *bias*.
7. It was easy to *cajole* him into *dissipating* his energy in foolish ways.
8. False *alibis exasperate* a judge.
9. They finally *elicited* from him a confession of the plan to *disrupt* our club.
10. *Anguish* over her husband's death slowly *emaciated* her once-attractive face.

UNIT 7

1. He was *niggardly* in granting permits, but he never had to *revoke* one.
2. The *reticent* secretary *scrutinized* every visitor.
3. "'Twas a land *transfigured*," he recited and his face went *pallid* because he had forgotten the next phrase.
4. Are girls more apt to *prevaricate* than boys? Are they more inclined to *vacillate*?
5. His *pious* character will *vindicate* him in time.
6. Her ambitions were *vitiated* because she was not *provident* enough.
7. His sudden decision to *renounce* his career rendered his friends *inarticulate* with surprise.
8. *Intermittent* breezes made the hot day seem less *monotonous*.
9. It *gratified* the nurse to see that her *juvenile* patient was better.
10. There was a *skeptical* look in his *protuberant* eyes.

UNIT 8

1. "I trust your *veracity*," he answered with a *benign* smile.
2. You are too *complacent* about the *utility* of your product.
3. She had a strange *presentiment* that the cabinetmaker was *culpable*.
4. His *cogent* manner was a *subterfuge*.
5. The promptness with which *retribution* overtook the man was *incredible*.
6. Her father thought the *pseudonym inane*.
7. The idea that his *prostration* was due entirely to heat was a *fallacy*.
8. His fit of *irresolution* ended in an *eccentric* course of action.
9. *Indolence* led him to neglect the *incipient* stages of the ailment.
10. It seemed *futile* to hope that such a *metamorphosis* could take place.

UNIT 9

1. *Indictment* of the leader started an *altercation*.
2. *Confiscation* will only *aggravate* the general dissatisfaction.
3. Orders *inundated* the company in *prodigious* numbers.
4. His wife would not *sanction* the *hazards* of flying.
5. The witness gave an *abridged* account *corroborating* the report.
6. He *acquiesces* in our beliefs about the *resurrection*.
7. *Culinary* training teaches one to *garnish* food attractively.
8. He has an *incorrigible* dislike for *diffident* persons.
9. *Inscrutable* joy made him more *obsequious*.
10. *Inveterate* fears surged up in him because he knew how *inexorable* the underworld could be.

UNIT 10

1. The G-men seemed almost *ubiquitous*, so great was their *vigilance*.
2. When there is a kidnaping to solve they are *implacable* and unbelievably *ingenious*.
3. *Belligerent* dictators think *carnage* is glorious.
4. The fighter's *lucrative* career ended in *oblivion*.
5. The *pernicious* idea that his race is superior is rank *heresy*.
6. The *miscreant* found no *respite* from his foes.
7. The *intrepid* halfback let his enthusiasm for football become a *detriment* scholastically.
8. He grew *morose* as he watched the *interment* of the bodies.
9. The man's *laconic* comments showed a *sanguine* attitude.
10. What is the *ostensible* reason for his *implacable* dislike?

THE VILLAIN OF PART TWO

Try devising "chapters" about the Villain of Part Two — or some of the class may write up the Hero while the others work on the Villain. The paragraphs may take the form of military citations or rogue's gallery descriptions.

Make a list of words pertaining to courts, criminals, trials, and the law in Part Two. Concoct a story employing some of them.

DIVISION TEST

Find the number of the definition that goes with each word.

A.

1. fortitude
2. prerogative

3. restitution
4. sequence
5. tenacity
6. opulence
7. precision
8. rancor
9. shambles
10. tranquillity

1. exactness
2. intense spitefulness or en-mity
3. courage (passive); endurance
4. scene of devastation
5. calmness, serenity
6. a right or privilege
7. nervousness
8. a tendency to hold fast
9. a bitter medicine
10. restoration, making amends
11. great riches, wealth
12. a series or order of succession

B.

1. affront
2. denizen
3. docket
4. illusion
5. irony

6. alien
7. bias

8. catalepsy
9. cupidity
10. façade

1. (mild) sarcasm
2. a foreigner or stranger
3. a tendency to fall in love
4. a deliberate insult
5. a fit (in which muscles stiffen and a person appears dead)
6. the chief front of a building
7. an abnormal desire to get wealth
8. an inclination or prejudice
9. an inhabitant or citizen
10. a shop near a wharf
11. a list of cases for trial
12. something deceptive or unreal a deception

C.

1. fluctuation	1. false teaching
2. irresolution	2. a foreboding
3. presentiment	3. a state of forgetfulness or of being forgotten
4. retribution	4. a wild uproar; a place of disorder
5. utility	5. the act of presenting or returning
6. abeyance	6. punishment or requital
7. heresy	7. watchfulness, caution
8. oblivion	8. indecision, vacillation
9. vigilance	9. usefulness
10. pandemonium	10. a holding or keeping inactive for a time; suspension
	11. (accumulated) wisdom
	12. rise and fall, a rolling to and fro

D.

1. allege	1. to come to a climax, reach the highest point
2. badger	2. to revive or bring back to life
3. conciliate	3. to violate or encroach upon
4. culminate	4. to declare, assert
5. dilate	5. to decorate or adorn
6. exaggerate	6. to enlarge or swell
7. infringe	7. to delay, postpone (from day to day)
8. jeopardize	8. to move slowly, slow down
9. procrastinate	9. to tease, annoy
10. resuscitate	10. to endanger
	11. to overstate, magnify
	12. to pacify, reconcile

E.

1. cajole
2. deprecate
3. dissipate
4. embezzle
5. exhort
6. gratify
7. prevaricate
8. revoke
9. vacillate
10. vitiate

1. to fall in value
2. to take by fraud
3. to please or afford pleasure to
4. to debase or render worthless
5. to disapprove of
6. to waver or be changeable
7. to urge, advise earnestly
8. to coax, wheedle, or deceive by flattery
9. to vary from the truth, quibble
10. to have a good time
11. to squander or scatter
12. to call back (a power or privilege); cancel or repeal

F.

1. acquiesce
2. corroborate
3. inundate
4. abridge
5. accelerate
6. appall
7. acquit
8. bequeath
9. depreciate
10. discriminate

1. to condense, shorten
2. to set free, declare not guilty
3. to verify or confirm
4. to decide quickly
5. to make a distinction or observe differences
6. to agree (by not objecting)
7. to quiet down
8. to flood or flow over
9. to increase the speed
10. to give by will
11. to decrease (in value)
12. to horrify, dismay

G.

1. alacrity
2. coincidence
3. consternation
4. dilemma
5. epithet
6. capricious

7. facile
8. impetuous
9. insidious
10. mellifluous

1. treacherous, deceitful
2. subject to whims, changeable
3. a shoulder ornament
4. swift, rapid
5. horror, dismay, panic
6. a descriptive title or appellation
7. rash, hasty, headlong
8. honeyed
9. a predicament, plight
10. easily done, skillful
11. eager readiness, briskness
12. an occurrence which matches remarkably and unexpectedly some other event or circumstance

H.

1. morbid
2. prosaic
3. stringent
4. venomous
5. wizened

6. competent
7. disconsolate

8. formidable
9. inflexible
10. mercenary

1. poisonous or malicious
2. hard to overcome; menacing
3. unwholesome, diseased
4. capable, qualified
5. actuated chiefly by desire for money (or reward)
6. shriveled, withered
7. incapable of yielding or bending
8. sad, dejected
9. dull, commonplace
10. well-written
11. strict, rigid, severe
12. having to do with soldiers or an army

1. plebeian
2. punctilious
3. spontaneous

4. trite
5. water-logged
6. intermittent
7. niggardly
8. pious
9. reticent

10. vicious

1. exact in conduct; particular
2. smooth, velvety
3. occurring at intervals; periodic
4. harmful, evil
5. godly, religious
6. dark-colored, ill-smelling
7. stale, worn out
8. inclined to be silent, reserved
9. water-soaked (until it will no longer float)
10. stingy, miserly
11. common, ordinary
12. arising from within; natural; self-generated

J.

1. benign
2. complacent
3. eccentric
4. inane
5. incredible
6. diffident
7. inscrutable
8. obsequious
9. belligerent
10. implacable

1. unbelievable
2. shy, timid, modest
3. warlike, quarrelsome
4. kindly, gentle
5. (too) submissive, servile
6. slow, deliberate
7. relentless, irreconcilable
8. self-satisfied
9. mysterious, incomprehensible
10. queer, odd, or peculiar
11. proud, haughty
12. empty, senseless

SUPPLEMENTARY TEST

This test is based on words introduced in the illustrative sentences and small-type notes.

Find the number of the definition that goes with each word:

A.

1. allegation
2. acme
3. quandary
4. audacity

5. innuendo
6. torpor

7. chaos

8. perspicacity
9. sequel
10. abattoir

1. confusion or disorder
2. boldness or daring
3. keenness of penetration
4. an assertion, that which is asserted
5. a wise decision
6. a dilemma or state of perplexity
7. something which follows (necessarily); continuation
8. a slaughterhouse or shambles
9. an insinuation
10. a dressing room
11. sluggishness, numbness, dullness
12. the highest point or culmination

B.

1. animus
2. commiseration
3. tyrant
4. lassitude
5. punctilio
6. cliché
7. specter

8. culprit
9. alias

10. epitome

1. pity, compassion
2. exactness in conduct or forms
3. wretchedness
4. an offender
5. a proverb or wise saying
6. a summary or summing up
7. an oppressive monarch or despot
8. a ghost or apparition
9. hostile intention; moving spirit
10. weariness
11. an assumed name
12. a hackneyed literary phrase

1. truculent
2. posterior
3. rancid
4. prolix
5. precipitate
6. pecuniary

7. peremptory
8. bellicose
9. punctual
10. petulant

1. financial, pertaining to money
2. enlarged, swollen
3. quarrelsome, inclined to fight
4. fierce, savage
5. eager to make peace
6. positive, dictatorial, imperative
7. cross, ill-humored
8. sudden, rash, overhasty
9. tedious, wordy, verbose
10. prompt, done at the exact moment
11. chemically sour
12. rear, later, situated behind

D.

1. evanescent
2. banal

3. puerile

4. parsimonious
5. infallible
6. utilitarian
7. quiescent
8. propitious
9. uxorious
10. nefarious

1. saintly or angelic
2. valuing things on the basis of practical usefulness
3. favorable, of favorable influence
4. childish
5. very wicked
6. commonplace, hackneyed
7. incapable of error
8. belonging to the working class
9. stingy, miserly
10. excessively submissive to one's wife
11. calm, tranquil, inactive
12. fading quickly, fleeting

E.

1. disparage
2. mortify
3. diversify
4. sequester
5. facilitate

1. to follow in haste
2. to go before or ahead of
3. to make amends or reparation
4. to vary, give variety to
5. to hurl headlong, bring to a crisis

6. precede

7. languish
8. precipitate
9. rescind

10. atone

6. to humiliate or humble painfully
7. to enjoy music immensely
8. to droop or pine away
9. to seclude or cause to withdraw into obscurity
10. to speak slightingly of
11. to repeal or make void
12. to make less difficult

CAN YOU PRONOUNCE THEM?

Being able to pronounce words correctly is as important today as knowing what they mean. Below are some of the most treacherous words from Part Two. The location of each by page number is given in order that you may look back if you are in doubt.

The pronunciation of all basic words is given in the list at the back of the book.

WORD WEALTH

PART THREE

It Often Happens

1. Writers and scientists __?__.

2. Dynamite charges __?__.

3. A court decides to __?__ the body.

4. One's dreams and plans come to full __?__.

5. One pays __?__ to a superior mind.

6. Life reaches an __?__ for someone.

PRETEST

Find the number of the definition that goes with each word.

VERBS

1. abscond	1. to belittle
2. cavil	2. to work together
3. collaborate	3. to flow forth or originate
4. condone	4. to make a musical sound
5. construe	5. to flee secretly
6. contemplate	6. to dig up; disinter
7. demur	7. to plot secretly
8. deter	8. to quibble
9. detonate	9. to restrain through fear
10. disparage	10. to interpret
11. emanate	11. to object or hesitate
12. exhume	12. to explode (loudly, suddenly)
	13. to forgive (especially by seeming to overlook)
	14. to intend or to meditate

NOUNS

1. arrogance	1. (acts of) respect, loyalty
2. audacity	2. respect, courteous submission
3. calumny	3. a puzzle
4. cartel	4. boldness
5. deference	5. an internal injection
6. dissension	6. shrewdness
7. elixir	7. strife, discord
8. enigma	8. slander, false accusation
9. exuberance	9. haughty pride
10. fruition	10. combination to control prices
11. homage	11. a medicinal liquid
12. hypocrisy	12. a situation from which there is no escape; a deadlock
13. impasse	13. a bearing of fruit, realization
	14. abundance, overflowing supply
	15. pretense of being what one is not, sham

STUDY GUIDE—VERBS

1. ABSCOND . . . to flee secretly, especially to avoid arrest

The treasurer tried to abscond with all the money.

2. CAVIL . . . to quibble or find fault without good reason

She would begin to cavil when she could not have her own way.
These cavils relieved her feelings.

Cavil also means *to raise foolish or frivolous objections.*

3. COLLABORATE . . . . to work together

Two authors collaborated in writing "The Valiant."
The collaboration of Gilbert and Sullivan resulted in a series of light operas.
Collaboration with the enemy was severely punished.

Note: *Collaborator*, usually a scientific or literary co-worker, was applied after World War II to those in liberated countries who had co-operated actively with the enemy. Cf. *collusion.*

4. CONDONE . to forgive (especially by seeming to overlook)

Untidiness is a fault which employers are not willing to condone.
His mother should not condone such deviltry.

5. CONSTRUE . . . . to interpret

He failed to speak to me. Shall I construe this as an affront?
It is construable in two or three ways.

6. CONTEMPLATE . . . . . . to intend or to meditate

We contemplate moving to another part of the city in the spring.
The hour spent in quiet contemplation was not wasted.
There is a contemplative [accent the second syllable] air about her all the time.

7. DEMUR . . . . to object or hesitate

Seeing what was ahead, Alice thought best to demur.
There was another demurrer in the group, Vera.

A *demurrer* in law is a plea for the dismissal of a case.

8. DETER . . . . to restrain through fear; discourage

The fate of his comrade will deter him.

Is capital punishment as effective a deterrent as life imprisonment?

9. DETONATE (DET-ŏ-nāte) . . **to explode (loudly, suddenly)**

The stuff detonates with a roar.
The detonation of a stick of dynamite can be heard for miles.

10. DISPARAGE . . . . . **to belittle, speak slightingly of**

The coach was too wise to disparage a beginner's attempts.
Disparagement would have discouraged a good prospect.
In French, *disparage* once meant *to marry unequally.*

11. EMANATE . . . . **to flow forth or originate**

The deepest courtesy emanates from within.
The energy in coal was once an emanation from the sun.
Light is emanative.

12. EXHUME . . **to dig up (something that has been buried);**
disinter

He wanted to exhume the body for an autopsy. The court ordered the exhumation.
Exhume comes from Latin *ex, out of,* plus *humus, ground.*

STUDY GUIDE—NOUNS

1. ARROGANCE . . . . **haughty pride**

The coach could not endure the captain's arrogance.
Success made the man arrogant.
The President was accused of arrogating (assuming unduly) to himself more power than the Constitution intended.
Other forms of pride: *presumption, disdainfulness, superciliousness.*

2. AUDACITY . . . . **boldness**

Lew Sarett had the audacity to walk unarmed past a grizzly on a narrow ledge.
Byrd was an audacious (ô-DAY-shŭs) explorer.
Review *effrontery* (II, 1). Watch for *temerity* (rash boldness).

3. CALUMNY . . . **slander, false accusation (willfully made)**

Few politicians escape calumny.

His enemies calumniated him, and their calumnious stories were believed.

Ugly words all: *defamations, aspersions, innuendoes* (II, 2).

4. CARTEL . . . . combination to control output and prices

Several large cartels were operating before the war.

A *cartel* is similar to a pool or trust but international in scope.

5. DEFERENCE . . . . respect, courteous submission

He showed deference for his father's opinion, even though he could not agree.

His deferential manner made men like him.

Veneration is the highest degree of respect and reverence.

6. DISSENSION . . . . strife, discord

The party was upheaved and split by internal dissension.

Six senators dissent (disagree) from the majority report of the committee. They will give the reasons for their dissent publicly.

Query: Do you know what *Dissenters* were in England after the Reformation?

7. ELIXIR (ē-LICK-sĕr) . . . . a medicinal liquid

The *elixir of life* was an imaginary liquid which would prolong life indefinitely.

Nature's elixir flows into trees and plants each spring and transforms them.

In poems and stories an elixir has magic properties.

8. ENIGMA (ē-NIG-må) . . . . a puzzle

The fate of the missing dog is the enigma of the week.

No one understood the teacher's enigmatic remark.

9. EXUBERANCE . . . . . abundance, overflowing supply

The exuberance of spring is inspiring.

How can one help feeling exuberant (abounding in good spirits) in May?

Do you wish to live exuberantly?

Exuberance is used especially of good spirits.

Cf. *effusive, prolific, luxuriant.*

10. FRUITION . . . . **bearing of fruit, realization**

The honor brought the fruition of a lifetime of hopes, fears, dreams, and persevering efforts.

11. HOMAGE (HŎM-ăj) . . . . **(acts of) respect, loyalty**

The gift expressed the homage of a grateful son.
Such heroism deserves our homage.
Homage is respect shown by outward actions.

12. HYPOCRISY . . **a pretense of being what one is not, sham**

His hypocrisy soon appeared.
How humans do hate a hypocrite!
A hypocritical smile is no promise of friendship at all.
A *hypocrite* is an *impostor, dissembler, cheat, liar.*

13. IMPASSE (ĭm-PAS, *a* as in *ask*) . . **a situation from which there is no escape; a deadlock**

The strike situation has reached an impasse.
His friends and money gone and his health broken, he faced an impasse.

FIRST SENTENCE SET

Copy the *italicized* words and opposite each write an appropriate definition.

1. There was no one to *condone* his deed when he *absconded* with money.
2. We cannot *collaborate* if either of us is going to *cavil* about who actually did the work.
3. I *contemplate* no action which an enemy might *construe* as cowardly.
4. She *demurred* at the idea of *exhuming* the body.
5. He often *disparaged* the man's judgment. Rebukes failed to *deter* him.
6. The spark which *detonates* the charge *emanates* from a battery behind the boulder.
7. His *arrogance* is exceeded only by his *audacity.*

8. *Dissension* over his father's will led to the *calumny* which you heard.
9. In spite of my *deference* for his opinion, I refuse to believe that such an *elixir* exists.
10. The operations of the *cartel* are an *enigma* to us all.
11. Enterprises launched in the *exuberance* of youth came to *fruition* years later.
12. He faced an *impasse* because he had not the *hypocrisy* to pay unfelt *homage*.

SECOND SENTENCE SET

1. His *arrogance* made it impossible for them to *collaborate*.
2. She had the *audacity* to *condone* her fault.
3. A gentleman would not *disparage* anyone with such *calumny*.
4. *Deference* for his mother's feelings *deterred* him.
5. The *dissension* was *construed* as an indication of enmity.
6. She *demurred* at the idea of encouraging *cartels*.
7. I do not *contemplate* having any need for such an *elixir*.
8. The reason why he *absconded* was an *enigma* for several days, but it turned out that he faced an absolute *impasse* in his business.
9. Why do you *cavil* at such refreshing *exuberance?*
10. *Exhuming* the body kept the other plot from coming to *fruition*.
11. Punctured *hypocrisy detonates* like dynamite.
12. *Homage emanates* from the king's subjects.

OBITER DICTA

Assume that you are a judge, a legislator, or an editorial writer. Compose an opinion on a recent murder, political scandal, legislative program, or some other current issue which involves disparagement, calumny, dissension, hypocrisy or an impasse. You may cavil, condone, or demur. Perhaps something should be exhumed.

Couples

Which verb in the pretest does each of these nouns suggest?

Slaves?	English exams?
Governor or President?	Invitations?
Garbage?	Errors?
Sins?	The attic?
Strikes?	Despots?

PRETEST

Find the number of the definition that goes with each word.

VERBS

1.	emancipate	1.	to burn to ashes
2.	expiate	2.	to seize forcibly (and wrongly)
3.	impale	3.	to pierce or thrust through
4.	impeach	4.	to serve as go-between
5.	incinerate	5.	to become sick
6.	mediate	6.	to yield temporarily to circumstances; to avoid committing oneself
7.	paraphrase	7.	to exercise self-control
8.	pique	8.	to correct, set right
9.	reciprocate	9.	to displease, wound the pride of; stimulate
10.	rectify	10.	to atone or make amends for
11.	relegate	11.	to send away or banish
12.	temporize	12.	to call in question, discredit
13.	usurp	13.	to pay back, exchange favors
		14.	to liberate, release (from bondage)
		15.	to state in one's own words

ADJECTIVES

1.	amorous	1.	conceited, self-assertive
2.	astute	2.	fortunate, well-chosen
3.	authentic	3.	loving, fond
4.	bumptious	4.	unintentional
5.	credulous	5.	harmless
6.	erratic	6.	genuine
7.	fastidious	7.	smooth and velvety
8.	felicitous	8.	daintily particular
9.	heinous	9.	hostile, unfriendly
10.	inadvertent	10.	shrewd, crafty, keen of mind
11.	inimical	11.	too willing to believe
12.	innocuous	12.	capable of going without food for long periods
		13.	hateful, atrocious
		14.	irregular, unstable

1. EMANCIPATE . . . **to liberate, release (from bondage)**

Electricity emancipates a woman from household drudgery.

Lincoln is called the Great Emancipator because of the part he played in the emancipation of the slaves.

2. EXPIATE . . . . . . **to atone or make amends for**

Years of toil will not expiate his crime.

His expiation took the form of a bouquet of flowers.

3. IMPALE . . . . **to pierce or thrust through**

Watch Bobby carefully impale a fresh worm on the hook and cast in his line.

The savages followed the impalement and burning of their captive with a wild dance.

Impaled by his own admissions, the prisoner was soon convicted.

Transfix is a synonym of *impale:* She stood transfixed (as if pierced) at the horrible sight.

4. IMPEACH . . . . . . **to call in question, discredit**

You cannot impeach his honesty.

Washington was a man of unimpeachable (irreproachable) honor.

Impeachment (trial for misconduct in public office) of the governor was demanded.

5. INCINERATE . . . . **to burn to ashes**

It is best to incinerate garbage.

This incineration is effected in an incinerator.

Cremation is one way to dispose of a corpse.

Cremate means the same as *incinerate,* but it applies to corpses and is done in *crematories.*

Note: Have you read "The Cremation of Sam McGee"?

6. MEDIATE . . **to serve as go-between or harmonizing agent**

A minister and a lawyer were asked to mediate in the bus strike. They formed a mediation board which had power to settle the dispute.

Cf. *mediator, intermediary.*

See also *arbitrate — to settle* (a dispute by discussion or by means of an umpire).

7. PARAPHRASE . . . . . to state in one's own words

The newspapers paraphrase the decisions of the Supreme Court.
"Paraphrase this passage from the speech for tomorrow," the
teacher said.

A *paraphrase* is a "translation" or restatement of a passage in other words.

8. PIQUE (PEEK) . . . . displease, to wound the pride of; stimulate

The insinuation will pique her.
The book piqued his curiosity because of its color.
He found her in a state of pique (mild anger).
The piquant flavor (agreeably sharp or keen) of the punch was
to my liking.

These are valuable words because hard to define. See a dictionary for more
complete definitions.

9. RECIPROCATE . . . to pay back or exchange favors or courtesies

Now that the Briggses have entertained you, you must reciprocate in a few weeks.
Reciprocation of presents at Christmas has reached enormous
proportions.

Query: What are reciprocal trade agreements? What is reciprocity in
trade?

10. RECTIFY . . . . to correct, set right

The storekeeper promised to rectify his error. Rectification
proved difficult.
"Ring in redress [righting of wrongs] to all mankind."
The leaders of the revolution were determined to redress the
evils of the government.

Rectitude is moral uprightness or integrity.

11. RELEGATE . . . . to send away or banish

We shall relegate "Spike" to the basement until he can let the
cat alone.
The relegation of old cars to junk yards makes the highways
quieter.

Relegation is usually to a worse place.

---

12. TEMPORIZE . . to yield temporarily to circumstances; to avoid committing oneself

Politicians frequently temporize. So do girls who have two Romeos.

13. USURP (ŭ-ZÛRP) . . . . to seize forcibly (and wrongly)

A beggar tried to usurp the throne.
Brother usurped sister's place at the table.
The usurper of a kingship often makes his act of usurpation seem perfectly legal. Can you cite an example?
You may *usurp* only an office, a place, powers, or rights.

STUDY GUIDE—ADJECTIVES

1. AMOROUS . . . . loving, fond

They lavish amorous glances on each other.
Such amorousness makes everything else seem unimportant.

2. ASTUTE . . . . shrewd, crafty, keen of mind

The quarterback was astute enough to sense the weaknesses of the other team.
The astuteness of one G-man enabled him to escape and led to the capture of five kidnapers.

3. AUTHENTIC . . . genuine, from an authoritative source

The will is authentic.
The historical authenticity (correctness) of the novel makes it worth reading.
We have affidavits to authenticate (prove the genuineness of) the letter from Hawthorne to his wife.

4. BUMPTIOUS . . . . conceited, self-assertive

College sophomores have a treatment for bumptious freshmen.
It removes their bumptiousness in one application.

5. CREDULOUS . . . . too willing to believe

Ignorant persons are often credulous.
The credulousness (credulity) of the old man was amazing.
Cf. *incredible* (unbelievable).

---

6. ERRATIC . . . . **irregular, unstable**

It is hard to tell what an erratic person is going to do next.
His erratic habits alienated the confidence of his friends.
Recall: *err, errant, errata* (I, 2), etc.

7. FASTIDIOUS . . . . **daintily particular**

He is very fastidious in selecting his clothes.
Her fastidiousness about where she eats annoys her husband.
Fastidious also means *overnice* or just *fussy*. Cf. *punctilious* (II, 5).

8. FELICITOUS . . . . **fortunate, well-chosen**

You arrived at a felicitous moment, for I just received a check
from home.
Sinclair Lewis expresses himself with rare felicitousness.
Do not forget to felicitate (congratulate) the bridegroom.
Marital *felicity* (happiness) means married bliss or blissful marriage.

9. HEINOUS (HAY-nŭs) . . . . **hateful, atrocious**

How could she be guilty of such a heinous crime?
The heinousness of the offense cannot be overstated.
Cf. *odious* (hateful), *nefarious* (wicked), *villainous* (wicked), *flagrant* (openly
wicked), *atrocious* (blackly wicked), *monstrous* (hideous, huge).

10. INADVERTENT . . . . **unintentional**

An inadvertent error in addition caused considerable trouble.
He lost a friend through inadvertence (negligence).
Advertise, to turn (attention) *toward*, is a relative.

11. INIMICAL . . . . **hostile, unfriendly**

The manufacturer was inimical to labor unions.
Late hours are inimical to good school work.

12. INNOCUOUS . . . . **harmless**

Kittens are innocuous creatures.
The innocuousness of most American snakes is not generally
realized.
Noxious means harmful or injurious: Carbon monoxide is a noxious gas.

FIRST SENTENCE SET

Copy the *italicized* words and opposite each write an appropriate definition.

1. The pirate sought to *expiate* his crimes by *emancipating* all of his slaves.
2. She could not *impeach* his motives after he tried to *rectify* the mistake.
3. He *incinerated* rather than cooked the fowl when he *impaled* it on a spit over the fire and then forgot it.
4. The man's unwillingness to *mediate piqued* the labor leader.
5. You may *reciprocate* by showing me how to *paraphrase* a poem.
6. Father decided to *temporize* when Mother proposed to *relegate* the dog to the kitchen.
7. A dictator is too *astute* to *usurp* absolute power openly and immediately.
8. The *amorous* deeds and *felicitous* speeches of the hero in the story are not historically *authentic*.
9. Because he is *credulous*, flattery makes him unbearably *bumptious*.
10. His *erratic* tastes would irritate a *fastidious* person.
11. The offense is less *heinous* because it was *inadvertent*.
12. Criticisms of the government that would be considered *innocuous* in this country are deemed highly *inimical* in some countries.

SECOND SENTENCE SET

1. His *amorous* glances at other girls *piqued* her.
2. It was *astute* of the speaker to express his desire to *emancipate* labor from long hours and low pay.
3. The idea of *impeaching* the governor was based on reports which are not *authentic*.
4. The coach *relegated* the youth to the bench because he was too *bumptious* to co-operate with the team.

5. You are *credulous* if you think the man was really *impaled* by the spear.
6. *Erratic* efforts are *inimical* to success.
7. She *paraphrased* the passage in graceful and *fastidious* language.
8. The man picked to *mediate* was a *felicitous* selection.
9. The clerk tried to *rectify* his *heinous* mistake.
10. An *inadvertent* remark showed that he intended to *expiate* his sin if he could.
11. Her *innocuous* remark revealed a desire to *temporize*.
12. We do not care whether they *reciprocate* if they insist on *usurping* our rights.
13. The decision to *incinerate* the city's garbage was a wise one.

LIFE AT HOME

Brothers, sisters, parents, cousins, boyfriends, girlfriends, and pets make good practice material for this unit and for a bit of review. Discuss their traits. Tell of a prank perpetrated by or on one of them. Did the victim retaliate — or merely reciprocate?

Opposites

Can you supply one from the pretest for each of the words below?

Veracity   Crafty, artful

Tradition or established custom   Clear, distinct

Prejudice   Brave

Celebrity   Reverent

Scarcity   Wordy, verbose

PRETEST

Find the number of the definition that goes with each word.

NOUNS

1. innovation	1. a principal city
2. metropolis	2. an (unfounded) preference
3. mortality	3. a broad, comprehensive view
4. nonentity	4. enthusiastic applause
5. overture	5. a new custom, device, or style
6. panorama	6. excess
7. paroxysm	7. a nobody
8. perjury	8. a complete change (of circumstances)
9. predilection	9. death (rate)
10. profusion	10. proper conduct; correctness of behavior
11. propriety	11. falsified testimony (in court)
12. surfeit	12. a sense of relief and release
13. vicissitude	13. an offer, proposition, or opening (of negotiations or of an opera)
	14. a spasm
	15. abundance

ADJECTIVES

1. lambent	1. very wicked
2. lugubrious	2. easily changing or very variable
3. mobile	3. suave, bland, oily, smooth
4. naïve	4. irreverent, blasphemous
5. nebulous	5. tiresome, wearying
6. nefarious	6. cowardly
7. pusillanimous	7. reclining or leaning
8. recumbent	8. softly radiant
9. sacrilegious	9. hazy, vague, shadowy
10. succinct	10. provisional, experimental
11. tentative	11. doleful, dismal
12. unctuous	12. quaint, unusual
	13. terse, concise
	14. artless, innocent

STUDY GUIDE—NOUNS

1. INNOVATION . . . . . **a new custom, device, or style**

The use of frozen-food lockers is a recent innovation.
Great men are innovators (bringers of new ways or customs).

2. METROPOLIS . . . . **a principal city**

Cleveland is an important metropolis.
Sauk Center did not have metropolitan ideas.

A *metropolis* is *principal* in terms of population and civilization.
Metropolis is Greek for *mother-city.* Cf. *cosmopolitan.*

3. MORTALITY . . . . **death (rate)**

Typhoid was once a disease of high mortality.
The infant mortality rate is high in Ethiopia.
He fell mortally (fatally) wounded.
His uncle is a mortician (undertaker).
Is European civilization moribund (in a dying condition)?

Death words (*mors, mortis = death*): *moribund, mortuary, post mortem.* Study
mortify, mortmain, amortize. Review *immortal(ity)* (I, 4).

4. NONENTITY . . . . **a nobody**

The person who holds the position is considered a nonentity.

5. OVERTURE . . **an offer, proposition, or opening (of negoti-
ations or of an opera)**

The strikers made overtures of peace.
The orchestra played the overture to *Carmen.*

6. PANORAMA . . . . . . **a broad, comprehensive view**

The panorama that unrolled as we drove along was magnificent.
The panorama of his whole life passed through his mind in a
few seconds.
A panoramic camera takes a series of views as it rotates.

The second *a* is pronounced as in *far.*
Other pan (*= all*) words: *panoply, Panhellenic, Pantheon, pantheism, panto-
mime, pandemonium* (II, 2).

7. PAROXYSM . . . . **a spasm**

Paroxysms of rage shake his little frame whenever he is informed
that it is time to go to bed.

8. PERJURY . . . . **falsified testimony (in court)**

The witness was guilty of perjury.

"At Love's perjuries, they say, Jove laughs."

He was too honest to perjure himself for any inducement. He simply would not be a perjurer.

9. PREDILECTION . . . . . **an (unfounded) preference or a partiality**

She has a predilection for tall boys with dark hair and brown eyes.

Jerome imagined that the coach would be predisposed (inclined beforehand) in his favor because of his curly hair.

Predilection is the opposite of *prejudice*, an unreasonable dislike.

10. PROFUSION . . . . **abundance**

Vegetation grows in the wildest profusion near the equator.

He overwhelmed us with profuse apologies for oversleeping.

Profuse suggests *lavish* and *prodigal*.

11. PROPRIETY . . . **proper conduct; correctness of behavior**

An etiquette book discusses matters of propriety.

The propriety of asking boys for dates was discussed.

Cf. *decorum* (II, I).

12. SURFEIT . . . . **excess**

Surfeit of success made him vain.

A Thanksgiving dinner surfeits the stoutest eater.

The cloying pleasures of an ancient palace are vividly described in the book.

The market is glutted with used cars.

Degrees of satiety: 1. *suffice* 2. *satisfy* 3. *satiate* (I, 6) or *sate* 4. *surfeit* 5. *cloy* (sicken with sweetness) 6. *glut* (fill disgustingly full)

13. VICISSITUDE . . . **a complete change (of circumstances)**

The vicissitudes of life did not disturb his quiet complacency.

Adolescence is full of vicissitudes.

The plural, which is more often used than the singular, means *ups and downs* or *irregular changes*.

STUDY GUIDE—ADJECTIVES

1. LAMBENT . . . . **softly radiant**

A lambent light gleamed in her eyes.
Lambent moonlight flooded the room.
The dictionary gives other meanings of *lambent*.

2. LUGUBRIOUS . . . . . . **doleful, dismal, funereal**

"The Song of the Shirt" is a lugubrious poem.
There are some who enjoy the lugubriousness of a funeral.
Do you ever use a lugubrious tone of voice?

3. MOBILE (MO-bil) . . . . **easily changing or very variable**

Her features are mobile, her ideas are mobile, and her tastes are mobile.
The mobility of his countenance showed that he was agitated.
An immobile face betrays no feeling.
Mobilize means *to call* (move) *into service,* especially troops. Cf. *immobilize.*

4. NAÏVE (nä-EVE) . . . . **artless, innocent**

The Chinaman looked very naïve.
She smiled with the naïveté [nȧ-eve-TAY] (innocent simplicity) of a child.
Cf. *ingenuous, unaffected, unsophisticated.*

5. NEBULOUS . . . . **hazy, vague, shadowy**

He was a dreamer whose head was perpetually swimming with nebulous projects.
The nebulousness of his farm policy caused him to lose the election.
Query: What are the starry nebulae of the Milky Way? What is the nebular hypothesis?

6. NEFARIOUS . . . . **very wicked**

Kidnaping is a nefarious crime. Because of its nefariousness the Lindbergh law was passed.
Cronies of *nefarious: heinous* (Unit 2), *iniquitous, atrocious* (II, 10), *detestable.*

7. PUSILLANIMOUS . . . . cowardly

It was pusillanimous to try to shift the blame for failure to someone else.

It comes from the Latin words *pusillus, petty,* and *animus, soul.*

8. RECUMBENT . . . . reclining or leaning

The recumbent figure on the couch was my aunt.

Noun forms: *recumbency, recumbence.*

9. SACRILEGIOUS (săk-rĭ-LEE-jŭs) . . irreverent, blasphemous

In Scotland it was once considered sacrilegious to whistle on Sunday.

The use of an organ in a church was once deemed a sacrilege.

Sacrilegiousness was punished severely in Geneva during the sixteenth century.

10. SUCCINCT . . . . terse, concise

The answer was admirably succinct.

Succinctness is a quality to cultivate. It is the opposite of prolixity, verbosity, and garrulousness.

Partners of *succinct: laconic* (brief, II, 10); *sententious* (compact or salty). Review *brevity* (I, 2).

11. TENTATIVE . . . . . . provisional, experimental

This is a tentative draft of the plan.

Our tentative method is to separate the two ingredients by gravity, but we hope ultimately to find a chemical process.

12. UNCTUOUS . . . . suave, bland, oily, smooth

His unctuous, saintly manner elicits favors which he does not deserve.

The unctuousness of the clergyman was both comforting and soothing.

The orator spoke with great unction (a manner which betokens deep emotion).

FIRST SENTENCE SET

Copy the *italicized* words and opposite each write an appropriate definition.

1. Parking meters were an unwanted *innovation* in the *metropolis*.
2. *Mortality* removed a *nonentity* in politics.
3. That particular *overture* stirred *paroxysms* of rapture in his soul.
4. The juror's *predilection* for the witness vanished when he found that she was guilty of *perjury*.
5. The *vicissitudes* of fortune left him only a *profusion* of debts.
6. A sense of *surfeit* came over him as *panorama* followed panorama in endless succession.
7. He exceeded the bounds of *propriety* in mentioning so many *lugubrious* details.
8. Her *lambent* eyes and *mobile* features made her a striking personality.
9. They are too *naïve* to realize how *nefarious* the plan is.
10. Even *nebulous* fears serve to terrify a *pusillanimous* nature.
11. Was it *sacrilegious* to remain *recumbent* while the flag was passing by?
12. With *unctuous* courtesy he stated their *tentative* proposition in a form that was admirably *succinct*.

SECOND SENTENCE SET

1. Have you a *predilection* for *innovations?*
2. The *vicissitudes* of winter weather affected the southern *metropolis* very little.
3. Is the *mortality* lower for *unctuous* men?
4. He is a literary *nonentity*, full of *nebulous* dreams that are laughably *naïve*.
5. *Lambent* moonlight played mysteriously on the *panorama* before them.
6. *Paroxysms* of fear shook his *pusillanimous* frame.

7. It was *perjury* to say that he was in a *recumbent* position when found.
8. *Nefarious* trickery lurked beneath their *overtures*.
9. How could one feel *lugubrious* in the midst of such a *profusion* of flowers?
10. His sense of *propriety* would resent anything *sacrilegious*.
11. His *mobile* tastes sprang from a temperament often swept by *surfeit* of emotion.
12. His opinion of the *tentative* plan was *succinct* and pointed.

MUSIC AND DATES

A fitting opportunity is provided by this unit to discuss:

1. A concert you attended (and, we hope, enjoyed).
2. Dates and dating — or your preferences and dislikes in regard to dates.

Draw freely upon previous units for any words that you need — and a few you did not realize you needed until you looked back.

We Visit Africa

1. We arrived during the summer __?__.

2. The jungle trails proved __?__.

3. The luxuriance of tropical foliage stirred our __?__ appre-

   ciation.

4. We tried to study a tribe which was in the process of __?__.

5. The witch doctor, however, waved a __?__ and uttered

   an __?__.

6. Forming a __?__ with a neighboring tribe, he undertook to

   drive us out.

7. We could not linger because our orders were very --?--.

PRETEST

Find the number of the definition that goes with each word.

NOUNS

1. anathema
2. atoll
3. barrage
4. coalition
5. fetish

6. gestapo
7. incarnation
8. incubus
9. migration

10. paragon
11. patriarch
12. quisling
13. solstice

1. a moving or journey
2. a many-sided figure
3. a nightmare
4. a disgraceful failure
5. an object worshiped for its magical power
6. a traitor ruler
7. a perfect model or pattern
8. a coral island
9. point at which the sun is farthest from the equator
10. a solemn ban or curse
11. a combination or alliance
12. ruthless secret police
13. a volley (of missiles)
14. an aged wise man
15. embodiment (in human form)

ADJECTIVES

1. adroit
2. aesthetic
3. amphibious
4. captious
5. chimerical
6. exotic

7. explicit
8. ineffable
9. logistic
10. mediocre
11. relevant
12. sinuous

1. of medium quality
2. unspeakable, inexpressible
3. strange, foreign
4. clever, skillful
5. bright and shimmering
6. pertaining to the moving, quartering and supply of troops
7. pertinent
8. capable of relieving pain
9. fault-finding, hard to please
10. beauty-sensitive
11. twisting, winding, devious
12. definite, plain
13. fantastic, delusive
14. adapted to both land and water

STUDY GUIDE—NOUNS

1. ANATHEMA (à-NATH-ĕ-mà) . . . . a solemn ban or curse

Anathemas did not discourage the reformer.
His enemies like to anathematize the President.
An *execration* (II,9) is a *profane curse* — it has no religious sanction.

2. ATOLL (AT-ŏl) . . . . a coral island, usually in the Pacific

Tarawa is now one of the most famous of the Pacific atolls.
Atoll is a word which came into wide usage during World War II.

3. BARRAGE (pronounced like garage) . . volley (of missiles)

A barrage of rotten apples convinced the cow that small boys
are cruel and treacherous.
At dawn the enemy laid down an artillery barrage.
Shrapnel is a barrage of steel balls. Cf. *salvo* (I, 1) and *fusillade* (fū-zǐ-LADE)

4. COALITION . . a combination or alliance (of opposing
parties, usually temporary)

A coalition of conservative Republicans and Southern Democrats
defeated the measure in the Senate.
The crystals will coalesce (fuse, unite) if you heat them.
The new president proposed a coalescence of the two societies.
Cf. *consolidation, amalgamation;* and *miscegenation.*

5. FETISH (FEE-tǐsh) . an object worshiped for its magical power

Is it true that a sense of humor "is becoming something of a
fetish"?
Fetishism still prevails in parts of Africa.
Any object of unreasoning idolatrous devotion is a fetish.
Query: What are some civilized forms of fetishism?

6. GESTAPO (gĕ-STAH-po) . . . . . ruthless secret police

Gestapo methods were employed against enemy aliens.
Gestapo is an acronym for Geheime Staats Polizei, a Nazi organization which
became a symbol of terroristic methods.

7. INCARNATION . . . . . embodiment (in human form)

Uncle Joe is the incarnation of mischievousness.

His son acts like a demon incarnate.

Latin *caro, carnis* means *flesh.* See note under *carnage* (II, 10.)

8. INCUBUS . . . . . **a nightmare or any depressing burden**

An incubus of fear haunted the killer day and night.

France was staggering under an incubus of debt.

Accent the first syllable.

9. MIGRATION . . . . **a moving or journey**

The migration of the desert tribe to the mountains took place because of drought.

Wild ducks migrate northward each spring. So do other migratory fowl.

A new home or a temporary abiding place is the object of a migration.

10. PARAGON . . . . **perfect model or pattern**

She is a paragon of beauty.

He is a paragon of courtesy.

11. PATRIARCH . . . . **an aged wise man**

The patriarch had lived in the desert all his life. He possessed the patriarchal wisdom of his ancient progenitors.

A *patriarch* is also the founder or head of a family.

12. QUISLING (KWIZ-ling) . . . . **a traitor ruler**

The usurper was a quizling.

The present ruler is a quisling because, even though he is a native, his primary loyalty is to a foreign power.

Quisling is one of the newest words derived from the name of a man. Cf. *boycott, cardigan, derrick, guillotine, shrapnel, nicotine.*

13. SOLSTICE . . . **point at which the sun is farthest from the equator**

The winter solstice (December 21 or 22) was only a few days off.

Solstice may mean simply *the furthest limit.*

Query: What are the dates of the summer solstice?

STUDY GUIDE—ADJECTIVES

1. ADROIT . . . . **clever, skillful**

His method of managing his sister was very adroit. He also possessed great adroitness in solving puzzles.

Synonyms of *adroit: dexterous, deft, ingenious.*

2. AESTHETIC . . . **beauty-sensitive; pertaining to a feeling for beauty**

Much has been written about the aesthetic aspects of literature.

Aesthetics is the science of the beautiful in nature or art.

3. AMPHIBIOUS . . . . . **adapted to both land and water**

Frogs and beavers are amphibious creatures.
The armed forces planned an amphibious operation.

Amphibious comes from the Greek *amphi, both kinds,* and *bios, life.*

4. CAPTIOUS . . . . **fault-finding, hard to please**

The invalid was captious. Her captiousness antagonized everyone.

The in-laws: *petulant, peevish, caviling, carping, hypercritical.*

5. CHIMERICAL (kĭ-MĔR-ĭ-kăl) . . . . **fantastic, delusive**

Her fears are as chimerical as the hallucinations of insanity.

A *chimera* (kĭ-MĒ-ra) is a frightful, foolish creature of the imagination.

6. EXOTIC . . . . **strange, foreign**

The odor of exotic flowers drifted in from the garden.

7. EXPLICIT . . . . **definite, plain**

The plan for the amphibious landing was unusually explicit.

8. INEFFABLE . . . . **unspeakable, inexpressible**

The ineffable stillness of evening slowly enveloped the scene.

Anything *ineffable* is too sacred for utterance.

9. LOGISTIC . . . **pertaining to the moving, quartering, and supply of troops**

The Quartermaster Corps provided logistic support.
Logistics is more complicated than it used to be.

10. MEDIOCRE . . . . . . of medium quality, commonplace

His singing is very mediocre.
Their lives were spent in quiet mediocrity.

11. RELEVANT . . pertinent; having to do with the case in hand

When we are discussing essays, almost any topic is relevant.
In Latin class, however, a remark about baseball is decidedly
irrelevant.
The relevance (relevancy) of the precedent was questioned.

12. SINUOUS . . . . twisting, winding, devious

Sinuous trails interlace the mountains to inveigle hikers. Because of this sinuousness (sinuosity) is is easy to get lost.
Sinus in Latin means *a curve.* A sinus in one's head is a natural cavity.

FIRST SENTENCE SET

Copy the *italicized* words and opposite each write an appropriate definition.

1. The postwar *coalition* of manufacturers drew an *anathema*
   from buyers.
2. Natives hurled a *barrage* of rocks from behind a heathen *fetish*
   when our forces first landed on the *atoll.*
3. The island *quisling* promptly organized a little *gestapo.*
4. The *patriarch* objected to the proposed *migration.*
5. The monster was to him the *incarnation* of evil, and its nearness among those *sinuous* streets haunted him like an
   incubus.
6. The *amphibious* plan created unusual *logistic* problems.
7. A *paragon* of loveliness, she spent the long days of the summer
   solstice among her *adroit* admirers.
8. When it comes to *aesthetic* factors, she is very *captious.*
9. His notions are *chimerical.* He must be more *explicit.*
10. Her tastes are *exotic,* her abilities *mediocre,* but her comments
    are *relevant.*
11. The *ineffable* beauty of the moonlit landscape awed us.

SECOND SENTENCE SET

1. It was *adroit* of the newspaper editors to form a *coalition* opposing *gestapo* methods.
2. Bird songs delight the *aesthetic* ear of the *patriarch*.
3. *Mediocre* playing makes any coach *captious*.
4. *Chimerical* dreams are *fetishes* by which he shapes his plans.
5. The charges against the local *quisling* were very *explicit*.
6. The *logistic* failures deserved *anathemas* from the high command.
7. A re-echoing *barrage* of gunfire broke the *ineffable* calmness of the night.
8. The reasons for planning the *migration* during the winter *solstice* were highly *relevant*.
9. The governor of the *atoll* looked like an *incarnation* of Uncle Sam.
10. The *sinuous* movements of *exotic* dancers dominated the dream.
11. The *incubus* of far-flung *amphibious* warfare hung over the Pacific for many months.
12. Who is the *paragon* of United States Presidents?

ALL AT SEA

Imagine yourself on an atoll in the Pacific and produce a paragraph about the joys and sorrows of your existence. You may be able to include relevant remarks about the island-hopping campaigns of 1941–1945.

A month in the mountains can be spent so as to employ ten or more of the words, particularly if your imagination is good and you are adroit in your selection of summer reading.

We Write a Story

1. The plot was suggested by an __?__ of ours two years ago.

2. It came to us during moments of __?__.

3. The __?__ or villain betrays himself by being too __?__.

4. The heroine traps him by being very __?__ also, thus encouraging him to talk.

5. The story states no moral, but it shows how character can __?__.

PRETEST

Find the number of the definition that goes with each word.

VERBS

1. assuage
2. converge
3. degenerate
4. extenuate
5. instigate
6. mitigate
7. mollify
8. negotiate

1. to make less serious, diminish
2. to appease or pacify
3. to collapse suddenly
4. to deteriorate, grow worse
5. to soothe, soften or lessen
6. to embarrass or annoy
7. to make milder or to lessen
8. to tend toward one point
9. to provoke or incite
10. to put through or to deal with

NOUNS

1. cynic
2. escapade
3. malefactor
4. plagiarism
5. reverie

6. vagary

1. an adventure or prank
2. the stealing of ideas
3. a mental wandering or whim
4. a fugitive or refugee
5. a sarcastic person who sees the worst in everything
6. belief in demon powers
7. a wrongdoer or criminal
8. deep musing; a daydream

ADJECTIVES

1. aggressive
2. allergic
3. forensic
4. garrulous
5. gregarious
6. irascible
7. militant
8. occult
9. succulent
10. truculent
11. turbulent

1. inclined to go in herds
2. juicy
3. warlike
4. disorderly, tumultuous
5. ready to take the initiative
6. confused, bewildered
7. talkative
8. secret, magical, supernatural
9. alert and enterprising
10. irritably sensitive
11. irritable, hot-tempered
12. fierce, savage
13. pertaining to public debate

STUDY GUIDE—VERBS

1. ASSUAGE (ă-SWAYJ) . . . **to soothe, soften or lessen**

The sympathy of someone who understood served to assuage Junior's disappointment.

Medicine has done much toward the assuagement of pain.

Cousins of *assuage: alleviate, allay, pacify, mitigate.*

2. CONVERGE . . **to come together or tend toward one point**

Meet me where the three paths converge.

The convergence of their lives was gradual.

Draw three convergent lines.

3. DEGENERATE . . . . . . **to deteriorate, grow worse**

Bad company caused Edgar to degenerate fast.

His parents could do nothing to arrest this process of degeneration. He had an uncle who was a degenerate.

4. EXTENUATE . . . . . **to make less serious, diminish**

"Circumstances simply do not extenuate your crime," the judge declared firmly. The culprit had cited his nervous condition in extenuation of the act.

5. INSTIGATE . . . . **to provoke or incite**

Did a false message instigate the attack?

At the instigation of the leader, the culprit concocted a false alibi.

The instigator is as guilty as the actual miscreant.

Inciters: *impel, goad, spur, tempt.*

6. MITIGATE . . . . **to make milder or lessen**

Lake Ontario tends to mitigate extremes of climate along its shores.

The governor would not consider mitigation of the sentence.

Assuage deals more with feelings than *mitigate.*

7. MOLLIFY . . . . **to appease or pacify**

A stick of candy will mollify Junior when he is angry or injured.

The mollification of an angry dog is not so easy.

8. NEGOTIATE . . . . . **to put through or to deal with**

The Secretary of State is trying to negotiate a new treaty with China.

The mine operators refused to negotiate with the strikers. Later they relented, but negotiations broke off when the strikers made known their demands.

STUDY GUIDE—NOUNS

1. CYNIC . . . . . **a sarcastic person who sees the worst in everything**

"I would not sit in the scorner's seat
  Or hurl the cynic's ban."

That writer is frequently cynical (sarcastic).

Many dislike his books because of his cynicism.

2. ESCAPADE . . . . **an adventure or prank**

Old Bill liked to describe his cowboy escapades in New Mexico.

3. MALEFACTOR . . . . . . **a wrongdoer or criminal**

The malefactor was a Hindu.

Male- (bad) words to identify: *malediction, malefaction, maleficent, malevolent, malfeasance, malformation, malice, malign.*
Accomplices: *culprit, felon, miscreant* (II, 10).

4. PLAGIARISM (PLAY-jǐ-à-rǐsm) . . . **the stealing of ideas or the ideas stolen**

The writer is guilty of unconscious plagiarism. He does not realize that he is a plagiarist.

Composers sometimes plagiarize from the old masters and present the music as their own.

It comes from the Latin word *to kidnap!*

5. REVERIE . . . . **deep musing; a daydream**

The professor was in the midst of a reverie.

The doctor, in the course of his ruminations, remembered a similar case.

Reverie comes from the French *rever, to dream.*
Cf. *ruminate, to muse* or *meditate.*
Note: *Ruminate* means literally *to chew the cud,* and ruminants are hoofed animals that chew the cud.
Review *meditate* (I, 2) and *contemplate* (Unit 2).

---

6. VAGARY (vǎ-GARE-y) . . . a mental wandering or whim

The volumes veiled the vagaries of a visionary.
In other words, they contained capricious cogitations.
Vagrant thoughts drifted through my mind.
The suspect was held on a charge of vagrancy.

Cf. *capricious* (II, 3), *vague* (I, 4), and *nebulous* (Unit 3) as well as *vagrant* (wandering) and *vagrancy*.
Query: Legally, what is a vagrant?

STUDY GUIDE—ADJECTIVES

1. AGGRESSIVE . . . . pushing, ready to take the initiative

Businessmen are usually aggressive. They have to be.
The inventor resented the aggressiveness of his employer.
The League of Nations failed to prevent armed aggression.

Aggressive also means *quick to attack*. Cf. *forward* and *officious* (I, 9).

2. ALLERGIC . . . . irritably sensitive

She is allergic to cat's fur.
Women are often allergic to masculine egotism.
Hay fever is the result of an allergy.

Allergy is a medical term, but *allergic* has come to denote social irritation.

3. FORENSIC . . . . pertaining to public debate, oratorical

Daniel Webster is remembered for his forensic talents.

4. GARRULOUS (GARE-you-lus) . . talkative (especially about trifles)

Old persons are sometimes garrulous. Garrulity is often annoying.

The Talkative Family: *loquacious* (II, 4), *voluble, diffuse, glib, fluent, verbose, prolix.* See *gobbledygook* (page 311), a popular word for "talking or writing which is long, pompous, vague, involved, usually with Latinized words." Look up *flapdoodle*.

5. GREGARIOUS . . . . inclined to go in groups or herds

Sheep are very gregarious animals.
Gregariousness is a trait of high-school pupils.
Hermits are not at all gregarious.

6. **IRASCIBLE** . . . . **irritable, hot-tempered**

Bad weather always made him irascible.
"Little people are commonly choleric." (KOL-ēr-ĭk)
She grew petulant when he did not come.
The officer was irate.

Three wrathful synonyms: *choleric* (hot-tempered), *petulant* (cross), *irate* (enraged).

7. **MILITANT** . . . . **warlike**

It is a militant organization.
Poor eyesight militates (contends) against success in college.

Cf. *hostile* (I, 7), *belligerent* (II, 10), *bellicose*.

8. **OCCULT** . . . . **secret, magical, supernatural**

The palmist appeared to possess occult powers of some sort.
All kinds of occultism allured her.

Accent the second syllable of *occult*. Cf. *recondite*.

9. **SUCCULENT** . . . . . . **juicy (literally and figuratively)**

Al brought home a pail of succulent berries.
The succulence of ripe fruit tempted two boys to climb a fence.

10. **TRUCULENT (TRUK-û-lent)** . . . . . . **fierce, savage**

A pair of truculent eyes watched alertly in the darkness.
The truculence of the woman's manner made everybody hate her.

Cf. *ferocious* (II, 2).

11. **TURBULENT** . . . . **disorderly, tumultuous**

The mob grew turbulent as the orator continued his harangue.
The turbulence of the ocean did not disturb Esther's inner serenity.

FIRST SENTENCE SET

Copy the *italicized* words and opposite each write an appropriate definition.

1. He would let no one try to *assuage* his grief or *extenuate* his fault.

2. A rebel general *instigated* the plan to *converge* on the city from three directions simultaneously.
3. Keeping active *mitigates* somewhat the tendency to *degenerate* physically.
4. Germany tried to *negotiate* a new treaty which would *mollify* her neighbor.
5. The *vagaries* of the *cynic* grew tiresome.
6. One of the *malefactors* was recognized after the *escapade*.
7. In moments of *reverie* he is *allergic* to noise.
8. The charge of *plagiarism* brought forth an *aggressive* defense.
9. *Forensic* displays and *occult* mysteries allure them.
10. Men are *gregarious* but not *garrulous*.
11. His *turbulent* spirit and *irascible* temper made him *truculent*.
12. Fido snapped at my *succulent* legs with *militant* fierceness.

SECOND SENTENCE SET

1. *Succulent* fruit allured them into the *escapade*.
2. Napoleon had a *turbulent, aggressive* nature.
3. Nothing would *mollify* the *cynic* or *mitigate* his bitterness.
4. A writer who resorts to *plagiarism* has *degenerated*.
5. A mischievous sophomore *instigated* the experiment to test the professor's faith in *occult* knowledge.
6. The *malefactor* remained *truculent* toward his captors.
7. All eyes *converged* on the *irascible* tiger.
8. Britain tried to *negotiate* a trade agreement with her *militant* neighbor.
9. His *forensic* efforts are full of *vagaries*.
10. After a few hours of *reverie* she grew *garrulous*.
11. Being *allergic* to snobs does not *extenuate* homicide.
12. He became *gregarious* in order to *assuage* his sorrow.

PARAGRAPH PROVOCATION

Many of the words in this unit will fit into an account of a salesman who goes from door to door and isn't too honest.

Guess What

(With the aid of the words in the pretest)

Everybody dislikes it.

Sheep-counters suffer from it.

English teachers talk about it.

War lords hate them.

It promises too much.

PRETEST

Find the number of the definition that goes with each word.

NOUNS

1. allegory
2. connoisseur
3. coterie

4. debutante
5. disparity
6. insomnia
7. olfactories

8. ostentation

9. pacifist
10. panacea
11. precursor

12. protégé
13. quintessence

1. sleeplessness
2. a cure-all
3. one under the guardianship of another
4. mercilessness, cruelty
5. a social set, clique
6. the organs or sense of smell
7. an expert judge (in matters of taste)
8. the pure essence or perfect representative
9. a forerunner, harbinger
10. a place where doves are kept
11. a story in which a teaching is conveyed symbolically
12. vainglorious display
13. one who opposes war
14. inequality, disproportion
15. young society girl

ADJECTIVES

1. bourgeois
2. bucolic
3. dogmatic
4. effete
5. efficacious
6. fatuous
7. impeccable

8. phlegmatic
9. preternatural
10. superannuated
11. taciturn
12. tantamount

1. unexcitable, stolid
2. spent, exhausted
3. rustic, rural
4. belonging to the middle class
5. equivalent
6. having nutritive value
7. vain and silly; complacently stupid
8. habitually silent
9. practical but crusty
10. unduly positive
11. blameless, faultless
12. unfit because of age
13. extraordinary, abnormal
14. powerful, effective

STUDY GUIDE—NOUNS

1. ALLEGORY . . a story in which a teaching is conveyed symbolically

Pilgrim's Progress is the most famous allegory in the English language.

The *Idylls of the King* have an allegorical (symbolical) meaning.

The characters of an allegory are personified virtues or vices.

Church pageants are frequently allegorical.

2. CONNOISSEUR (kŏn-ĭ-SUR) . . an expert judge (in matters of taste)

When a connoisseur speaks, his judgment is final.

3. COTERIE (KO-tĕ-rĭ) . . . . . a social set, clique (kleek)

Their little coterie is most unfriendly to strangers.

High-school pupils are particularly fond of cliques.

4. DEBUTANTE (dĕb-you-TAHNT) . . . . young society girl (who is about to make or has just made her first appearance in society)

The debutante was dressed in lavender.

She made her debut in the fall.

The foreign pianist made his debut in Paris.

Cf. *debut* (dă-BÜ or dĕ-BÜ) — any first attempt. The *ü* is pronounced as in the French *lune* or German *für*.

5. DISPARITY (*a* as in *act*) . . . inequality, disproportion

The disparity between their ages is very great.

The two fighters are on a parity as far as weight goes.

What is the par value of the stock?

Cf. *par* (normal value) and *parity* (equality).

6. INSOMNIA . . . . sleeplessness

Extreme nervousness is one cause of insomnia.

The somnolence of the audience was not flattering to the speaker.

The somnambulist had a narrow escape when he walked across the railroad trestle.

Look for sleep (*somn-*) in: *somnolent* (drowsy), *somnambulist* (sleep-walker), *somniferous* (sleep-inducing), and *somniloquence* (talking in one's sleep).

7. OLFACTORIES . . . . . **the organs or sense of smell**

Their proximity to a tannery made them regret that they were endowed with olfactories.

The olfactory nerve is one used in smelling.

8. OSTENTATION . . . . **vainglorious display**

The newly rich frequently indulge in ostentation.

The peacock is the most ostentatious of birds.

Synonym of *ostentation: pretentiousness.*

9. PACIFIST . . . . **one who opposes war (and militarism)**

The pacifist pleaded for arbitration of international disputes.

The Quakers are noted for their pacifism.

According to the Kellogg Pact, nations were to seek solutions to their quarrels only by pacific (peaceful) means.

Pacification of the angry mob was not easy.

Query: Why was the Pacific Ocean so named?

What is the best way to pacify a crying baby?

10. PANACEA . . . . **a cure-all**

Each agitator has his own special panacea for the ills of the country.

Patent medicine is no panacea for physical ailments.

See Pan (= all) words in a dictionary. Review those in Unit 3.

11. PRECURSOR . . . . **a forerunner, harbinger**

Paleness is a precursor of illness.

Robins are the harbingers of spring.

12. PROTÉGÉ (PRO-tĕ-zhay) . . . **one under the guardianship of another**

Joe gradually became the coach's special protégé (charge).

Protégée, like *fiancée*, is feminine.

13. QUINTESSENCE . **the pure essence or perfect representative (of some quality or qualities)**

The quintessence of the essay is stated in a few sentences at the beginning.

She is the quintessence of modesty.

Quintessence is a high-powered word. Related nouns: *acme, epitome, paragon* (Unit 4).

STUDY GUIDE—ADJECTIVES

1. BOURGEOIS (boor-ZHWAH) . . belonging to the middle class; somewhat commonplace

Bourgeois ideals do not include love of beauty for its own sake. Smugness is apt to be a bourgeois fault.

In France, *bourgeois* refers to shopkeepers, who are neither gentlemen nor peasants.

Classes of Society
1. aristocratic or patrician
2. bourgeois
3. proletarian

Note: The proletariat is the laboring class.

2. BUCOLIC (bŭ-COL-ĭk) . . . . rustic, rural

We were received with bucolic courtesy.

3. DOGMATIC . . . . unduly positive

The scientist was careful not to be dogmatic in his statements. Uncle Henry likes to dogmatize.

4. EFFETE . . spent, exhausted (but not in any temporary sense)

Roman civilization gradually became effete.

5. EFFICACIOUS . . powerful, effective, producing (or able to produce) the desired results

The medicine is highly efficacious. It is famous for its efficacy.

The word is not used of persons. *Effectual* and *efficient* are cousins.

6. FATUOUS . . . . . vain and silly; complacently stupid

Helen grew weary of fatuous remarks. Their fatuousness nauseated her.

Cf. *infatuate, infatuation.*

7. IMPECCABLE . . . . blameless, faultless

His behavior throughout the campaign was impeccable. Technical impeccability is not enough in an artist.

8. PHLEGMATIC . . . . unexcitable, stolid

"Haste not, rest not" is sometimes the motto of a phlegmatic nature.

Phlegmatic is a type of temperament, the opposite of *volatile.*

---

9. PRETERNATURAL. . . . . . **extraordinary, abnormal**

A preternatural stillness preceded the approach of the cyclone.

It is halfway between natural and supernatural.

10. SUPERANNUATED . . **unfit because of age; retired on a pension**

Superannuated employees are treated well by the company.

The superannuation of aged persons gave employment to ten young men.

11. TACITURN . . . . . **habitually silent, uncommunicative**

John Alden was a taciturn youth.

Coolidge considered his taciturnity a distinct asset.

Mother gave her tacit consent to the plan.

Tacit means *implied but not stated.*

Synonyms of *taciturn: reticent* (II, 7), *reserved.*

12. TANTAMOUNT . . . . **equivalent**

Recommendation by a congressman is tantamount to appointment.

The word is not used of objects.

FIRST SENTENCE SET

Copy the *italicized* words and opposite each write an appropriate definition.

1. The *fatuous debutante* did not understand the *allegory.*
2. The men form a little *coterie* of *connoisseurs.*
3. His *insomnia* was due to *disparity* between the amount of work and of play in his life.
4. The *pacifist* was fond of *ostentation.*
5. The *panacea* may be *efficacious*, but it is offensive to one's *olfactories.*
6. The death of his *protégé* was the *precursor* of other misfortunes.
7. She was the *quintessence* of *bucolic* gracefulness.
8. He was *dogmatic* about the virtues of his plan to aid *superannuated* office workers.

9. War leaves a country *effete*.
10. He is *phlegmatic* and *taciturn* — *impeccable,* too — in performing his duties.
11. His unusual powers and *preternatural* intelligence are *tantamount* to genius. His *bourgeois* background gave him great stability.

SECOND SENTENCE SET

1. The *allegory* had a *bucolic* flavor.
2. The approval of such a *connoisseur* is *tantamount* to acceptance.
3. The *coterie* of *debutantes* discussed *insomnia*.
4. The coach's *phlegmatic protégé* is the *quintessence* of agility.
5. The man is *dogmatic* in disapproving of the *disparity* in their ages.
6. The activities of the *pacifist* were financed by a group of *superannuated* nurses.
7. The *olfactories* of the dog were *preternaturally* sensitive.
8. *Fatuous ostentation* disgusts them. It is not a *bourgeois* trait.
9. No such *panacea* will help an *effete* nervous system.
10. Is there an *efficacious* remedy for such *taciturn* tendencies?
11. With *impeccable* logic he demonstrated that wind is the *precursor* of cool weather.

LOVE STORY

A debutante who was a pacifist or in love with one will make a suitable topic for the words in this unit. Insomnia is inevitable, and one or the other may resort to ostentation. The adjectives may be divided between the two. Include a few words from previous units if you can do so without overloading the sentences.

Your Kingdom for a Simile

As auspicious as __?__.

As grotesque as __?__.

As incongruous as __?__.

As portentous as __?__.

As tangible as __?__.

As volatile as __?__.

PRETEST

Find the number of the definition that goes with each word

ADJECTIVES I

1. auspicious
2. effeminate
3. egregious
4. equitable
5. equivocal

6. expedient
7. fortuitous
8. grotesque
9. incongruous
10. intrinsic

11. latent
12. maudlin
13. meretricious

1. weakly emotional, very sentimental
2. discordant, ill-matched
3. outstanding, remarkable
4. noisy, disorderly
5. deceptively alluring, gaudily ornamented
6. real, true, actual
7. having a melodious voice
8. promising, favorable
9. womanish, weak, or soft
10. indefinite, obscure, having a double meaning, ambiguous
11. distorted and fantastic
12. dormant, hidden
13. occurring by chance, casual
14. advisable, advantageous
15. fair, just, impartial

ADJECTIVES II

1. pastoral
2. portentous
3. recondite
4. sadistic
5. salient
6. salubrious
7. sardonic
8. saturnine

9. stoical
10. tangible
11. urbane
12. volatile

1. biting, bitter, sneering
2. cruel, fond of cruelty
3. unmoved by pleasure or pain
4. spicy, comical, or droll
5. ominous, foreshadowing evil
6. gloomy, grave
7. airy, changeable, lighthearted
8. obscure, too difficult for the ordinary mind
9. real, substantial, palpable
10. having a salty taste
11. healthful, wholesome
12. suave and polished
13. pertaining to shepherds or rural life
14. prominent, conspicuous

STUDY GUIDE—ADJECTIVES I

1. AUSPICIOUS . . . . **promising, favorable**

It was an auspicious year in which to launch a new business.
The auspiciousness of the weather promised a fine trip.
The apparent favor of the headman of the tribe was a propitious sign.

Propitious means *favorable* in the sense of an influence.

2. EFFEMINATE . . . . **womanish, weak, or soft**

Roman nobles became effeminate as the centuries went on.
The effeminacy of the man was evident.

Query: What makes a man effeminate?

3. EGREGIOUS (ĕ-GREE-jŭs) . . . **outstanding, remarkable**

He made an egregious fool of himself.
He came to realize only slowly the egregiousness of his blunder.

The word is used in an uncomplimentary sense.
Synonym: *flagrant*.

4. EQUITABLE . . . . **fair, just, impartial**

An equitable settlement of the claim was arranged out of court.
   No one questioned its equitableness.
Equity prevailed throughout the land.

Accent the first syllable of *equitable*. *Equity* (justice) is the parent word.

5. EQUIVOCAL . . . **indefinite, obscure, having a double meaning, ambiguous**

His meaning was too equivocal to be trusted, especially since
   everyone knew that he liked to trap the unwary with his
   equivocations.
The wording of the contract is ambiguous in two or three places.
   Ambiguousness can be very costly.

Do you ever equivocate to avoid embarrassment?

6. EXPEDIENT . . **advisable, advantageous (but not necessarily right)**

Is preparedness the most expedient way to avoid war?
The expediency of the plan was evident, but it nevertheless
   seemed unjust.
Bombing cities is an expedient (device) designed to cut off supplies before they reach the front.

7. FORTUITOUS . . . . occurring by chance, casual

A fortuitous encounter with a beggar provided a valuable clue.
The fortuitousness of the visit made it all the more pleasant.

8. GROTESQUE . . . . distorted and fantastic

Surrealism (a form of modern art) seems grotesque at first. A
similar grotesqueness is seen in some forms of modern music.

Cousins of *grotesque: absurd, incongruous,* and *bizarre.*

9. INCONGRUOUS . . . . . . discordant, ill-matched

It was most incongruous to see the mayor wielding a pick and
shovel.
The incongruousness of a huge woman with a tiny husband
made everyone titter.
Incongruity (disproportion) is said to be the basis of humor.
Anger and serenity are incompatible.

Incompatible means *incapable of being harmonized.* Incompatibility is a cause
of unhappiness in marriage. *Incongruous* is not often used of persons.

10. INTRINSIC . . . . real, true, actual

Silver coins have an intrinsic value almost equal to their face
value.
His intrinsic qualities will come to the surface in time.

11. LATENT (LAY-tĕnt) . . . . dormant, hidden

Her latent powers began to unfold in the new environment.
Coal contains latent heat.

12. MAUDLIN . . . . weakly emotional, very sentimental

Much maudlin sympathy was wasted on the killer.

Note: *Sentiment* is genuine feeling, but *sentimentality* is an overdone, ar-
tificial, or insincere counterfeit.

13. MERETRICIOUS . deceptively alluring, gaudily ornamented

She lavishes upon her friends a meretricious sympathy which is
almost maudlin at times.
The meretriciousness of the scheme gave it temporary success.

STUDY GUIDE—ADJECTIVES II

1. PASTORAL . . . . pertaining to shepherds or rural life

He liked pastoral poetry and pastoral music.

Pastor originally meant *shepherd*. *Minister* is now preferred in designating the head of a church.

2. PORTENTOUS . . . . . ominous, foreshadowing evil

Sailors think a morning rainbow portentous.

Some think that a black cat portends disaster.

The comet was regarded as a portent (omen) of evil.

Query: What scientific basis can you suggest for the rainbow fear?

3. RECONDITE . . obscure, too difficult for the ordinary mind to understand

Relativity is a recondite topic. So is nuclear fission.

The Rosicrucians love to delve in the metaphysical and recondite.

Kin words: *abstruse, occult* (II, 5), *mystical, esoteric.*

4. SADISTIC . . . . cruel, fond of cruelty

He displayed a sadistic delight in mistreating animals.

The sadistic horrors of Dachau were almost incredible.

Sadism is love of cruelty.

5. SALIENT (SAY-lĭ-ĕnt) . . . . . prominent, conspicuous

He outlined briefly the salient features of his plan.

See a dictionary for other meanings.

6. SALUBRIOUS . . . . healthful, wholesome

Salubrious mountain air brings color to the cheeks.

The salubriousness of the climate drew many settlers.

7. SARDONIC . . . . biting, bitter, sneering

A sardonic laugh echoed through the prison.

Dyke smiled sardonically.

Sardonic is a stronger word than *sarcastic* or *derisive.*

8. SATURNINE . . . . gloomy, grave

With saturnine heaviness he awaited the inevitable.

Here is another type of temperament to go with *phlegmatic.*

9. STOICAL . . . . **unmoved by pleasure or pain**

His stoical manner stirred our admiration.
Stoicism was cultivated as a virtue by the Indians.
The Stoics taught uncomplaining endurance of life's vicissitudes.

Stoicism implies restraint and is therefore an acquired trait. Cf. *insensitive, impassive, unemotional, undemonstrative, apathetic* (I, 8), *stolid.*

10. TANGIBLE . . . . **real, substantial, palpable**

What we need is tangible proof.
His evidence has all the tangibleness of a ten-ton truck.
Faith and hope are intangible qualities.

Literally, *tangible* means *capable of being felt or touched.*

11. URBANE . . **suave and polished (with a touch of elegance)**

Uncle Richard is very urbane. Urbanity is a family trait.

Note: *Urban* (of or pertaining to a city), *urbanize* (to make citylike), and *suburban* (pertaining to the outlying districts) are closely related. Watch for them.

12. VOLATILE . . . . **airy, changeable, lighthearted**

Nothing ever troubles a volatile nature very deeply or very long.
The volatility of the French makes them very responsive.

Volatile means *easily evaporated* when applied to a liquid, such as ether. File with *phlegmatic* and *saturnine* as a "temperament" word.

FIRST SENTENCE SET

Copy the *italicized* words and opposite each write an appropriate definition.

1. His *auspicious* start gave evidence of *intrinsic* ability.
2. He is an *egregious* example of an *effeminate* man.
3. It was an *equitable* settlement of a most *equivocal* agreement.
4. A *fortuitous* comment revealed her *latent* interest in music.
5. Does modern art seem *grotesque* and *incongruous?*
6. *Maudlin* tears were a *meretricious* device to elicit sympathy.
7. *Pastoral* poetry seldom deals with *recondite* secrets.

8. Dark hair, a low forehead and ferocious eyes were *salient* features of the *sadistic* sailor's appearance.
9. In such a *salubrious* climate, wise habits of living are no less *expedient*.
10. His *sardonic* comments showed a *saturnine* temperament.
11. *Portentous* clouds gave *tangible* proof of a storm ahead.
12. Uncle's *urbane* manner matches his niece's *volatile* spirits.
13. Dentists like their patients to be *stoical*.

SECOND SENTENCE SET

1. Her *stoical* eyes were incapable of *maudlin* tears.
2. The *salient* ideas are stated in an *equivocal* manner.
3. In the *salubrious* air of the mountains, his *latent* talent emerged.
4. He thought it *expedient* to sell the stock which had little *intrinsic* value.
5. He regarded as *portentous* such a *fortuitous* circumstance as the appearance of a raven.
6. The speaker made a *sardonic* remark about *pastoral* music.
7. His *saturnine* nature found a certain satisfaction in *grotesque* stories.
8. Himmler's mild manner and *sadistic* acts seemed *incongruous*.
9. Such *meretricious* excuses fooled no one. It was an *egregious* mistake to resort to them.
10. He is *urbane* in address and *equitable* in his judgments. Some think him *effeminate* at first.
11. Such *tangible* evidence of prosperity is an *auspicious* sign.
12. Her *volatile* nature recoils from anything *recondite*.

CRYSTAL GAZES

With proper attention to intrinsic qualities and latent abilities, write a few sentences for a class prophecy. Be ready to read them if called upon, and employ words from previous units judiciously, if possible.

Extremities

Find a pair of opposites in the first list on the next page.

..?.. and ..?..

Which word best contradicts:

Sweetness?	Beneficial?
Embarrassment?	Unlawful?
Open, unconcealed?	Spontaneous?
Disconnected?	Obedient?

PRETEST

Find the number of the definition that goes with each word.

NOUNS

1. amenity
2. capitulation
3. comity
4. dilettante
5. dourness

6. escarpment
7. hyperbole
8. intuition

9. nonchalance
10. optimism
11. pertinacity

12. pessimism
13. stratosphere

1. easy unconcern
2. sourness
3. a pleasing act
4. poetic exaggeration
5. upper atmosphere (40,000 feet or more)
6. a surrender
7. a kind of poem
8. the inclination to look on the bright side of things
9. disregard for others' rights
10. unyielding perseverance
11. politeness (especially between nations)
12. instinctive knowledge
13. a dabbler (in the fine arts or in science)
14. a cliff or steep slope
15. the inclination to look on the dark side of everything

ADJECTIVES

1. calorific
2. clandestine
3. coherent
4. deleterious
5. immutable
6. impervious
7. iridescent
8. legitimate
9. perfunctory
10. preposterous
11. recalcitrant
12. specious

1. impenetrable
2. connected or united
3. lawful
4. absurd
5. plausible-appearing; deceptive
6. of enormous importance
7. unchangeable, unalterable
8. heat-producing
9. stubborn, refusing to comply
10. secret, stealthy
11. halfhearted or mechanical
12. retiring, clannish, shrinking
13. glistening with colors
14. harmful, injurious

STUDY GUIDE—NOUNS

1. AMENITY (-MEN- rhymes with *pen*) . . . **a pleasing act**

Each bit of courtesy is an amenity that makes life less prosaic. The amenities of society serve the same purpose that pneumatic tires on cars do.

2. CAPITULATION . . . . **a surrender**

His wife accepted Jonathan's capitulation as a matter of course. The major was instructed to capitulate to prevent excessive loss of life.

Recapitulation means *a summary;* so does *capitulation* sometimes.

3. COMITY (COM- as in *comma*). . . **politeness (especially between nations in recognizing each other's laws and customs)**

A high degree of comity exists between the United States and Canada.

4. DILETTANTE (dĭl-ĕ-TAN-tĭ) . . . **a dabbler (in the fine arts or in science)**

The youth became something of a dilettante at college, but he never learned much more than the names of two dozen painters and the rudiments of sketching.

5. DOURNESS . . . . **sourness or fierceness**

The man's dourness earned him no friends. His dour attitude scared children.

Dourness rhymes with *poorness.*

6. ESCARPMENT . . . . **a cliff or steep slope**

The guns were mounted along an escarpment near the shore.

Watches have an *escapement.*

7. HYPERBOLE . . . . **poetic exaggeration**

An example:
"The dawn came up like thunder."

See *hyperbola* if you like mathematics.

8. INTUITION . . . . **instinctive knowledge**

He knew by a kind of intuition that she would not be there.

Do you believe in a woman's intuition?

Is the intuitive reaction of a child a reliable indication of a person's character?

Intuition is based on insight or spiritual perception rather than reasoning.

9. NONCHALANCE . . . . **easy unconcern**

It must have been the nonchalance of the daring young man on the flying trapeze.

A nonchalant manner is sometimes a studied disguise.

Accent the first syllable of *nonchalance*.

10. OPTIMISM . . **the inclination to look on the bright side of things; hopefulness**

The optimism of the invalid was unfailing.

Optimists are apt to be healthy, but it is hard to tell whether they are optimistic because healthy or vice versa.

Review *sanguine* (II, 10).

11. PERTINACITY . . . . **unyielding perseverance, obstinacy**

That salesman has the pertinacity of a bulldog. A salesman has to be pertinacious.

12. PESSIMISM . . . **the inclination to look on the dark side of everything; opposite of optimism**

Pessimism and dyspepsia have a strange affinity for each other.

"Nothing discourages a pessimist like refusal of things to go wrong."

A pessimistic viewpoint: Life is so tragic that no one gets out of it alive.

13. STRATOSPHERE . **upper atmosphere (40,000 feet or more)**

Planes fly in the stratosphere to an increasing extent.

STUDY GUIDE—ADJECTIVES

1. CALORIFIC . . . . **heat-producing**

The calorific value of each kind of food is of great importance to corpulent persons.

Caloric means *pertaining to heat*.

2. CLANDESTINE . . . . **secret, stealthy**

The clandestine plot had been taking shape for several weeks when the spy was caught.

Review *surreptitious* (II, 7).

3. COHERENT . . . . **connected or united**

At last she was able to give a coherent account of what had happened.

The clay formed a coherent mass.

The particles cohere readily under the influence of a magnet.

Cohesion and *coherency* are the noun forms. Watch them in use.

4. DELETERIOUS (dĕl-ē-TEE-rĭ-ŭs). . . . **harmful, injurious**

The medicine has a beneficial effect at first, but in the end it is deleterious.

The deleteriousness of the drug caused it to lose favor with the public.

Disease germs are pernicious and sewer gas is noxious.

Two other killers, *pernicious* (II, 10) and *noxious*, have similar meanings.

5. IMMUTABLE . . . . **unchangeable, unalterable**

The laws of the Medes and Persians were immutable.

The immutability of the laws of nature is taken for granted.

Cf. *mutate* (to change or modify), *mutation* (a change or variation), *mutable* (variable).

6. IMPERVIOUS . . . . **impenetrable**

Paraffin is impervious to water. Its imperviousness makes it useful in sealing jars.

Impervious is followed by *to*.

7. IRIDESCENT . . . **glistening with colors (like a rainbow)**

Diamonds and dewdrops are iridescent.

Have you observed the iridescence of fine mist in the sunlight?

Iris is the Greek word for *rainbow*.

8. LEGITIMATE . . . . **lawful**

The procedure is entirely legitimate.

The excuse was legitimate.

The legitimacy of the marriage was not questioned.

The new law legitimizes (makes lawful) the sale of opium.
See a dictionary for derived meanings of *legitimate*.
Opposites: *illegitimate, illegitimacy.*

9. PERFUNCTORY . . . . . . **halfhearted or mechanical**

The speech sounded very perfunctory.
The men worked very perfunctorily.

10. PREPOSTEROUS . . . . **absurd**

The demands were preposterous.
The preposterousness of perpetual-motion machines is obvious
to scientists.

11. RECALCITRANT . . . . **stubborn, refusing to comply**

We finally had to start a fire under the recalcitrant mule.
The recalcitrance of Congress annoyed the President.
Literally, *recalcitrant* means *kicking back.*

12. SPECIOUS (SPE- rhymes with *free*) . . **plausible-appearing; deceptive**

He possessed extraordinary skill at inventing specious excuses.
The speciousness of the idea did not occur to us.
Cousins: *plausible* (I, 3) *ostensible* (II, 10), *meretricious* (III, 7).

FIRST SENTENCE SET

Copy the *italicized* words and opposite each write an appropriate definition.

1. The *dilettante* observes all the *amenities* punctiliously.
2. Such a diplomatic *capitulation* could occur only when a
   high degree of *comity* existed between the two nations.
3. His *dourness* grew a shade darker when he saw how near
   he was to the *escarpment.*
4. It took no *intuition* to decide that the remark was a *hyperbole.*
5. Can you distinguish between *optimism* and mere *nonchalance?*
6. He had the *pertinacity* to cling to his *pessimism* no matter
   how bright the outlook grew.

7. Special equipment is needed for *stratosphere* flying.
8. Saccharine has no *calorific* value and is not *deleterious*.
9. Give a *coherent* account of the *clandestine* escapade.
10. The *iridescent* gem is *impervious* to scratches.
11. You have a *legitimate* right to know all about the will. Its provisions are *immutable*, however.
12. He is *perfunctory* at best and sometimes *recalcitrant*.
13. It is *preposterous* to think the professor can be fooled by such *specious* reasons.

SECOND SENTENCE SET

1. The *dilettante* computed the *calorific* value of each meal.
2. *Intuition* told Aunt Carrie that some *clandestine* plan was being concocted.
3. His reasons for the *capitulation* were very *coherent*.
4. The *deleterious* effects of a medicine he was using contributed to his *pessimism*.
5. His *optimism* was deep and *immutable*.
6. The substance is *impervious* to moisture, and the low temperatures of the *stratosphere* will not harm it.
7. The mist at the base of the *escarpment* became *iridescent* in the sunlight.
8. It is *preposterous* to believe that they have *legitimate* reasons for remaining *recalcitrant*.
9. His *specious* zeal appears only when someone is watching. At other times he is very *perfunctory*.
10. It is no *hyperbole* to say his *pertinacity* is like granite.
11. He executed with *nonchalance* the *amenities* expected.
12. The diplomat's *dourness* strained the *comity* between the two nations.

FOR EXAMPLE

Illustrate 15 or more of the words from incidents in personal experience or in your reading. Use a sentence for each, and be as definite as you can.

Kinds

1. What kind of laughter do you discover?

2. What kind of son — very famous at that?

3. What kind of automobile?

4. What kind of music?

5. What kind of ideas?

6. What kind of government?

Was a little juggling necessary to find the most appropriate word for each?

Find the number of the definition that goes with each word.

VERBS

1. abrogate	1. to secretly aid or approve another in wrongdoing
2. adulterate	2. to make ineffective
3. alleviate	3. to imitate an Irishman
4. amplify	4. annul, do away with
5. bereave	5. to withdraw
6. connive	6. to decorate with flowers
7. effervesce	7. to deprive of someone very dear; make desolate
8. hibernate	8. to launch (a new policy); install in office
9. inaugurate	9. to lighten or lessen
10. nullify	10. to overspread or spread through
11. reprieve	11. to give off gas in bubbles
12. secede	12. to cheapen or debase
13. suffuse	13. to postpone punishing
	14. to pass the winter
	15. to make larger or fuller

ADJECTIVES

1. bigoted	1. spiritual, airy, exquisite
2. clement	2. lavish, wasteful
3. convivial	3. coarse, uproarious
4. coquettish	4. frank, sincere, noble
5. ethereal	5. narrow-minded, intolerant
6. ingenuous	6. jovial, gay
7. mundane	7. lower, lying beneath
8. nether	8. dull, stupid, inert
9. obsolete	9. haphazard, confused
10. prodigal	10. mild, merciful
11. promiscuous	11. out of use, outmoded
12. ribald	12. skillful in giving anaesthetics
	13. flirtatious, fond of trifling
	14. earthly, worldly

STUDY GUIDE—VERBS

1. ABROGATE . . . . **annul, do away with**

The new law abrogates an older one.
Abrogation of the treaty was inevitable.
Cf. *revoke* (II, 7), *repeal, nullify, rescind, cancel, annul.*

2. ADULTERATE . . **to cheapen or debase (with harmful or inferior ingredients)**

Gasoline was once used to adulterate kerosene.
The pure food and drug laws limit the adulteration of foods.
Penalties are prescribed for the use of adulterants.

3. ALLEVIATE . . . . **to lighten or lessen**

A nurse tries to alleviate pain.
Alleviation of poverty is one of the dreams of society.
Review: *mitigate, assuage* (Unit 5).

4. AMPLIFY . . . . **to make larger or fuller**

Will you amplify the account which you have already written?
He will have ample (abundant, large) leisure.
Apparatus for the amplification of sound will be installed in the auditorium.

5. BEREAVE . . . . **to deprive of (someone very dear), make desolate**

If death should bereave them of a son, it will be years before they recover from this bereavement.
Bereft of health, he could work no longer.
Many notes of sympathy came to the bereaved (sorrowing) parents.
Bereave takes the preposition *of;* its Saxon ancestor meant *to rob.*
Bereft is used of abstract qualities; *bereaved,* of persons.

6. CONNIVE (kŏ-NIVE) . . **secretly aid or approve another in wrongdoing**

George thought that his father would connive at the prank he had perpetrated on his sister. Because of this connivance he hoped to escape punishment.
Connive is followed by *at* or *with.* Literally, it means *to wink.*

7. EFFERVESCE . . . . to give off gas in bubbles (fizz) or bubble with liveliness

Soda water effervesces.

She has an effervescent (sparkling, lively) disposition.

Her effervescence is refreshing.

The Latin meaning of *effervesce* is *to boil out* Cf. *fervent, fervency, fervor, fervid.*

8. HIBERNATE . . . . to pass the winter

The banker hibernates in Florida.

Animals are in hibernation already.

Hibernal (wintry) winds are usually chilling.

The opposite of *hibernate* is *aestivate*. When referring to animals, *hibernate* implies a state of torpor or drowsiness.

9. INAUGURATE . to launch (a new policy); install in office

The company will inaugurate a new investment plan next year.

We could not attend the inauguration of the officers.

Everyone now can hear the President give his inaugural address.

10. NULLIFY . . . . . . to make ineffective; invalidate

A move was on foot to nullify the law.

You will nullify the effect of the medicine if you do not stay in bed.

Nullification of the measure failed.

Cf. *null:* The contract became null and void.

11. REPRIEVE . . . . to postpone punishing

The governor refused to reprieve the man.

All hopes of a last-minute reprieve were vain.

Vacation was a two-week reprieve (temporary escape) from the monotony of operating a machine.

12. SECEDE . . to withdraw (from membership in a political or religious body)

Lincoln believed that a state may not secede from the Union.

In other words, secession is impossible.

13. SUFFUSE . . . . . . to overspread or spread through

A blush suffused her cheeks, and tears came to her eyes.

The suffusion of new life through trees and flowers is an annual miracle.

STUDY GUIDE—ADJECTIVES

1. BIGOTED . . . . narrow-minded, intolerant

Mr. Morgan was very bigoted when it came to politics, and he cared little how many enemies his bigotry made.

Mr. Morgan was a bigot, in other words.

2. CLEMENT (accent first syllable) . . . . . mild, merciful

The weather was clement.

The jury recommended clemency.

She is very lenient with her children. Perhaps she shows too much leniency.

Review *lenient, lenity, leniency* (I, 7).

3. CONVIVIAL . . . . jovial, gay

The party was a convivial affair.

Even grandfather joined in the conviviality.

He is a congenial (agreeable) companion.

Jack and his father are congenial (kindred, sympathetic) spirits.

Congenial merely means kindred, agreeable, or sympathetic.

4. COQUETTISH . . . flirtatious, fond of trifling with love

Her coquettish ways (i. e., coquetry — CO-kĕt-rĭ) please men for a while, especially those who like coquettes.

Sometimes *coquettish* means *coy* because coyness is *pretended* bashfulness.

5. ETHEREAL . . . . spiritual, airy, exquisite

Shelley's poetry is known for its ethereal quality.

Poe etherealized (idealized) the women about whom he wrote poems.

6. INGENUOUS . . . . frank, sincere, noble

"I'd do the same thing myself," was the ingenuous response.

He had all the ingenuousness of youth at its best.

A new actress from abroad plays the part of the ingénue (ân-zhå-NÜ) in the story.

Do not confuse *ingenuous* with *ingenious*. An ingénue is an unsophisticated girl or an actress who plays the part of one.

7. MUNDANE . . . . earthly, worldly

The mundane affairs of life do not worry a genius.

Secular music (not religious or sacred) is abundant. Opposites: *earthly—heavenly; secular—sacred; terrestrial—celestial; temporal—eternal.*

8. NETHER . . . . **lower, lying beneath**

The nether layers were unaffected.

Ulysses explored the nether region of the earth.

9. OBSOLETE . . . . **out of use, outmoded**

The Model-T Ford has long been obsolete.

The obsoleteness of armor began with the invention of gunpowder.

Machinery in a modern factory becomes obsolescent (passing out of use) before it wears out. Although this rapid obsolescence is costly, it is less costly than the operation of the obsolescent equipment.

Decadent (on the decline) and *decadence* apply more to ideas, systems, and standards than to objects.

10. PRODIGAL . . . . **lavish, wasteful**

The fullback burns up energy with prodigal extravagance.

The prodigality of a Roman feast is described in *Quo Vadis*.

11. PROMISCUOUS . . **haphazard, confused, undiscriminating**

Do you ever toss your clothes into a promiscuous heap?

The promiscuousness with which many nationalities have mingled in this country is bewildering.

12. RIBALD (RIB-ăld) . . . . . . **coarse, uproarious**

Ribald laughter greeted the remark of the drunken truck driver.

For several hours ribaldry ran riot in the tavern.

FIRST SENTENCE SET

Copy the *italicized* words and opposite each write an appropriate definition.

1. Nothing *abrogates* his right to visit the parents whom fate has *bereaved* of a daughter.

2. Nothing should be allowed to *adulterate* the joy of a person who spent her life trying to *alleviate* suffering.

3. Will you *amplify* your confession by telling why you *connived* at your brother's prank?

4. "We'll *hibernate* on the French Riviera!" she *effervesced.*
5. The case *inaugurates* an attempt to *nullify* the law.
6. A blush *suffused* his face when he was accused of urging his church to *secede* from the denomination.
7. He directed a *clement* smile at the *bigoted* politician.
8. She is very *coquettish* when feeling *convivial.*
9. She approached her *ingenuous* escort with *ethereal* grace.
10. Red flannel *nether* garments are now *obsolete.*
11. His *prodigal* spending showed his inexperience in *mundane* matters.
12. The president *reprieved* him on condition that he would not mingle with *promiscuous* groups of *ribald* roisterers.

SECOND SENTENCE SET

1. A *bigoted* merchant wants pure-food laws *abrogated.*
2. She *adulterates* her *ingenuous* charms with *coquettish* byplays.
3. Alterations will *alleviate* strain on the *nether* timbers.
4. Will you *amplify* your knowledge of the plan to *secede?*
5. *Mundane* considerations did not trouble the *bereaved* father.
6. The theater owners *connived* with the city authorities in an attempt to *nullify* the vote on daylight-saving time.
7. In *convivial* company she *effervesces* like soda water.
8. She planned to *hibernate* in the *ethereal* climate of California.
9. The new president whom we are to *inaugurate* is a very *clement* gentleman.
10. With *promiscuous* unconcern the governor *reprieved* prisoners.
11. He spends money with *prodigal* recklessness on himself and his *ribald* companions.
12. The contentment which *suffused* her being vanished abruptly when she saw that the car was an *obsolete* model.

PERSONS WE COULD DO WITHOUT

Nominate for oblivion several persons, or types of persons suggested by the words of the unit. Explain facetiously, lugubriously, or unemotionally — but in any event, unequivocally.

We Graduate

The author of this book thinks that vocabulary is of __?__ importance because it enables one to think and express himself with greater __?__. Though our first glimpse of this book was accompanied by a definite touch of __?__, that soon passed, and we leave it with a feeling of __?__. We feel sure that we are more __?__ and better able to meet each __?__ which arises because we have a finer command of the English language.

Q. E. D.

PRETEST

Find the number of the definition that goes with each word.

NOUNS

1. acumen	1. a (clever) teller of stories
2. adamant	2. rate of movement
3. avocation	3. stone of impenetrable hardness or anything unyielding
4. clarity	4. a solemn agreement, compact
5. covenant	5. an urgent need
6. exhilaration	6. infamy, disgrace (public)
7. exigency	7. a rebellious feeling (against lawful authority)
8. franchise	8. dizziness, giddiness
9. ignominy	9. a prisoner on parole
10. raconteur	10. keenness of insight
11. sedition	11. a hobby or diversion
12. tempo	12. harshness, meanness
13. vertigo	13. clearness
	14. invigoration, enlivenment
	15. the right to vote; a business privilege

ADJECTIVES

1. anonymous	1. universal, widely inclusive
2. catholic	2. peaceful, calmly happy
3. derogatory	3. inborn, existing inseparably in something
4. halcyon	4. supreme, chief
5. indigent	5. easily managed, docile
6. inherent	6. able to do many things well
7. maritime	7. windy, stormy, violent
8. paramount	8. of unknown authorship
9. strident	9. uncomplimentary, disparaging
10. tractable	10. needy, destitute
11. ulterior	11. pertaining to the movies
12. versatile	12. connected with the sea
	13. harsh, shrill
	14. more remote, beyond what is expressed or implied

STUDY GUIDE—NOUNS

1. ACUMEN (*å*-CUE-měn) . . . . . **keenness of insight**

His acumen in business is extraordinary.

Her acumen is a great help to her husband.

2. ADAMANT . . **stone of impenetrable hardness or anything unyielding**

On matters of moral principle, Lincoln was adamant.

The boy displayed adamantine (tĭn) courage.

3. AVOCATION . . . . **a hobby or diversion**

An avocation is as necessary as a vocation.

This is the usual, not the only meaning.

4. CLARITY . . . . **clearness**

The clarity of the atmosphere in the Rockies makes distances deceptive.

Writing helps to clarify (make clear) one's ideas.

The clarion (trumpet-clear) call to arms brought many volunteers.

5. COVENANT . . . . . . **a solemn agreement, compact**

The church covenant was read.

Many nations ratified the covenant of the League of Nations.

6. EXHILARATION . . . . . **invigoration, enlivenment**

The exhilaration of success transformed her.

Mountain air exhilarates one.

The fresh breeze proved exhilarating.

7. EXIGENCY . . . . **an urgent need**

He yielded to the exigencies of the moment. The need for action was exigent.

An *exigency* names a need arising out of a situation, whereas an *emergency* is the situation itself.

Accent the first syllable of *exigency*.

8. FRANCHISE . . . **the right to vote; a business privilege granted by a government**

The franchise was extended to Negroes.

The enfranchisement of women was a forward step in western civilization.

There is no one left to enfranchise in this country except children, aliens, and convicts.

The city refused to renew the bus company's franchise.

9. **IGNOMINY** . . . . **infamy, disgrace (public)**

A man who was a victim more than a villain did not deserve such ignominy.

Was the social credit experiment an ignominious failure?

Accent the first syllable of *ignominy*.

10. **RACONTEUR** (rá-kôn-TUR) . . **a (clever) teller of stories**

Uncles frequently make excellent raconteurs.

It is an imported French word, not yet naturalized.
Note: The feminine is *raconteuse*.

11. **SEDITION** . . **a rebellious feeling (against lawful authority)**
or incitement of rebellious feeling

Sedition precedes a revolution.

The man was imprisoned in Germany for distributing seditious literature.

Cf. *mutiny, anarchy, insurrection, treason*.

12. **TEMPO** . . . . **rate of movement**

Gay music has a lively tempo.

The tempo of modern life was too much for his nerves.

Query: Do you live at a rapid, medium, or slow tempo?
Literally, *tempo* means *time*.

13. **VERTIGO** . . . . **dizziness, giddiness**

A vertigo seized him as he started.

The medicine has a vertiginous (dizziness-causing) effect.

Vertigo is a relative of the Verto (to turn) family: *avert, invert, revert, convert,* etc.

STUDY GUIDE—ADJECTIVES

1. **ANONYMOUS** . . . **nameless, of unknown authorship**

The author of the anonymous letter was traced.

Hawthorne's first stories were anonymously published. This anonymity delayed recognition of his talent.

2. CATHOLIC . . . . universal, widely inclusive

He was a man of catholic interests.
The catholicity of the book's appeal will make it a best seller.
Curio: *catholicon* means *a panacea* or *cure-all*.

3. DEROGATORY . . . . uncomplimentary, disparaging

Derogatory remarks irritated him.

4. HALCYON (HAL-sĭ-ŭn) . . . . peaceful, calmly happy

The halcyon days of autumn stirred something deeply poetic within him.

This word is based on a legend. See a dictionary.

5. INDIGENT (accent the first syllable) . . . needy, destitute

Money was collected to help the poor and indigent of the parish.
Because of his parents' indigence, he could not have an education.

6. INHERENT . . . inborn, existing inseparably in something

Her inherent dislike for snakes offered an irresistible temptation to her brother.
Freedom and equality inhere in a democratic form of government.
The inherence of mutual distrust among nations is a great pity.

Synonyms of *inherent: innate, inbred, ingrained, intrinsic.*

7. MARITIME . . connected with the sea (or situated near it)

The strike of maritime workers ended.
The maritime villages of New England harbor many legends of the sea.

Seafaring adjectives: *marine, nautical, naval.*

8. PARAMOUNT . . . . supreme, chief

The paramount need for better housing was emphasized.
Her husband's safety was her paramount concern.
Cf. *preeminent.*

9. STRIDENT . . . . harsh, shrill

The strident wail of a fire engine penetrated the stillness unpleasantly.

10. TRACTABLE . . . . **easily managed, docile**

The mare proved tractable.
The tractability of the workers grows out of a co-operative spirit.

11. ULTERIOR . . . **more remote, beyond what is expressed or implied**

Mother had ulterior reasons for wanting him to spend the summer at camp.

12. VERSATILE . . . . . . **able to do many things well**

An executive must be versatile.
Her versatility makes her friends envious.

FIRST SENTENCE SET

Copy the *italicized* words and opposite each write an appropriate definition.

1. He had the *acumen* to choose an *avocation* that would advance him in his work.
2. The *clarity* of her ideas made her *adamant* in refusing.
3. No *exigency* justifies our violating such a *covenant*.
4. The *raconteur* fairly radiated *exhilaration*.
5. Should a criminal suffer the *ignominy* of losing the *franchise?*
6. A feeling of *vertigo* unnerved him at the very mention of the penalty for *sedition*.
7. The *derogatory* letter was *anonymous*.
8. He spent the *halcyon* years of his life indulging his *catholic* tastes in literature.
9. An *inherent* sympathy for the *indigent* led her to help in a home for superannuated *maritime* workers.
10. Elimination of *strident* downtown noises is a *paramount* need.
11. He lives at an even *tempo* and is very *tractable*.
12. The youth was *versatile* enough to unearth proof of the doctor's *ulterior* motives.

SECOND SENTENCE SET

1. The *anonymous* pamphlet was designed to stir up *sedition*.
2. There should be a more *catholic* regard for the sacredness of international *covenants*.
3. Someone made a *derogatory* remark about his skill as a *raconteur*.
4. The *halcyon* days of harvest produce a quiet *exhilaration*.
5. He was *adamant* in his refusal to help *indigent* persons, whatever their *exigencies*.
6. Lack of *acumen* was *inherent* in the family.
7. Is sailing a popular *avocation* in the *maritime* provinces?
8. Intelligent use of the *franchise* is a *paramount* function of citizenship.
9. The *strident* wail of a locomotive brought on an attack of *vertigo*.
10. With sudden *clarity* she realized that she would be suspected of *ulterior* designs.
11. He is too *versatile* and *tractable* to be unemployed long.
12. He preferred the slow *tempo* of everyday living to the risk of *ignominy*.

MAY AND SEPTEMBER

Youth has exhilaration. Age has its halcyon years but sometimes brings ignominy, as in the case of Benedict Arnold. Both eras of life have their exigencies.

Write of youth and age, noting that words like *tempo* and *vertigo* may be applied ingeniously to either — or devise a biography employing most of the words of this unit together with a few from earlier units, if possible. You might combine the two ideas and write about a May-and-September romance.

What was the effect on each?

Where did they plan to live?

What was her paramount characteristic?

What was his?

FINAL TESTS

Copy the *italicized* words and opposite each write an appropriate definition.

UNIT 1

1. Nothing could *deter* him from letting the charge *detonate* too soon.
2. All the *calumny emanates* from one source.
3. Why *disparage* his attempts to bring the peace plan to *fruition?*
4. Out of *deference* for her husband's wishes, she *demurred.*
5. They will *collaborate* on the solution of a new scientific *enigma.*
6. His tendency to *cavil* at the delay produced *dissension.*
7. The manager was inclined to *condone* the youth's *audacity.*
8. Their *arrogance* was *construed* as outright defiance.
9. He *absconded* soon after his *hypocrisy* became known.
10. The police, having reached an *impasse,* decided to *exhume* the body of the victim.

UNIT 2

1. His sister can think of such *felicitous* words with which to *paraphrase* poems.
2. He is *astute* enough to *mediate* in any dispute.
3. The remark *impeached* his honesty and *piqued* all of his friends.
4. Jack *impaled* the can with his toy sword before *relegating* it to the ash heap.
5. That account of Lincoln's order to *emancipate* the slaves is *authentic.*
6. It being impossible to *rectify* the wrongs, he sought some way to *expiate* them.
7. *Bumptious* ways are *inimical* to his best interests.

8. He *reciprocated* with *amorous* words.
9. His *fastidious* ideas about diet led him to *usurp* the task of planning menus.
10. His *erratic* ways appeared *innocuous* as long as he was not employed.

UNIT 3

1. The *lambent* firelight made his features appear *lugubrious*.
2. The *tentative* draft is too *nebulous*.
3. Her *mobile* features and *naïve* manner give her extraordinary charm.
4. It is *pusillanimous* to run away from one's foes, however *nefarious* they may be.
5. His *unctuous perjuries* were soon detected.
6. The *recumbent* figure appeared to be suffering from a *surfeit* of Christmas food.
7. His *predilection* for *succinct* answers is quite natural.
8. The *metropolis* is flooded with a *profusion* of light.
9. The *innovation* offended her sense of *propriety*.
10. We doubled up in *paroxysms* of laughter as he described the *vicissitudes* of a salesman's career.

UNIT 4

1. He was *adroit* enough to ignore the *anathema*.
2. She unleashed a *barrage* of *captious* questions.
3. The agreement which members of the *coalition* sign is very *explicit*.
4. The *ineffable* charm of Poe's poems has at times an *exotic* flavor.
5. The *patriarch* guarded the *fetish* with reverence.
6. The scientist was searching among Pacific *atolls* for new forms of *amphibious* life.
7. The coach's fear that his *paragon* would be disqualified or injured haunted him like an *incubus*.
8. The *migration* of the birds northward began soon after the winter *solstice*.

9. Could he give any *relevant* explanation for such *mediocre* playing?
10. A dozen *chimerical* plans coursed through his mind as he threaded the *sinuous* trails.

UNIT 5

1. The *malefactor* grew less *irascible* as the hour of execution approached.
2. As a youth he had begun to *degenerate* through *turbulent* companions.
3. Lawyers found nothing to *extenuate* his crime or *mollify* the judge.
4. The judge refused to *mitigate* the penalty for this crime which the culprit had been able to *negotiate*.
5. He sank into a *reverie* as the priest sought to *assuage* his bitterness.
6. He realized the folly of being a *cynic* and of having a *truculent* attitude toward society.
7. A fake medium who claimed *occult* powers had *instigated* his crime.
8. A *garrulous* relative came to pity him and deplore the *escapades* which had culminated in murder.
9. It was his too-*aggressive* spirit plus the *vagaries* of the medium which had finally brought him to this.
10. Memories which *converged* with horrible vividness made him unable to enjoy that last *succulent* meal.

UNIT 6

1. He was *dogmatic* about the value of his *panacea*.
2. "Is capitalism *effete?*" the *debutante* asked.
3. Have you an *efficacious* cure for *insomnia?*
4. His *olfactories* told the *connoisseur* that something was wrong.
5. The *disparity* in salaries did not disturb his *phlegmatic* nature.

6. Is the *preternatural* color of her cheeks a *precursor* of illness?
7. There was no *ostentation* about the *bucolic* informality with which they were received.
8. His *fatuous* smile is *tantamount* to an insult.
9. The *taciturn* youth is an ardent *pacifist*.
10. Her son regarded her as the *quintessence* of *impeccable* matronly elegance.

UNIT 7

1. The coach thought it *expedient* to avoid too *auspicious* a beginning.
2, 3. The group included an *effeminate*-looking lawyer, a *saturnine* artist, a *volatile* society girl, and an *urbane* bank manager.
4. The professor has made *tangible* progress in exploring *recondite* branches of astronomy.
5. His *sardonic* comments border on the *grotesque*.
6. A *fortuitous* circumstance led us to suspect the *latent* wealth of the country.
7. It was an *equitable* decision, and it contained not a single *equivocal* phrase.
8. Saying that her book has no *intrinsic* value was an *egregious* blunder.
9. The *salubrious* climate of the South has several *salient* virtues.
10. Acting requires a *meretricious* imitation of *stoical* behavior.

UNIT 8

1. Such *amenities* should not seem *perfunctory*.
2. Her *capitulation* was as *specious* a trick as the gift of the wooden horse to the Trojans.
3. The *dilettante* in art thought my drawings simply *preposterous*.
4. The man's *dourness* caused many to act *recalcitrant*.

5. With *pertinacity* he continued to carve out steps in the side of the *escarpment*.
6. It is a *hyperbole* to talk about kites reaching the *stratosphere*.
7. She claimed that her *optimism* was based on *intuition*.
8. His *nonchalance* enabled him to tell a *coherent* story.
9. In his *pessimism* he fears that an *immutable* fate will wreck his dreams.
10. *Clandestine* misdeeds have a *deleterious* effect on character.

UNIT 9

1. None of the old laws was *nullified* under the new king's *clement* sway.
2. His *convivial* temperament helped to *alleviate* the heaviness in her heart.
3. A new ardor *suffused* her being. *Mundane* details did not matter now.
4. An *ingenuous* German *inaugurated* the first youth hostels.
5. It seemed impossible that such *ethereal* eyes could *connive* at injustice.
6. He was thought *bigoted* because he did not want to *secede*.
7. "I will *reprieve* you this time!" she declared with a *coquettish* smile.
8. *Obsolete* words constitute one of his *promiscuous* interests.
9. Their *ribald* mockery could be heard in the *nether* regions of the house.
10. The liquid *effervesces* if anything has been put in to *adulterate* it.

UNIT 10

1. His *acumen* makes him *versatile*.
2. He is *adamant* in his determination to avoid *ignominy*.
3. There were *ulterior* reasons why he took up music as an *avocation*.
4. With unusual *clarity* he saw that saving the Union was the *paramount* objective.

5. The *exigencies* of war increased the *tempo* of production.
6. *Vertigo* gave way to a feeling of *exhilaration*.
7. City authorities were *tractable* about renewing the bus company's *franchise*.
8. The *raconteur* was executed for stirring up *sedition*.
9. The *anonymous* protest was traced to an *indigent* farm hand.
10. His *inherent* serenity harmonized well with the *halcyon* epoch in which he lived.

HAPPILY EVER AFTER?

By way of review it is suggested that you compile The Romance of Part III, answering in your capricious tale such questions as the following:

What was he like? (Use adjectives and illustrate)
What was she like? (Use adjectives and illustrate)
Were they compatible? Why not? (Use verbs)

Perhaps, like Macbeth and Lady Macbeth, they perpetrated a heinous crime, absconded with money, usurped a throne, or committed perjury. Prolong the affair as much as you like. Make it lugubrious if you must, but try to be succinct, and do not let description degenerate into strings of loosely-assorted adjectives. Avoid a stilted or overloaded style.

If you are not romantically disposed, a biography of either the Hero or the Villain of Part III will be acceptable. So will a rogues' gallery or hall of fame, consisting of pungent, disconnected sentence paragraphs. A series of comments on radio programs you like or dislike is another good pretext for a creative review of Part Three.

DIVISION TEST

Find the number of the definition that goes with each word:

A.

1. audacity
2. dissension
3. elixir
4. fruition
5. hypocrisy
6. metropolis
7. overture
8. paroxysm

9. profusion
10. surfeit

1. a pretense of being what one is not, sham
2. a painful disease of the joints
3. excess
4. abundance
5. a magic password
6. strife, discord
7. a principal city
8. an offer, proposition, or opening (of negotiations or of an opera)
9. boldness
10. a spasm
11. a medicinal liquid
12. bearing fruit, realization

B.

1. barrage
2. fetish
3. incarnation
4. migration
5. patriarch
6. connoisseur
7. disparity
8. olfactories
9. panacea
10. protégé

1. an expert judge (in matters of taste)
2. one under the guardianship of another
3. a volley (of missiles)
4. an aged wise man
5. a cure-all
6. embodiment (in human form)
7. an act of worship
8. a moving or journey
9. inequality, disproportion
10. the organs or sense of smell
11. an unpleasant (but wholesome) odor
12. an object worshiped for its magical power

C.

1. capitulation
2. dourness
3. hyperbole
4. optimism
5. pessimism
6. adamant

7. covenant
8. exigency

9. raconteur
10. tempo

1. amassing of money
2. a solemn agreement, compact
3. a (clever) teller of stories
4. rate of movement
5. poetic exaggeration
6. the inclination to look on the dark side of everything; opposite of optimism
7. an urgent need
8. a stone of impenetrable hardness
9. an animal related to the fox
10. a surrender
11. the inclination to look on the bright side of things; hopefulness
12. sourness

D.

1. cavil

2. construe
3. demur
4. disparage

5. exhume

6. expiate
7. incinerate
8. paraphrase
9. rectify
10. temporize

1. to dig up (something that has been buried); disinter
2. to correct, set right
3. to smooth out
4. to yield temporarily to circumstances; to avoid committing oneself
5. to quibble or find fault without good reason
6. to act hastily
7. to object or hesitate
8. to atone or make amends for
9. to burn to ashes
10. to state in one's own words
11. to interpret
12. to belittle, speak slightingly of

E.

1. converge
2. instigate

3. mollify

4. adulterate
5. amplify

6. effervesce
7. nullify
8. secede
9. abscond

10. emanate

1. to provoke or incite
2. to make ineffective; invalidate
3. to withdraw (from membership in a political or religious body)
4. to flee secretly
5. to come together or tend toward one point
6. to appease or pacify
7. to make larger or fuller
8. to do wrong
9. to give off gas in bubbles (fizz) or bubble with liveliness
10. to flow forth or originate
11. to imitate
12. to cheapen or debase (with harmful or inferior ingredients)

F.

1. astute
2. credulous
3. fastidious
4. inadvertent
5. innocuous
6. lugubrious
7. nebulous
8. pusillanimous
9. succinct
10. unctuous

1. harmless
2. hazy, vague, shadowy
3. weak-minded
4. too willing to believe
5. terse, concise
6. daintily particular
7. cowardly
8. suave, bland, oily, smooth
9. doleful, dismal
10. unintentional
11. shrewd, crafty, keen of mind
12. sharp, sarcastic

G.

1. aesthetic
2. explicit
3. ineffable

4. chimerical
5. sinuous

6. exotic
7. irascible
8. garrulous
9. gregarious
10. militant

1. fantastic, delusive
2. irritable, hot-tempered
3. inclined to go in groups or herds
4. trusting, faithful
5. beauty-sensitive, pertaining to a feeling for beauty
6. twisting, winding devious
7. strange, foreign
8. warlike
9. definite, plain
10. talkative (esp. about trifles)
11. unspeakable, inexpressible
12. puzzling, mysterious

H.

1. truculent

2. dogmatic

3. fatuous
4. phlegmatic
5. superannuated
6. tantamount
7. intrinsic
8. equitable
9. fortuitous
10. latent

1. vain and silly; complacently stupid
2. unfit because of age; retired on a pension
3. equivalent
4. occurring by chance, casual
5. fond of horsemanship
6. fierce, savage
7. unexcitable, stolid
8. dormant, hidden
9. clumsy, awkward
10. real, true, actual
11. fair, just, impartial
12. unduly positive

I.

1. meretricious
2. recondite
3. salubrious
4. sardonic
5. tangible

6. volatile
7. clandestine
8. immutable
9. iridescent
10. preposterous

1. biting, bitter, sneering
2. glistening with colors
3. unchangeable, unalterable
4. having Scottish ancestors
5. deceptively alluring, gaudily ornamented
6. secret, stealthy
7. absurd
8. real, substantial, palpable
9. airy, changeable, lighthearted
10. obscure, too difficult for the ordinary mind to understand
11. explosive
12. healthful, wholesome

J.

1. specious
2. clement
3. ethereal
4. mundane
5. prodigal

6. ribald
7. catholic
8. indigent
9. maritime
10. tractable

1. particular or fussy
2. spiritual, airy, exquisite
3. plausible-appearing; deceptive
4. universal, widely inclusive
5. connected with the sea (or situated near it)
6. mild, merciful
7. earthly, worldly
8. easily managed, docile
9. needy, destitute
10. lavish, wasteful
11. coarse, uproarious
12. heavy, huge, ponderous

SUPPLEMENTARY TEST

This test is based on words introduced in the illustrative sentences and small-type notes.

Find the number of the definition that goes with each word.

A.

1. demurrer
2. anarchy
3. presumption
4. temerity
5. aspersion
6. ingress
7. impostor
8. intermediary
9. rectitude
10. panoply

1. bold forwardness
2. armor or any splendid, enveloping array
3. a plea for the dismissal of a case
4. one who deceives by false pretensions
5. shyness
6. a go-between
7. slander, false report
8. apparatus for transferring
9. foolhardiness, rash boldness
10. entrance or access
11. moral uprightness, integrity
12. lawless condition of society; absence of government

B.

1. nebula
2. fusillade
3. aesthetics
4. felon
5. parity
6. somnambulist
7. paragon
8. recapitulation
9. cohesion
10. fervor

1. a discharge of a large number of firearms at once
2. a criminal or wicked person
3. a uniting or sticking together
4. equality
5. zeal, intensity of feeling
6. a summary
7. a cloud of stars or luminous gas
8. a many-sided figure
9. a perfect model or pattern
10. a sleepwalker
11. the science of the beautiful in nature or art
12. the study of explosives

C.

1. prolific
2. reciprocal
3. odious

4. flagrant

5. tacit
6. cosmopolitan
7. moribund
8. sententious
9. caviling
10. voluble

1. terse, energetic in expression
2. openly wicked
3. done by each for the other, mutual
4. raising foolish or frivolous objections
5. fond of digging
6. hateful
7. talkative
8. fruitful
9. in a dying condition
10. implied but not stated
11. very polite or courteous
12. without local or national prejudices

D.

1. choleric
2. abstruse
3. somnolent
4. incompatible
5. illegitimate
6. mutable

7. congenial
8. innate
9. pre-eminent

10. bizarre

1. soapy
2. fantastic, grotesque
3. inborn
4. variable, inconstant
5. incapable of being harmonized
6. difficult to understand, deep in meaning
7. willing to buy or sell
8. drowsy
9. kindred, agreeable, sympathetic
10. very superior, outstanding
11. hot-tempered
12. unlawful

E.

1. transfix
2. cremate
3. redress
4. satiate
5. cloy

1. to make void
2. to satisfy or surfeit
3. to return or go back
4. to fasten on a garment
5. to do away with a wrong or injury

6. mutate
7. annul
8. aestivate
9. revert
10. equivocate

6. to spend the summer
7. to pierce or impale
8. to change or undergo change
9. to use double meanings
10. to burrow in the ground
11. sicken with sweetness
12. to burn to ashes, especially a corpse

CAN YOU PRONOUNCE THEM?

Being able to pronounce words correctly is as important today as knowing what they mean. Below are some of the most treacherous words from Part Three. The location by page numbers is given in order that you may look back if in doubt.

The pronunciation of all basic words is given in the list at the back of the book.

APPENDIXES

APPENDIX ONE

A SECRET PROCESS

How would you like a magic passkey or master key which will unlock at sight the meanings of dozens of long words and scores of "hard" words wherever you meet them all the rest of your life? Among its values are these:

1. It will help you understand better than anyone who doesn't possess this magic key nearly everything that you read and hear.

2. It will add a wealth of meaning to hundreds of words which you see and use every day because it will show you "what makes the wheels go round." That's just as much fun with words as it is with old alarm clocks or radio sets.

3. It will help you remember new words by linking them up in chains — endless chains, in fact. You will not confuse *inhale* with *exhale* or *introvert* with *extrovert*, or other such pairs of terms.

4. It will help you in spelling to know how words are put together. *Misspell* and *accommodate* could hardly be different.

Let's see how this key works. The list below contains twenty-four words, all of which you should understand immediately. Some you will recognize as familiar, but could you define them accurately enough to pass a test, getting sixteen and possibly eighteen right?

1. prearrange	9. intercept	17. provocation
2. biweekly	10. millennium	18. subaqueous
3. aqueduct	11. subservience	19. exhalation
4. octogenarian	12. introspection	20. incursion
5. antedate	13. regression	21. retractable
6. circumnavigate	14. infidel	22. polysyllable
7. geology	15. astringent	23. suffuse
8. quadruped	16. retentivity	24. superfluous

Perhaps your teacher will come back to this list after your master key has been cut by the machinery of the lessons which follow.

HERE'S THE SECRET

Many words have three parts:

1. A prefix or beginning
2. A root or stem. This is the middle, base part, or " chassis."
3. An ending or suffix

A few dozen prefixes and roots are used hundreds and hundreds of times in all sorts of words and all kinds of combinations, but they keep their original meanings almost unchanged if they contribute to one's understanding of the word at all. Hence, **if one knows the meanings of a few dozen prefixes and roots,** he will grasp the significance of words like those listed above when he encounters them. A *knowledge* of these roots and prefixes, then, *is* the Magic Key.

HERE'S THE PROCESS

Take apart the words *retraction, prearrangement,* and *superfluity,* for example, and this is what one gets:

re-tract-ion   pre-arrange-ment   super-flu-ity

The meanings, part by part, are:

Prefixes: *re-* back, again   *pre-* before, ahead   *super-* over, above
                                    of time

Roots: *-tract-* draw (pull)   *-arrange-* arrange[1]   *-flu-* flowing

Suffixes: *-ion* act of   *-ment* act or fact   *-ity* state or condition

That makes the words mean:

retraction — act of drawing back or withdrawing (a statement)
prearrangement — fact of arranging (perhaps the hour for meeting someone) ahead of time
superfluity — state of flowing over or above, i.e., an overflowing or unnecessary amount

Now apply it to three sentences:

     The newspaper printed his retraction of the statement that all Democrats are idiots.

---

[1] This "root" really consists of a root (*-range*) plus a prefix (*ar-*). It means *to put in order,* but the two parts have rusted together so completely that it seems useless to pry them apart.

All of the cars arrived at the same instant as if by prearrangement.

In his speech he avoided superfluity of words.

Wouldn't it have been easier to look up the whole word in a dictionary instead of pulling it to pieces? Yes, definitely, as far as those three words are concerned.

BUT

Look what a toe hold you have on:

react	predict	superfine	attract	fluid
reform	prepay	superheat	protract	influence
readjust	premeditate	supercharger	distract	effluence
reaffirm	prelude	superior	detract	affluence
reunite	premonition	supernal	traction	confluence

That's just the beginning. You'll be seeing many of them again soon. Before you start, however, there's a

20% DISCOUNT ON ALL WORDS

Suffixes either have no meaning at all most of the time or else the meaning is so obvious that few endings need to be studied intensively. Yet, before you scornfully disregard them, observe what they can do to a child:

> child (noun)
> childish (adjective)
> childlike (adjective)
> childhood (noun)

— You guessed it, perhaps. In addition to showing sometimes the user's likes and dislikes, they determine what part of speech a word will be. If the root is the chassis of a word, the suffixes are the body styles.

Now for Lesson I.

LESSON ONE

PRETEST

We Learn to Count

What is the meaning of the italicized prefix in each sentence? It will be a number in each case.

1. To *bi*sect an angle is to cut it in __?__ parts.

2. A *cent*ime is one __?__th of a franc.

3. A *non*agenarian has reached the age of __?__ty.

4. An *octo*genarian has reached the age of __?__ty.

5. *Mono*theism is belief in __?__ god.

6. A *tetra*hedron is a solid having __?__ surfaces.

7. A *cent*enarian is __?__ years old or more.

8. A *tri*reme was an ancient boat having __?__ rows of oars.

9. A *quinque*reme, on the other hand, had __?__ rows.

10. A *sex*tant is one __?__th of a circle.

11. Nebraska has a *uni*cameral legislature (__?__-chambered)

12. A *sept*ennial is the __?__th anniversary.

13. A *quadr*uped has __?__ feet.

14. *Hept*archy means government by __?__ rulers.

15. *Du*plicity is __?__ dealing.

16. A *pent*athlon is an athletic meet having __?__ events.

17. A *tri*logy consists of __?__ books or plays.

18. A *deca*logue is a set of __?__ laws.

19. A *mill*ennium lasts __?__ years.

20. A *kilo*gram is __?__ grams.

What is the meaning of the italicized root used in the sentence? It will be a word from the list at the left.

shut	1. To inter*cept* a message is to __?__ it before it reaches the one to whom it should go.
keep or save	
foot	2. A con*fid*ant is someone you __?__ very much.
come	
breaking	3. A *pedo*meter will __?__ one's __?__ mileage.
do	4. To inter*vene* in a quarrel is to __?__ between the parties fighting.
take or seize	
send	5. Do not contra*dict* (__?__ the opposite).
measure	6. E*mot*ion is a __?__ of the feelings.
moving	7. A *fact*otum is a __?__-it-all.
trust	8. To e*mit* a yell is to __?__ it forth.
love	9. An in*fract*ion is a __?__ of the rules.
say	10. To con*serve* one's energy means to __?__ it.

STUDY GUIDE—PREFIXES

UNI– . . . . MONO– . . . . one

*Uni*ty (*one*ness) prevailed.
We studied *uni*cellular (*one*-celled) animals.
He raised his *mono*cle (*single* eye-glass).
The *mono*logue (*one* person talking) continued.

Cf. *unite, unify,* (to make as *one*), *monopoly* (only *one* selling), *monoplane* (*one*-winged plane).

DU(O)– . . . . . BI– . . . . two

They sang a *du*et (music for *two*).
*Du*plicate (*two*fold) prizes were given.
*Bi*monthly (every-*two*-months) payments are expected.
Man is a *bi*ped (*two*-footed creature).

NOTE: *di-* means *two* in words like *dicotyledon,* a plant having two seed leaves. Do not confuse with *dia-* (through, between, or across) in words like *dialect, diameter, diaper, diapason, diocese, dielectric.*

TRI– . . . . TRI– . . . . three

*Tri*plets were born.
Type it in *tri*plicate (*three*fold).
It is a *tri*ennial (every-*three*-years) event.

Cf. *Trinity* (*three* parts of the Godhead), *trisect* (cut in *three* parts).

QUAD(RI)– . . . . TETRA– . . . . four

*Quadru*plets (*four* babies at one birth) are rare.
A *quadr*ant is *one fourth* of a circle.
A *quadr*angle is a *four*-cornered court or lawn surrounded by buildings, usually in a college.
A *tetr*arch (TEE-trark) ruled *one fourth* of a province.
Lead *tetr*aethyl (*four* ethyls) is used in gasoline.

Cf. *quadruplex, quadruplicate.*

QUIN(QUE)– . . . PENTA–. . . . . five

The Dionnes are called *QUIN*-tu-plets. (Note accent on first syllable.)
Our basketball *quin*tet played well.
A *penta*style is a building with *five* columns in front.
*Pente*cost comes the *fiftieth* day after the second day of the Passover.

SEX– . . . . . . HEX– . . . . six

A *sex*tet is a group of *six* (musicians, usually).
A *sex*agenarian is a person in his *six*ties.
A *hex*agon is a *six*-sided figure.

SEPT(EM)– . . . . HEPT– . . . . seven

*Septem*ber was really the *seventh* month until the beginning of the year was changed from March to January.
A *sept*uagenarian is a person in his *seven*ties.
A *hept*agon has *seven* sides. It is *hept*angular because it has *seven* angles.

OCTO– . . . . . . OCTA– . . . . eight

An *oct*et sang.
An *octa*gon is a figure having *eight* sides.
An *octa*ve is the *eight* tones of a musical scale.
*Octo*ber was once the *eighth* month.

NON(A)– . . . . NOV(EM) . . ENNEA . . nine*

A *nona*gon is a *nine*-sided figure.
A *nona*genarian is in his *nine*ties.
*Novem*ber was the *ninth* month in early Roman days.
A *nov*ena is a nine-days' act of devotion (Catholic).
An *ennea*d is a group of nine, esp. nine gods.
Note: *Nov(a)* — and *novo* — mean *new,* as in *novelty.*

DECEM, DECI(M)– . . DEC(A) . . . . ten

A *deca*de is a *ten*-year period.
The Ten Commandments comprise the *Deca*log (*Deca*logue).
To *deci*mate an army is to destroy every *tenth* man or a considerable part of.
Note: *Deci* — usually means a *tenth,* as in *deci*meter. Cf. *decem*vir, *deci*mal, *deca*syllable, *deca*thlon.

CENT(I)– . . . . . HECTO– . . . . . one hundred

A *centi*pede has *one hundred* legs.
A *cent*ury is *one hundred* years.

* The examples given are practically the only ones, and the entry is included merely for the sake of completeness.

A *hecto*graph makes *one hundred* copies.
A *hecto*meter is *one hundred* meters.

MILL(E)– . . . MILLI– . . . KILO– . . one thousand

A *milli*ard is a *thousand* millions.
A *milli*on is a *thousand* thousand.
A *milli*gram is *one thousandth* of a gram.
A *kilo*gram is a *thousand* grams.

NOTE: These *thousand* prefixes occur chiefly in units of the metric system. In this system, *milli-* means *one thousandth* and *cent-* *one hundredth*.

STUDY GUIDE — ROOTS

1. –CEIVE– . . . . . –CEPT– . . . . to take or seize

He managed to inter*cept* (*take* or *seize* between sender and receiver) the message.
Are you an ex*cept*ion (one *taken* out from)?
Here are the other words so common that the root has lost much of its original meaning:

receive — reception	inception
deceive — deception	precept
conceive — conception	susceptible
perceive — perception	accept

2. –DIC– . . . . . –DICT(A)– to say (often in sense of command)

A *dicta*tor arose.
He issued an e*dict* (*command*).
A *dicta*torial manner is one like that of a dictator.
A dictaphone is a mechanical ear that records *dicta*tion.
Cf. *indicate, addict, dictate.*

3. –FACT– . . . –FECT– . . . –FICT– to make or do

A *fact*ory is a place to *make* something.
To manu*fact*ure is literally to make by hand (*manu-*).
*Fict*ion is *make*-believe.
Cf. *confection, affect(ion), effect.*

---

4. –FID(E)– . . . . **faith, trust**

*fid*elity — *faith*fulness
in*fid*el — one having no *trust* (in God)
per*fid*y — breach of *faith*, disloyalty
con*fid*ence — *faith* in something

5. –FRACT– . . . . **to break**

A *fract*ured (broken) leg resulted.
In*fract*ion (breaking) of the rules will be punished.
Cf. *fraction, refract, diffract.*

6. –METER– . . . . **a measure or measurer**

The gas *meter* leaks.
The speed*o*meter (speed *measurer*) is broken.

7. –MIT(T)– . . . . –MISS– . . . . . **to send, sent**

emit — *send* forth   e*miss*ion
dis*miss* — *send* away   dis*miss*al
trans*mit* — *send* across   trans*miss*ion
*miss*ion — a *sending*   com*miss*ion
*miss*ionary — one *sent*   com*mitt*ee

NOTE: Some of these show how the meaning is affected by prefixes which
you have not studied yet.

8. –MOV– . . . . . –MOT– . . . . **to move**

*mot*ive — idea which *moves* one (to act)
pro*mot*e — *move* forward
e*mot*ion — *moving* forth of feelings
Cf. *move, motion, motor, promotion, motivation.*

9. –PED– . . . . . . –POD– . . . . **foot**

*ped*estrian — one who journeys on *foot*
Cf. *equestrian* — one who journeys on a *horse.*
*ped*icure — care of the *feet*
The burden im*ped*es (puts *foot* against or hinders) his progress.
Cf. *pedal, pedestal, impediment, chiropodist.*

10. –POS– . . . . . –PON– . . . . **to place**

To com*pos*e is to *place* together.
A com*pos*ition is a *placing* together of words, paints, or musical
notes.

Post*pone* (*place* later) the event.

Cf. *position* (a *placing*), *impost* (a tax *placed* on something), *proposition* (an idea *placed* or *put* forward).

11. –SERV– . . . . **to keep, save**

Why pre*serve* this any longer?
Did he re*serve* (*keep* back) it for you?
Cf. *reservation, preservation.*

12. –SIST– . . . . **(to make) to stand**

Will you as*sist* (*stand* to, help)?
She in*sists* (*makes a stand*) that I was there.

Cf. *consist, desist, exist, persist, resist, subsist, assistant, assistance, insistence.*

13. –VEN(I)– . . . . –VENT– . . . **to come, a coming**

The con*ven*tion (*coming* together) takes place soon.
Will the government inter*vene* (*come* between) in the labor dispute?

Cf. *convene, intervention.*

EXHIBITS

Study these carefully. Then test yourself on them or have a friend quiz you.

Births	Feet	Music
1. baby	1. monopode	1. solo
2. twins	2. biped	2. duet
3. triplets	3. tripod	3. trio
4. quadruplets	4. quadruped	4. quartet
5. quintuplets	8. octopus	5. quintet
6. sextuplets	10. decapod (lobster)	6. sextet
7. septuplets	100. centipede	7. septet
8. octuplets	1000. millepede	8. octet or double quartet

POETRY

Each line contains a certain number of *feet* or *measures*, each of which has one accented syllable.

1. monometer   Away'!
2. dimeter   Away' we go'!
3. trimeter   Away' we go' to school'!
4. tetrameter   Away' we go' to school' each day'!
5. pentameter   And thus' we take' our books' to school' each day'.
6. hexameter   On hol'idays' we take' no books' away' from school'!
7. heptameter   Except' on hol'idays' we take' our books' to school' each day'!
8. octameter   (Just double No. 4)

Now It's Your Turn to Concoct
A Meter Exhibit

Look up *triad* and *triolet* if you have time.

METRIC SYSTEM

(You'll have to *learn* it if you take much science. Remember that *cent-* means 1/100, *hecto-* means 100, *milli-* means 1/1000 and *kilo-* is 1000.)

Length

1 meter	= 39.37 inches
1 hectometer	= 100 meters
1 kilometer	= 1000 meters
1 centimeter	= 1/100 meter
1 millimeter	= 1/1000 meter

Weight

1 gram	= .0353 ounce
1 hectogram	= __?__ grams
1 kilogram	= __?__ grams
1 centigram	= __?__ gram
1 milligram	= __?__ gram

Multiplication

double
triple
quadruple
quintuple
sextuple
septuple
octuple
decuple
centuple

The Years

1. annual — occurring every year
2. biennial — occurring every two years
3. triennial
4. quadrennial
5. quinquennial
6. sexennial
7. septennial
8. octennial
10. decennial
100. centennial
150. sesquicentennial (See a dictionary.)
300. tercentennial
1000. millennial

Sides

1. *uni*lateral — having *one* side
2. *bi*lateral — having *two* sides
3. *tri*lateral — having *three* sides
4. *quadri*lateral — having *four* sides

Marriage

1. monogamy
2. bigamy

Look up *polygamy*.

Parts

*tri*partite — having *three* parts

*quadri*partite — having *four* parts
*quinque*partite — having *five* parts
*sex*partite — having *six* parts

Ancient Boats

1. *uni*reme — *one* row of oars
2. *bi*reme
3. *tri*reme
5. *quinque*reme

Numbers

million.....a thousand thousand..........1,000,000.... 6 ciphers
billion..............................1,000,000,000.... 9 ciphers
trillion.........................1,000,000,000,000....12 ciphers
quadrillion..................1,000,000,000,000,000....15 ciphers
quintillion................1,000,000,000,000,000,000....18 ciphers
sextillion..............1,000,000,000,000,000,000,000....21 ciphers
septillion......... .1,000,000,000,000,000,000,000,000....24 ciphers
octillion........1,000,000,000,000,000,000,000,000,000....27 ciphers
nonillion....1,000,000,000,000,000,000,000,000,000,000....30 ciphers
decillion.1,000,000,000,000,000,000,000,000,000,000,000....33 ciphers

Elderly Persons		Transportation	Radio
sexagenarian	60–70	1. unicycle	triode
septuagenarian	70–80	2. bicycle	pentode
octogenarian	80–90	3. tricycle	
nonagenarian	90–100		
centenarian	100 plus		

PRACTICE SET 1

What is the meaning of the italicized prefix or root?

1. A *sept*et is a group of __?__ performers.

2. An *octo*syllable is a word with __?__ syllables.

3. Disease *decim*ated the army (destroyed one __?__*th* of the men).

4. A *mono*rail track consists of __?__ rail.

5. A *quadri*lateral has __?__ sides.

6. To *quin*tuple a figure, multiply it by __?__.

7. *Du*plex means __?__ fold.

8. The audience sang in *uni*son (__?__ sound or tone).

9. *Tri*une means __?__ in one.

10. A *sex*partite object has __?__ parts.

11. A *bi*polar battery has __?__ poles.

12. *Tetra*meter has __?__ __?__ in a line.

13. A *mono*tonous voice is one which stays on __?__ tone most of the time.

14. An *octa*vo is a book in which the sheets have been folded into __?__ leaves.

15. A *tri*umvirate consisted of __?__ men.

16. A *deca*thlon is an athletic contest of __?__ separate events.

17. A *milli*gram is __?__ gram.

18. One *kilo*watt hour is consumed by a __?__-watt lamp operating for an hour.

19. What device used by photographers has *three feet*?

20. To sub*sist* on apples and graham wafers means literally to __?__ physically on them, or, in other words, to live on them.

21. A chrono*meter* is a time __?__r.

22. A chiro*pod*ist is a hand and __?__ specialist.

23. What is a word meaning to *take* something that is offered?

24. To con*fide* in a person is to __?__ that person with one's secrets.

25. What is a word which means to *keep* something for a long time? *pre* __?__.

PRACTICE SET 2

What is the meaning of the italicized prefix or root?

1. A *bi*plane has __?__ wings.

2. To *sex*tuple a number, multiply it by __?__.

3. A *quinque*partite arrangement has __?__ parts.

4. A *mono*syllable is a word of __?__ syllable.

5. A *sept*enary lasts or occurs once in __?__ years.

6. A *penta*hedron has __?__ surfaces.

7. A *tri*ennial event occurs once in __?__ years.

8. A *quadr*ennial event occurs once in __?__ years.

9. How many wheels does a *uni*cycle have?

10. *Heptameter* has __?__ __?__ in a line.

11. The machine has *du*al (__?__) controls.

12. *Quadru*plex telegraphy involves __?__ messages over one wire at the same time.

13. A *tetr*arch ruled one__?__*th* of a province.

14. An *octa*ngular figure has __?__ angles.

15. A *deca*syllable is a line of __?__ syllables.

16. The *Centi*grade thermometer has __?__ degrees or steps.

17. A *heca*tomb was the public sacrifice of __?__ oxen.

18. To re*mit* a sum of money is to __?__ it.

19. To re*pose* one's faith in God is to __?__ it in Him.

20. An alti*meter* is a height-__?__*r*.

21. *Ped*ate is a term in zoology which means __?__-like.

22. A word for much noisy *mov*ing about is com__?__.

23. A *break* in a bone is called a __?__*ure*.

24. The expression "bona *fide*" means "in good __?__."

25. Can you think of the word which means *make*-believe and rhymes with *diction*?

FINAL TEST

What is the meaning of the italicized prefix or root in each of the sentences below? It will be a number in most cases.

1. How many rows of oars did a *tri*reme have?

2. How many rows of oars in a *uni*reme?

3. How many wives does a *mono*gamous man have?

4. An *octo*pus has __?__ tentacles.

5. A *quint*et consists of __?__ persons.

6. A *deca*hedron has __?__ faces.

7. A *hecto*graph makes __?__ copies.

8. *Duo*tone means a __?__-tone effect in the same color.

9. A *bi*ped has __?__ feet.

10. The *tri*color is a flag of __?__ colors arranged in equal parts.

11. A *centi*pede has __?__ legs.

12. A *centi*meter is __?__ meter.

13. To *quadr*uple a number is to multiply it by __?__.

14. A *quinqu*ennial event occurs once in __?__ years.

15. A *sex*ennial event comes once in __?__ years.

16. A *mille*pede has, literally, __?__ feet.

17. A *tetra*stich is a poem of __?__ lines.

18. A *sept*ilateral figure has __?__ sides.

19. A *kilo*meter is __?__ meters.

20. The *Penta*teuch consists of the first __?__ books of the Old Testament.

21. Per*fidy* is breach of __?__.

22. The ad*vent* of spring means the __?__*ing* of spring.

23. A __?__*ory* is a place where articles are *made*.

24. I shall dis*miss* (__?__ away) the class.

25. One's choice of words in *say*ing anything is known as his __?__*ion*.

LESSON TWO

PRETEST

A Thousand Times No

What is the meaning of each italicized prefix and root in the sentences below? It may be expressed by a word or words from the list which follows the sentences.

1. *Non*essentials are __?__ important.

2. To *mis*apply a statement is to apply it __?__.

3. To *ob*viate a difficulty is to make headway __?__ it.

4. He concealed his *anti*pathy (feeling __?__) us.

5. An *il*liberal thinker is __?__ generous toward the opinions of others.

6. *Contra*band goods are goods imported __?__ the law.

7. An *ab*erration is a wandering __?__ the truth.

8. A *counter*claim in a damage suit is an __?__ claim.

9. An *in*active stock is __?__ being bought or sold.

10. To *de*pose a ruler is to put him __?__ the throne.

11. *Im*mature corn is __?__ ripe.

12. To *sub*merge is to dip __?__.

13. To *ex*hale is to breathe __?__.

14. *Aqua*marine is the color of sea __?__.

15. To *aud*it a course is to __?__ it without receiving credit.

16. At the time of the *equi*nox, the days and nights are __?__.

17. To *eject* a person is to __?__ him __?__.

18. A *pend*ant is an object made to __?__ from above.

19. A *pli*able person is easily __?__.

20. *Absolution* is __?__ one __?__ guilt.

21. To *evoke* a response is to __?__ one __?__.

22. An a*string*ent will __?__ tissues of the body.

23. *Ten*acity is unusual ability to __?__ on.

24. The an*nunci*ation to Mary was a __?__.

25. A post *mortem* is an investigation after __?__.

Words:

near	under	contract	death
from	out, forth	listen to, hear	loosening
against	over, above	water	declaring
opposing	very	again	hold
not	wrongly	equal	back
down from, off	too	twisting	hang
really	cast	call	folded, i.e., bent

STUDY GUIDE—OPPOSITES AND NEGATIVES

1. ANTI-
2. COUNTER- . . . CONTRA- } against, opposing, opposed to, opposite
3. OB-

An *anti*dote is something acting *against* the effects of a poison
An *anto*nym is the *opposite* of a word.
*Anti*pathy is feeling *against* someone.
An *anti*septic is a medicine *opposed* to decay.
Cf. *antislavery, anti-war* pacts, *anti-labor* feeling

*counter*claim — an *opposite* or *opposing* claim
*counter*balance — *opposite* force or weight
*counter*plot — an *opposing* plot
*contra*dict — say the *opposite*
*counter*act — act *in opposition to*
See *counterfeit* and *counterirritant.*

An *ob*jection is an idea hurled *against* something.
An idea which *ob*sesses one literally sits *against* or besieges him.
To *ob*struct is to build *against*.
Your *op*ponent is one placed *against* you.
Anything which *op*presses, pushes or presses *against* one.
NOTE: Other meanings of *ob-* are not important enough to include.

4. NON- }
5. UN- } . . . . **not**
6. IN- }

*non*conductor — *not* a conductor of electricity
*non*pareil — *not* equaled, unsurpassed
Cf. *nonresident, nonsense, nonunion, nonmetal*, etc.

*un*feigned — *not* pretended
*un*sophisticated — *not* experienced in the ways of the world
*un*warranted — can*not* be proved or defended
Cf. *unconfirmed, ungenerous, ungovernable, unattached, unbearable, unceasing, uncompromising.*
NOTE: Sometimes *un-* carries the idea of reversing as in *untwist, untangle,* and *undress,* but this is not so common as the meaning given, and it is rarely misleading.

*in*eligible — *not* eligible
*in*capable — *not* capable
*in*convenient — *not* convenient
*in*consistent — *not* uniform or harmonious

Other examples: *inconclusive, inactive, inefficient, ineffective, inattention, inaudible, indestructible.*

NOTE: *in*– becomes *im*– before *m* and *p*, *il*– before *l*, *ir*– before *r*: *immovable, impossible, illogical, irreligious*, etc.

N.B. It has another equally important meaning. See next lesson.

7. MIS– . . . . **wrong(ly), incorrect(ly)**

> *mis*behave — behave *wrongly*
> *mis*calculate — calculate *incorrectly*
> *mis*chance — *bad* luck
> *mis*conduct — *wrong* conduct

STUDY GUIDE—DOWNS, OUTS, AND FROMS

1. AB–
2. DE– (down)
3. DIS– ⎫ . . away from, down from, out from, apart
4. EX– (out)
5. SE–

*ab*sence — being *away from*
*ab*rupt — breaking *away* (too quickly) *from*
To *ab*dicate is to declare (*dic*–) one's separation *from* (a throne).
To *ab*duct is to lead *away from* or kidnap.
What you *ab*hor you shrink *from*.

NOTE: Sometimes *s* is added, as in *absent*. Before *v*, the *b* is omitted as in *avert*.

*de*pend — literally, to hang *down from*
*de*populate — take the inhabitants *from*
*de*press — push or press *down*
*de*scend — climb *down*
*de*spise — look *down* on
*de*ter — frighten *away from*

*dis*miss — send *away*
*dis*aster — *separation from* (the protection of) one's guiding star
Cf. *disable, disarm, disapprove, discharge, discolor, discomfort, disconnect.*

*ex*cavate — to hollow *out*
*ex*cept — to take *out*, i.e., not consider or count
*ex*cerpt — something plucked *out from* (a book or speech)
*ex*communicate — to cut *off from* (membership in a church)

NOTE: *Ex-* is reduced to *e* before *d*, *g*, *l*, *m*, *n*, *r*, *v*, and one or two other consonants. It becomes *ef-* before *f* and sometimes *es-* or *ec-*. Look up two or three examples of each in addition to the ones given below if you have time.

Cf. *edict, educate, egress, elude, elect, emit, enounce, erupt,* and *evaporate.*

See *excoriate, exhume, ex libris, extant, extradite,* and *exodus* if you wish to *ex*tract (draw *out*) a few more word secrets.

*se*cede — go *apart*
*se*cure — without (*apart from*) care
*se*duce — to lead *apart* (from the path of right)
*se*clude — shut *apart*

5. SUB– . . . . **under, beneath**

NOTE: The *b* sometimes changes to agree with the first letter of the root to which the prefix is attached.

*sub*cellar — cellar *under* a cellar
*sub*agent — agent *under* an agent
*sub*contract — contract *under* a contract

STUDY GUIDE—ROOTS AND STEMS

1. –AQUE– . . . . –AQUA– . . . . **water**
   Have you an *aqua*rium?
   We studied sub*aque*ous life. (Long *a*, as in *ate*)
   *Aqua*planing is great fun.
   Do you like *aqua*tic sports?

2. –AUD– . . . . –AUDI– . . . . **hear, listen to**
   *audi*torium — a place for *hearing* programs
   *audi*tion — a *hearing*
   *aud*ience — a group of *hearers*

3. –EQU(I)– . . . . **equal**
   The rivers are *equi*distant from this point.
   *Equa*nimity is *equal*ness, *evenness,* or *calmness* of mind (*–anim–*).
   An *equa*ble climate does not vary much.
   Cf. *equilateral, equation, equipoise, equilibrium.*

---

4. –JECT– . . . . : : : : . . **cast or hurl**

A pro*ject*ile is an object *hurled*.
Ab*ject* means *cast* down or downcast.
An inter*ject*ion is an exclamation *hurled* between ideas.

Cf. *project(ion), inject(ion), deject(ion), object(ion), subject(ion).*

5. –MORT– . . . . **death**

A *mort*al wound is a *deadly* injury.
The *mort*ality rate is the *death* rate.
A post *mort*em is an investigation after *death* to determine the cause.

Look up *mortify, mortification.*

6. –NOUNCE– . . . **–NUNCI–** . . . . . . **declare**

De*nounc*ing graft is "*declaring* it down."
An an*nunci*ator *declares* or *announces* a call and tells where the porter is wanted.

Cf. *announce, pronounce, enunciate.*

7. –PEND– . . . . **–PENSE–** . . . . **hang or weigh**

To ex*pend* money is literally to *weigh* it out.
An inde*pend*ent person is one not (*in*–) *hanging* (–*pend*–) down from (*de*–) anything.
An ap*pend*age is something (i.e., arm or leg) *hanging* to the body.

Query: What is one's "pedal appendage"?

8. –PLI(C)– . . . . **–PLEX–** . . . . . . **fold**

A *pli*able person is easily *folded* or *bent*, i.e., *influenced*.
To im*plic*ate one in a crime is literally to *fold* him into it.
A com*plic*ated situation has many "*folds.*"

Cf. *supplicate, duplicate, triplicate, quadruplicate, multiplication, application,* etc.

9. –SOLV– . . . . . **–SOLUT–** . . . . . . **loosen**

dis*solve* — "*loosen*" a solid substance
solve — "*loosen*" a problem
*solv*ent — a liquid which will *loosen* or *dissolve* a solid
ab*solve* — *loosen* a person from (guilt)

Cf. *solution, soluble.*

---

10. **–STRING–** . . . **–STRICT–** . . . draw together, tighten

To re*strict* one's privileges is to *draw* back and thus limit or "tighten" them.

*String*ent laws are *tight* laws.

A *strict*ure of the intestine is a *drawing together* of the walls.

An a*string*ent *contracts* bodily tissues. It is the opposite of a laxative.

11. **–TAIN–** . . . **–TEN(T)–** . . . . hold

A re*ten*tive memory *holds* facts well.

A bulldog has great *ten*acity or *holding* power.

*Ten*ets are beliefs one *holds*.

Cf. *detain, retain, tenable, tenement, detention.*

12. **–VOC–** . . . **–VOCAT–** . . . . . . call

*voc*ation — a *calling* or occupation

con*voc*ation — a *calling* together or assembly

re*voke* — *call* back

in*voc*ation — a *calling* to (God)

Cf. *evoke, provoke, invoke, revocation.*

PRACTICE SET

What is the meaning of the italicized root or prefix in each sentence?

1. To *de*magnetize means literally to take the magnetism __?__.

2. One who *ob*trudes thrusts himself __?__ the wishes of someone.

3. A *non*assessable policy is one which is __?__ assessable.

4. A *counter*plot is a scheme __?__ a plot.

5. *Anti*-Semitic literature is directed __?__ the Jews.

6. *Un*attached means __?__ attached.

7. A *sub*cellar is a cellar __?__ a cellar.

8. __?__-the-beginning inhabitants are called *ab*origines.

9. A *mis*demeanor is a kind of __?__ conduct.

10. *Il*limitable stretches of desert are __?__ limited expanses.

11. To *se*gregate is to place in a flock __?__.

12. To *e*merge is to come __?__.

13. An *in*accessible spot is one __?__ easy to approach.

14. *Equi*poise involves __?__ weights.

15. "La *Mort*e D'Arthur" means "The __?__ of Arthur."

16. A con*ject*ure is a __?__ at the truth.

17. An *aud*itor, literally, is a __?__*er*.

18. Pro*nounce* means to __?__ a word correctly.

19. *Aqua*rius, a sign of the Zodiac, means __?__ -bearer.

20. A *pend*ulum is a weight to __?__ from a ceiling or clock.

21. The ap*plic*ation of a rule means to __?__ it to (fit) the situation.

22. Dis*solut*ion sometimes means the __?__ of the soul from the body, or death.

23. A con*strict*ion of the tube is a __?__*ing* together or __?__*ing*.

24. The beliefs which they __?__ are stated in six *ten*ets.

25. He will fight if there is sufficient pro*vocat*ion (lit. __?__*ing* forth).

If another practice set is desired, repeat the pretest. It will repay additional study.

FINAL TEST

What is the meaning of the italicized prefix or root in each sentence?

1. An *il*logical plan is one that is __?__ well reasoned out.
2. He remained *ob*durate (firmly __?__ the plan).
3. A *non*metal is __?__ a metal.
4. To *ab*stain is to keep oneself __?__ something.
5. A *counter*offensive is a campaign __?__ an attack.
6. His money supply is *in*adequate (__?__ sufficient).
7. To *de*prive is to take something __?__ a person.
8. *Anti*toxin is a substance __?__ a poison.
9. *Sub*soil is __?__ the main layer.
10. An *im*modest person is __?__ modest.
11. To *mis*rule a country is to govern it __?__.
12. To *mis*apprehend is to understand __?__.
13. When one is *ex*pelled, he is driven __?__.
14. A *se*cluded spot is one shut __?__.
15. Im*mort*al means not subject to __?__.
16. An inex*plic*able situation is one not easily *un*__?__*ed*.
17. An *equi*lateral figure has __?__ sides.
18. A con*voca*tion is a __?__*ing* together.

19. Im*pend*ing evil is misfortune that __?__s over one.

20. To ab*solve* a person is to __?__ him from blame.

21. *Subaqueous* plants are vegetation __?__ __?__.

22. A *ten*able belief is one which a person can readily __?__.

23. A pro*ject*ile is an object to __?__ forward.

24. A *strict*ure is a __?__*ing* together or __?__.

25. The *aud*itory nerve is one which enables a person to __?__

LESSON THREE

PRETEST

What is the meaning of each italicized prefix and root in the sentences below? It may be expressed in each case by a word or words from the list at the end of the exercise. Some sentences will require two, one for the prefix and the other for the root. A word may be used more than once.

1. To *append* a footnote is literally to __?__ (*–pend–*) it __?__ (*ap–*) the article.

2. A *col*loquy is a speaking __?__.

3. An *inter*regnum is a period __?__ reigns.

4. A *poly*syllable is a word which has __?__ syllables.

5. A *concourse* is a __?__ __?__.

6. A *demi*god is a __?__ god.

7. To *super*impose an object is to place it __?__ another.

8. His means of *egress* is his means of __?__ __?__.

9. An odor which *per*vades a room is spread __?__ the air.

10. An organ *pre*lude is a playing __?__ the service.

11. *Ante*diluvian means __?__ the flood.

12. To *pre*sage is to tell or give a warning __?__.

13. The *post*erior end is __?__.

14. To *recede* in the distance is to __?__ __?__.

15. To *dispel* a mist means to __?__ it __?__.

16. Re*tract*able landing gear is constructed so that the pilot can __?__ it back into the ship.

17. A *port*age makes it necessary to __?__ a canoe.

18. What does a *multiped* have that humans do not? __?__ __?__.

19. A *scribe* is one who __?__.

20. Sopori*fer*ous atmosphere is sleep-__?__.

21. *Vert*ebrae are so called because they __?__.

22. An intro*spect*ive person is one who likes to __?__ within himself.

23. A stone pillar is an in*flex*ible object; no one can __?__ it.

24. *Semi*civilized races are __?__ civilized.

25. A *spirometer* is a __?__ __?__r.

Words:

going	beforehand	between	look
through	before	half	bearing
out	running	writes	measurer
to, onto	together	away	bend
hang	five	carry	breath
go	behind	draw, pull	half
back	many	feet	against
over, above	drive	turn	

STUDY GUIDE—PREFIXES

1. AD– . . . . **to, toward**

NOTE: This prefix is especially apt to change its *d* to the first letter of the root to which it is joined. Sometimes the *d* is dropped before *s*.

*ad*here — to stick *to*
*ad*junct — (something) joined *to*
*ad*vertize — to turn (*–vert–*) attention *toward*
*ap*pease — to give peace *to;* pacify
*al*locate — to allot *to*

Cf. *allure, append, ascribe, addict, adjoining, astringent,* etc.

2. CON– . . . . . **SYN–** . . . . . **together, with**

NOTE: Remember that *con–* may appear as *col–, com–, co–,* and *cor–* as explained under *ad–* above. Also *syn–* becomes *sym–,* sometimes.

A *con*vention is a coming (*–vent–*) *together.*
A *col*loquy is a speaking *together* or conversation.
To *com*pare two objects is to equal (*–par–*) them *with* each other.
*Con*cord means heart(s) *together* or harmony.

Cf. *collect, co-operate, corroborate, correlate.*

*Sym*pathy is feeling (*–path–*) *with* someone.
*Sym*phony means sound (*–phon–*) *together.*
*Syn*chronous processes are timed (*–chron–*) *together.*
A *syn*thesis is a placing *together* of elements to create something new or different.

3. IN– . . . . **to, toward, into**

NOTE: It becomes *il–, im–,* and *ir–* as explained under *ad–* above. It also appears as *im–* before *b* and *p*.

*in*gratiate — make (oneself) pleasing *to*
*im*migrant — one who migrates *into* a country
*il*luminate — cast light *into* or *upon*
*im*bibe — drink *in*

Cf. *indwell, inject, inflame, influx, infuse, ingraft, ingrain, ingrown.*

4. INTER– . . . . **between or among**

Examples:
interchange, intercede, intercept (Lesson I), *interscholastic, intercommunicate*
interfere (strike between), *interlace, intermarriage, international, interpenetrate,* etc.

NOTE: *Intra–, intro–* mean *within*. *Intra*mural sports are games *within* the walls (*–mur–*) of one's own school. An introduction is literally a *leading within*.

5. MULTI– . . . . POLY– . . . . many or several

A *multi*graph makes *many* copies.
*Multi*farious devices are schemes having *much* variety.

Cf. *multimillionaire, multicellular, multitude.*

A *poly*gon is a *many*-sided figure.
A *poly*glot knows *many* languages.
*Poly*theism is belief in *many* gods.

Investigate *polygamy* and *polytechnic.*

6. PER– . . . . through

*per*ceive — see *through*
*per*colate – – strain *through*
*per*sist –– stand *through*, i.e., hang on
*per*meate — spread *through*
im*per*vious — no way *through*

7. POST– . . . . after, behind

To *post*date a check is to date it *after* or *later than* the time of writing.
The *post*erior end is behind.
An organ *post*lude is a playing *afterward.*

Cf. *postgraduate, postpone, postscript.*

8. PRE– . . . . . ANTE– . . before, ahead of time

The *pre*concerted plan was arranged (*–cert–*) together (*–con–*) ahead of time.
Murder is *pre*meditated (planned-*ahead-of-time*) killing.
An organ *pre*lude is a playing (*–lude–*) *before* the service.
A *pre*monition is a warning *beforehand.*
*Ante*meridian means occurring *before* noon.
An *ante*type is an *earlier* form from which a later form has developed.

Cf. *preplan, prepay, preheat, pre-exist, anteroom, antechamber.*

9. PRO– . . . . forward, favoring, before

*pro*mote — move *forward*
*pro*clivity — a natural tendency *forward* or *toward*
*pro*crastinating — *favoring* tomorrow, putting off until tomorrow

---

pro-Russian — *favoring* Russia

(See dictionary for occasional other meanings as in *proconsul* and *pronoun*.)

10. RE– . . . . **back(ward), again**

To *re*act is to act *backward* or against.

To *re*cognize is to know *again*.

When a condition *re*curs it happens *again*.

Cf. *reborn, readjust, reform, regain, refresh*.

11. SEMI– . . . . **DEMI–** . . . . **HEMI–** . . . **half**

A *semi*annual event occurs every *half* year.

Cf. *semicircle, semicivilized, semifinals*.

A *demi*god is a *half* god.

A *demi*volt is a *half* leap in horsemanship.

A *hemi*sphere is *half* a sphere.

Query: What is a *demi-tasse?*

12. SUPER– . . **HYPER–** . . **ULTRA–** . . **above, beyond**

(The latter two often imply an excess of that to which they are prefixed.)

A *super*eminent man is eminent *beyond* others.

*Super*abundance is *above* or *beyond* abundance.

*Super*nal beauty is *above* or *beyond* mere earthly loveliness.

Cf. *superheat, supercharger, superior*.

*Hyper*acidity is *excessive* acidity.

A *hyper*critical person is *excessively* critical.

An *ultra*modern person is *excessively* modern — or at least *beyond* one who is merely modern.

13. TRANS– . . . . **across**

*Trans*verse lines cut *across* or form a crisscross.

To *tra*verse a field is to go *across* it.

To *trans*cend is to climb *across* or beyond.

Cf. *transport, transship, transatlantic, transoceanic*.

STUDY GUIDE—A ROMAN ROOT FEST

1. –CEDE– . . . . **–CEED–** . . . **–CESS** . . . **go**

   –GRAD– . . . . **–GRESS–** . . . . **go or walk**

To pro*gress* is to *go* forward.

An ag*gress*ive attitude is a *going* toward (*ad–*) or pushing attitude.

A di*gress*ion is a *going* away from or wandering.
An ant*eced*ent is the word which *goes* before a pronoun and thus
identifies it.
To ex*ceed* the limit is to *go* out of or beyond.
Cf. *ingress, egress, regression, recede, precede, proceed, secede.*

2. –CUR(R)– . . . . –CURS– . . . . . . run(ning)

*Curr*ent literally means *running.* So does *course.*
To in*cur* dislike means to *run* into it.
An ex*curs*ion is a *running* out from (one's place of abode).
A *courier* is a *runner.*
Cf. *concourse,* a running together; *recur,* to run back, i.e., happen again.

3. –DUC(T)– . . . . lead

"Il *Duce*" meant The *Leader.*
A *duct*ile substance is easily "*led*" or shaped.
What light does your knowledge of prefixes and roots throw
upon meanings of common words like *induce, induct, deduce,
deduct, conduct, product, nonconductor,* and *duct?*
How many additional words can you list, using suffixes or end-
ings?
Review: *abduct, aqueduct, introduce.*

4. –FER– . . . . . –LAT(E)– . . . carry, bear, bring
–PORT–. . . . . –PORTAT– . . . .

Confer, refer, defer, interfere, transfer, translate, suffer, superlative,
and *relate* are just a few common derivatives. The practical
value of knowing roots appears in words like these:
col*late* — *bring* together (books or data for critical study)
sopori*fer*ous — sleep-*bearing* or *-giving*
odori*fer*ous — odor-*carrying*
Report, export, import, purport, porter, and *support* are a few of
the commonest from *–port–.*
A *port*age is a canoe *carry* between bodies of water.
De*port*ment is one's *carriage* or *behavior.*

5. –FLECT– . . . . –FLEX– . . . . bend

re*flect* — *bend* back
circum*flex* — *bent* around
To de*flect* a blow is to *bend* it away from one.
Cf. *flexible, inflexible, reflex, inflect.*

---

6. -FUS(E)- . . . . **pour**

To *refuse* is literally to *pour back*.
To *interfuse* is to *pour among*.
To *confuse* is to *pour together*.
The tonic will *infuse* (*pour in*) new life.

Review: *suffuse*, pour under.

7. -PEL- . . . . . . **-PULS-** . . . . . . **drive or push**

repel	repulsion
expel	expulsion
impel	impulsion

An *impulse* is a *pushing* (toward action) of some sort, and *impulsiveness* is a trait of those who yield often to impulses.

Cf. *pulsate*, throb; *dispel*, drive away.

8. -SCRIBE- . . . . . . **-SCRIPT-** . . . . . . **write, written**

ascribe	ascription	scrip
describe	description	script
inscribe	inscription	scripture
prescribe	prescription	
subscribe	subscription	
transcribe	transcription	

A *scribe* is one who *writes*.
A *script*orium is a room for *writing*.

9. -SPEC(T)- . . . . . **-SPIC-** . . . . **to look (at)**
-VIDE- . . . . . **-VIS-** . . . . **to see**

A *suspicious* person is always looking (*-spic-*) or peeking under (*-sus-*) what appears on the surface.
Introspection is *looking within* oneself.
The *prospect* (*forward look*) appears good.
A *circumspect* person is one who *looks about* (*circum-*) and is thus careful of appearances.

Cf. *expect, inspect, respect, conspicuous,* and their kin. *Spectator, spectacle, spectacular, specter* (ghost), *spectrum,* and *speculate* must not be overlooked.

To *provide* is to *see forward* or *ahead*.
A *visor* has to do with *seeing*, and a *vista* is a *sight* or *view*.

Cf. *vision, visible, visual, visit, visitor, revision, invisible.*

NOTE: The Greek word meaning to look gives us the ending of a dozen or more look-devices such as microscope, spectroscope, kaleidoscope, periscope, telescope, and stereoscope.

10. –SPIR(E)– . . . –HAL(E) . . . breathe or breath

An *aspirant* is one who *breathes* or *strives toward* something.
A *spirograph* is a *breath record.*
Perspiration is *breathing through* (the skin).

aspire — aspiration	inspire — inspiration
expire — expiration	respire — respiration

Cf. *spirit, spiritual, inspirit, spirited, despirited.*

If you have learned the prefixes well, you will never confuse *inhale* and *exhale* or any similar pair such as *prelude* and *postlude, immigrant* and *emigrant* or *egress* and *ingress.*

11. –TRACT– . . . . draw (in the sense of drag or pull)

at*tract* — *draw* to	attraction	tractor
dis*tract* — *draw* away from	distraction	traction

How many others can you list, together with their meanings?

12. –VERT– . . . . –VERS– . . . . turn

avert	aversion	averse
convert	conversion	converse
divert	diversion	diverse

Vertigo is a *turning* or *whirling* called dizziness.

PRACTICE SET

What is the meaning of the underlined prefixes and roots in the sentences below?

1. The function of a *co*herer was to make particles stick _ _ _ _.

2. The act of *exhal*ation (_ _?_ _*ing* _ _?_ _) was pleasant.

3. *Super*fluous praise is _ _?_ _ what is necessary or desirable.

4. A *demi*-tasse is _ _?_ _ a cup.

5. A *spect*er is something startling to _ _?_ _, i.e., a ghost.

6. *Pre*mature fruit is ripe _ _?_ _.

7. A *pro*-British attitude is one __?__ the British.

8. One who *transgresses* the law literally __?__ __?__.

9. To *re*habilitate men is to make them useful __?__.

10. To *cor*relate several activities is to tie them __?__.

11. An event which *ante*dated the voyage of Columbus occurred __?__ 1492.

12. A *tract*able person is easy to __?__ toward someone's point
of view.

13. An *ad*junct is something joined or added __?__ an arrangement.

14. A *post*script is something written __?__ the rest of the
letter.

15. A *semiannual* event occurs __?__ __?__.

16. *Intercession* is an act of __?__ __?__ a friend and someone
in authority.

17. To ex*pire* really means to __?__ one's last.

18. The *Scrip*tures are sacred __?__*ings*.

19. *Poly*technic training involves __?__ skills.

20. If *vi-* means way or path, to say that a person is *im*-
*per*vious to criticism means that it can find __?__
way __?__.

21. The in*cursion* of barbarians means their __?__ in, i.e.,
their inroads.

22. A *versatile* person is one who can __?__ his hand to almost
anything.

23. To *expel* a pupil is to __?__ him __?__.

24. *Revision* literally means __?__ a piece of work __?__.

25. To *deport* a person is to __?__ him __?__ the country.

For further exercise material, use the pretest again. The effort will be well repaid.

FINAL TEST

What is the meaning of each prefix, root or word italicized in the sentences below?

1. *Inter*stellar space exists __?__ the stars.

2. A *poly*gon has __?__ sides.

3. If a unicellular animal has one cell, a *multi*cellular animal has __?__.

4. How often does a *semi*weekly paper appear? Every __?__ week.

5. *Trans*verse lines are drawn __?__ the paper.

6. A *pre*meditated act is one planned __?__.

7. The literal meaning of *introduce* is to __?__ one __?__.

8. A *per*ennial is a plant which lasts __?__ the years.

9. A feeling of *repulsion* __?__s one __?__.

10. The *ante*rior end is toward the __?__.

11. If an auditorium is a room for hearing, what would a *scriptorium* be? A __?__.

12. *Con*cord means heart(s) __?__.

13. A *spiro*graph is a record of one's __?__.

14. The *re*currence of a disease is its happening __?__.

15. *Hyper*acidity is acidity __?__ normal.

16. If *retro*- means backward, what does retro*spect* mean? __?__.

17. A *pro*clivity is a natural tendency __?__ something.

18. To *retract* a statement is to __?__ it __?__.

19. A *super*normal person is __?__ normal.

20. A *post*lude is music played __?__ a service.

21. An *ultra*radical person is __?__ a radical.

22. To *deflect* a blow is to __?__ it __?__.

23. Odori*fer*ous plants are odor __?__.

24. To *revert* to a bad habit is to __?__ __?__ to it.

25. *Hali*tosis is unpleasant __?__.

PUZZLE PRACTICES

These puzzle exercises, no less than the lessons themselves, will help you remember and understand dozens of words which you could otherwise learn only in a more laborious manner or with which you would never have more than a surface acquaintance. They will make easier your conquest of those words which cannot be taught adequately or efficiently by such lessons as these.

PUZZLE 1

What word from the list below the exercise fits best in each sentence?

1. The car began to __?__. (lose speed — opposite of *accelerate*)

2. __?__ the vase in your drawing more. (move away from the center)

3. Can you __?__ the message? (take from a cipher or code)

4. He was afraid to __?__ a hen. (remove the head, *–capit–*, from)

5. Chlorine will __?__ a rose. (remove color from)

6. Why __?__ the idea? (cry down)

7. __?__ the tire before you fix it. (take the air from)

8. No armor will __?__ these bullets. (bend away)

Words:

decipher or decode	deflate	decapitate
decolor	decenter	deform
decry	deflect	decelerate

1. Ice will __?__ a plane. (deprive of ability to fly)

2. Never try to __?__ a burglar. (take the weapons away from)

3. Father and Mother __?__ of your going. (opposite of *approve*)

4. Your efforts produce only __?__. (lack of harmony)

5. Do you think the law should __?__ criminals? (deprive of power to vote)

6. The __?__ between their ages is great. (lack of equality)

Words:

discord	disapprove	disenfranchize
disarm	distinguish	disparity
disable	dismiss	

1. To hollow out is to __?__.

2. This will __?__ him from the charge of robbery. (free from blame)

3. To __?__ a body is to remove it *from the ground* after it has been buried.

4. A Latin expression often found on book plates is "__?__".

5. An __?__ is a person who has given up his native land or has been driven out.

6. It was difficult to __?__ small boys. (shut out)

Words:

exculpate	exhume	examine	excavate	exclude
ex libris	extinct	expatriate	expunge	

PUZZLE 2

How many of the missing words can you find?

1. We rode in a __?__ railroad. (across the Alps)

2. The *Queen Mary* is a __?__ liner. (across the Atlantic)

3. A blood __?__ saved his life. (pouring or carrying blood from one person to another)

4. If you __?__ the law, you will perish. (step across)

5. The steam engine brought about the __?__*ition* from medieval to modern times. (going across)

6. Can you __?__ this German sentence? (carry across from one language to another).

7. Will you __?__ this message? (send across)

8. Is it possible to __?__*mute* copper into gold? (change across)

9. A gardener __?__ tomatoes from a hot house to the garden. (moves across)

10. Be sure to nail the __?__ supports in place. (crosswise)

PUZZLE 3

What single word having the meaning described in parentheses after the sentence, belongs in each blank?

1. Two substances __?__. (act on each other)

2. The __?__ railroad went bankrupt. (between boroughs)

3. __?__ space is filled with fat. (space between cells)

4. He went out for __?__ basketball. (basketball between colleges)

5. __?__ among airliners is possible. (communication between airliners)

6. The __?__ of capital and labor is not always recognized. (dependence on each other)

7. __?__ distances are unbelievably vast. (among the stars)

8. __?__ between Negroes and whites seldom occurs. (marriage between Negroes and whites)

9. __?__ travel may some day be possible. (travel among planets)

10. __?__ commerce is affected. (commerce among states)

PUZZLE 4

Can you find all the missing words?

1. What does the weather man __?__? (say beforehand)

2. One who rules entirely by his own say-so is a __?__.

3. A machine for *what-you-say writing* is a __?__*graph.*

4. A term for a decree or royal order: e-__?__.

5. A person who habitually uses a drug is an __?__.

6. The grand jury will __?__ (say against) you if you seem to be guilty.

7. Kidnapers __?__ their victims. (lead away)

8. Can you __?__ him to try? (lead into, persuade)

9. The guide will __?__ a tour of the park. (lead with him)

10. A "water-leading" device: __?__.

PUZZLE 5

What single word belongs in each of the blanks below?

1. He decided to __?__ the check. (mark with a date later than the time of writing it)

2. A __?__ is a pupil who keeps on taking courses after graduation.

3. A *post*humous child is one born __?__ the death of its father.

4. *Pre*natal influences occur __?__ birth and *post*natal care comes ____ birth.

5. An under-the-sea boat is known as a __?__.

6. *Sub*cutaneous means __?__ the skin.

7. A person who works under (the direction of) another is a __?__.

8. *Super*fine means __?__ fine.

9. A __?__ power stole the gold from Silas Marner. (more than natural)

10. A *super*sonic radiation vibrates at a rate __?__ what can be detected by the human ear.

SUFFIXES

If you read "A Secret Process" you already know why very little has been said about the endings of words, though they are worthy of one lesson. Here it is. The suffixes below are arranged in groups. Those on the first list usually make nouns or name-words of the chassis or stems to which they are attached. Those on the second make a verb or action-word, those on the third an adjective, and the one in the fourth, innumerable adverbs. The fifth list contains odds and ends which commonly make more than one part of speech out of a word.

Where the meaning seems important or definite enough to bother with, it is given. Remember that suffixes are simply mountings, useful in classifying words but not in ferreting out twenty or thirty centuries of hidden meaning. Like the tails of animals they are more ornamental than useful.

GROUP I

Makers of nouns or name-words

–ability	—— capability, usability, habitability
–acity	—— tenacity, pertinacity, perspicacity, sagacity
–ance	—— resistance, importance, dominance
–(at)or	—— creator, liberator, factor, victor, perpetrator
–dom	—— kingdom, Christendom, freedom
–ence	—— preference, insistence, impertinence, conference, essence
–hood	—— manhood, womanhood, childhood
–ice	—— service, novice, avarice

-ism	—— communism, fascism, impressionism, surrealism
-ness	—— shyness, awkwardness, deceptiveness, foolishness, kindness
-ship	—— friendship, stewardship, relationship
-(t)ion	—— invention, prevention, dominion, suspicion, ascension
-tude	—— multitude, fortitude, servitude, gratitude
-(t)ure	—— fixture, creature, texture, manufacture
-ty	—— fealty, royalty, loyalty, liberty, poverty

GROUP II

Makers of adjectives or describing-words

-able	—— capable, tenable, usable, habitable, portable
-ful	—— meaningful, zestful, skillful, rueful, peaceful

(NOTE: Add another suffix, *-ness*, and make nouns of these.)

-(i)al	—— practical, superficial, electrical, mechanical, partial, manual, venial
-(i)ent	—— convenient, resilient, magnificent, beneficent

(NOTE: *convenience, resilience* (*-cy*), and *magnificence* are corresponding nouns.)

-(i)ous	—— perilous, seditious, precious, delicious
-ish	—— foolish, devilish, childish, womanish
-istic	—— realistic, materialistic, symbolistic, moralistic, futuristic
	Cf. *-ist* —— socialist, realist, moralist
	Cf. *-ism* —— socialism, realism, individualism
-ive	—— seductive, productive, pensive, subversive
-less (lacking)	—— conscienceless, reckless, hapless, headless, merciless, remorseless, defenceless

(NOTE: Add *-ness* to each.)

-ment	—— predicament, impediment, compliment, supplement
-(u)al	—— usual, manual, perpetual, factual

GROUP III

Makers of verbs or action words

-ate ——— complicate, fluctuate, investigate, decimate, enervate, perpetuate

(NOTE: See *-ate* in Group V.)

-(i)fy (make) ——— magnify, horrify, specify
-ize ——— burglarize, realize, sensitize, monopolize

GROUP IV

Maker of most adverbs or when-where-why-how words

-(i)ly ——— greedily, angrily, poorly, badly, quickly, shyly

GROUP V

Makers of various kinds of words

-age ——— adage, portage, savage, ravage, dotage
-ant ——— pleasant, savant, important, rampant
-ate ——— triplicate, duplicate, syndicate, sedate, fluctuate
-e ——— determine, reverse, converse, surprise
-ent ——— latent, patent, portent, independent
-ory ——— memory, factory, obligatory, sensory, advisory
-(r)ior ——— interior, exterior, anterior

EXERCISES

1. List additional examples of each suffix above. You might consult a rhyming dictionary if necessary.

2. Have a contest to see who can list the largest number of *–ists;* the largest number of *–isms*. A committee may be appointed to prepare a composite list for exhibition purposes from the papers turned in.

3. Using the following list of prefixes, roots, and endings, how many words can you construct? Be sure to check any doubtful words or spellings in a large dictionary.

Prefixes	Roots	Suffixes
ab–	–dict–	–ness
ad–	–duct– –duce–	–or
con–	–fact– –fect– –fict–	–(t)ion
de–	–mitt– –miss–	–able
ex–	–pel– –puls–	–ence –ance
		–ent –ant
in–	–ceive– –cept–	–ive
ob–	–ject–	
pre–	–serv–	
re–	–sist–	
sub–	–spect–	

This problem will take a long time if you do it systematically and resourcefully. To simplify it, divide the prefixes and roots into two parts. Use the first half of each, then the other half, and finally the first half of one and the second half of the other with all of the suffixes. This makes four exercises out of the material.

4. How many words can you add to this list of words which have a compound prefix or suffix?

nonproductiveness	insurrectionist
proprietorship	nonconductor
insufficiency	incomprehensibleness
preposterousness	independent
internationalism	multitudinous

Invent a Word

When Maury Maverick was in Congress, he needed a word to describe the kind of language too often found in legal documents and Government forms, especially during the war when there were so many complicated rules and restrictions. *Gobbledygook* was the result — suggested by turkeys strutting and gobbling with ridiculous pomposity back in his native Texas.

The word quickly became popular. *Gabble, chatter, jabber, argot, lingo, cant, echolalia* and similar words are useful enough, but none suggests stuffy pompousness in speech or writing quite so well as *gobbledygook*.

Hundreds of new words are invented annually. As many as 5000 emerged each year during the war. Most new words are soon forgotten, however. How many of the following, for example, are still familiar and valuable?

panzer	baka	Herrenvolk	posturing
commando	banzai	parapooch	leftwardness
bazooka	kamikaze	walkie-talkie	bibliotherapy
foxhole	gungho	dunkirked	genocide

Business and commercial activity have given us many new words like *lubritorium, simonize, winterize*. Someone has called such words "the robots of our language." Science is continually creating new words. *Curium*, a new element after the Curies, and *fission* in the nuclear sense are examples.

If you need a word and cannot find a suitable one, it is your privilege to invent one — but *please* turn to page 322 first.

TWO DOZEN MORE TECHNICAL
WORD BRICKS—LARGELY GREEK

STUDY GUIDE—PREFIXES

1. AUTO– . . . . **self-**

*auto*matic — *self*-operating
*auto*mobile — *self*-moving
*auto*maton — a mechanical (*self*-operative) man

2. BENE– . . . . . **EU–** . . . . **well, good**

*bene*faction — (*well* doing)
*bene*volence — (*well*-wishing)
*eu*genics — science of being *well* born
*eu*logy — a speaking *well* of someone, formal statement of praise

3. CIRCUM– . . . . . **PERI–** . . . . . . **around, about**

*circum*flex — bent *around*
*circum*gyrate — whirl *around*
*circum*locution — speaking *around* (a topic), talking in a circle
*circum*navigate — sail *around*
*peri*meter — the measure *around*
*peri*cardium — (a membrane) *around* the heart

4. EPI– . . . . **above, over, or upon**

The *epi*dermis is *above* or *upon* the dermis.
The *epi*glottis is *upon* the glottis.
An *epi*taph is an inscription *upon* a tomb.

5. GEO– . . . . **earth**

*Geo*logy is the study of *earth* (structure).
*Geo*graphy is *earth*-writing
*Geo*desy (gĕ-ODD-ĕ-sĭ) is the science of measuring the size and
   shape of the *earth*.

---

6. HYDR(O)– . . . . **water**

The *hydro*sphere is that part of the earth's surface consisting of *water*.
> *hydr*ous — containing *water*
> an*hydr*ous — not containing *water*

*Hydro*lysis is the breaking up of *water*.

7. MICRO– . . . . **very small, tiny**

*Micro*be means "*small* life."
A *micro*meter measures very *small* distances.
A *micro*scope is a device for seeing very *small* objects.
A *micro*phone handles very *small* sounds.

8. NEO– . . . . **new**

*Neo*n is literally the "*new*" gas.
A *neo*phyte is a "*new* growth," i.e., a beginner or novice.
A *neo*plasm is a *new* and abnormal growth within the body.
See *neolithic*.

9. ORTHO– . . . . RECT– . . . . . . **correct, right**

> *ortho*dox — *right* opinions or teaching
> *ortho*graphy — spelling (*right* writing)
> *rect*itude — up*right*ness
> *rect*ify — make *right*

10. PAN– . . . . OMNI– . . . . **all**

The *Pan*-American Union is an association of 21 American republics.
Pan-Germanism is a desire for the political unity of *all* Germans.
The *Pan*theon was sacred to *all* the gods.
An *omni*vorous appetite is one which is *all*-devouring.

11. PHOTO– . . . . **light**

> photosynthesis   photometer
> photo-electric   photo-engrave

12. TELE– . . . . **far off, at a distance**

> *tele*graph — *far-off* writing
> *tele*photo — *far-off* light, i.e., picture taking
> *tele*vision — *far-off* vision or seeing
> *tele*pathy — feeling (–*path*–) someone else's thoughts *at a distance*

1. –CIDE– . . . . **killing**

homi*cide* — *killing* a man
regi*cide* — *killing* a king
Cf. *infanticide, insecticide, parricide.*

2. –CLUDE– . . . . –CLUS– . . . . **shut**

in*clude* — in*clus*ion, *shutting* in
ex*clude* — ex*clus*ion, *shutting* out
se*clude* — se*clus*ion, *shutting* apart

3. –DOMIN– . . . . **rule, ruling**

The *domin*ant trait is a *ruling* trait.
To *domin*ate is to *rule.*
Cf. *domination, dominion.*

4. –FLU(EN)– . . . –FLUX– . . . . . . **flow(ing)**

con*fluence* — *flowing* together (of two rivers)
ef*fluence* — a *flowing* out from
Super*flu*ous comments are those *flowing* above or beyond and
   therefore unnecessary.

5. –GRAPH– . . . . –GRAM– . . . . **writing, record**

*graph*ology — study of (hand)*writing*
chiro*graphy* — hand *writing* (cf. *chiro*podist)
seismo*gram* — earthquake *writing* or *record*
Cf. *telegraph, monograph, monogram, heliograph, pantograph, geography.*

6. JURIS–, JUR(E)– . . . . **right or law**

*Juris*diction — authority (*right* to say)
*Juris*prudence — skill in *law* or *rights*

NOTE: Several very closely related sources are involved. The
   ones which follow carry the "I-swear" idea, which is one phase
   of both right and law: *conjure, perjure, adjure, injure,* and their
   variants.

7. MAGNA– . . . MEGA– . . . . . **large, great**

*magn*ify — make *large,* enlarge
*magn*itude — *large*ness

Magna Charta — The *Great* Charter (1215 A.D.)
*mega*lith — huge stone
*mega*lomania — crazy notion of one's own *greatness* or *bigness*

8. –MERGE– . . . . **–MERS–** . . . . **dip**

sub*merge*, *dip* under — submersion
im*merse*, *dip* into — immersion

9. –PHONE– . . . . **sound**

Examples: *telephone, phonograph, megaphone, phonetic, dictaphone,*
xylophone (ZYE-lŏ-fōn, wood-sound), *euphonious.*

10. –POLI(S)– . . . **–URB(S)–** . . . . **city**
–POLIT– . . . . **–CIVI(S)–** . . . . . . **citizen**

A metro*polis* is literally a "mother" *city.*
Sub*urb*an areas are "under" the *city* in the sense of being
dominated by it though they are not politically a part of it.
An *urb*ane person is of the *city* in that he is polished and
courteous.

Cf. *Annapolis, Minneapolis, political, politician, civil, civilian, civilize,* etc.

11. –SEQU– . . . . . **–SECUT–** . . . . **follow**

A *sequ*ence is a *series* or *following.*
Con*sequ*ences *follow* together as the result of one's actions.

Cf. *consecutive, sequel, execute, persecute, inconsequential.*

12. –VOLVE– . . . **–VOLUT–** . . . . **roll**

In*volut*ions are *rollings* in or folds.
A re*volut*ion is a *rolling* over or back in machinery or govern-
ments.
E*volut*ion is a *rolling* out from.

Cf. *involve, revolve, volume, voluble.*

PRACTICE SET

What meaning of the *italicized* word or fraction of a word
belongs in each blank?

1. An *auto*nomous group is a __?__-governing group.

2. A *euphonious* name is one which __?__s __?__.

---

3. A *neo*logism (nē-OL-ō-jĭzm) is a __?__ word or phrase.

4. A *photometer* is a __?__ __?__r.

5. *Hydro*therapy is the cure (–*therap*–) of diseases by means of __?__.

6. *Pan*chromatic film claims to respond uniformly to __?__ colors (–*chrom*–).

7. To *circumvent* a plot is to __?__ __?__ or thwart it.

8. An *ortho*gon is a parallelogram having __?__ angles.

9. The *telephone* literally is a device for reproducing __?__ __?__.

10. An *orthophonic* loudspeaker produces the __?__ __?__s.

11. A *periscope* is a device for __?__*ing* __?__ something which is between the object and the observer.

12. *Graph*ology is the study (–*ology*) of __?__.

13. A *magn*animous person is one who is __?__ of soul.

14. *Micro*chemistry is the chemistry of __?__ quantities.

15. An *omni*potent person is __?__-powerful.

16. *Geo*desy is the science of measuring the size and shape of the __?__.

17. *Urb*an life is __?__ life.

18. A *circumfluent* river is one which __?__ __?__ a piece of land.

19. *Civi*l rights are those of a __?__.

20. To *preclude* the possibility of trouble is to __?__ it off __?__.

21. The *sequel* to an occurrence is the incident which __?__s.

22. A task which de*volves* upon a person literally __?__s down upon him.

23. Fratri*cide* is __?__ a brother (*fratri–*).

24. A *beneficent* person is always __?__ __?__.

25. An *epi*logue is a poem or comment __?__ a play which has just been produced.

MISCELLANEOUS PUZZLES

Try These on Your Vocabulary

PUZZLE I

What single word best fits the description given in each sentence or in parentheses following the sentence?

1. The __?__ of a circle is a little more than three times its diameter.

2. Who was the first to __?__ the globe? (sail around)

3. Are you clever enough to __?__ your enemies? (come around, encircle)

4. Who is the most __?__ person you know? (prudent, looking carefully around)

5. The __?__ of the rectangle is 20 feet. (measure around)

6. The submarine carried a __?__ so that its commander could see what was happening above the surface. (device for *seeing around*)

7. The membrane around the heart is the __?__ *cardium.*

8. A courageous soul knows how to __?__ all difficulties. (climb across)

9. The typist will __?__ the lists. (write across)

10. The Federation of Churches is an __?__ organization. (among denominations)

PUZZLE 2

What word from the list below the exercise fits best in each blank?

1. A train announcer makes himself heard by means of a __?__.

2. A __?__ is a device for measuring minute distances.

3. Every radio performer stands in front of a __?__.

4. A very tiny organism is called a __?__.

5. A device for looking at exceedingly small objects is a __?__.

6. A __?__ is a new or abnormal growth.

7. A __?__ is a beginner or novice.

8. A __?__ implement belongs to the newer or late Stone Age.

9. The universe, if __?__, would have the earth as its center.

10. The word __?__ has to do with the internal heat of the earth.

Words:

megalith	geothermic	geometry
microphone	megaphone	microorganism
neoplasm	micrometer	microscope
geocentric	neophyte	neolithic

PUZZLE 3

What word from the list below the exercise belongs in each blank?

1. A remedy that claims to cure *all* ills is a __?__.

2. __?__ means *all* demons let loose at once.

3. A __?__ council is one representing *all* the *Greeks* or Greek-letter fraternities in a college.

4. A picture giving a view in *all* directions or in one that is very complete is called a __?__.

5. __?__ is the belief that *all* is God in some form.

6. __?__ is *all* acting with no talking.

7. A warrior in full __?__ is completely (*all*) armed.

8. An __?__ bill contains many and varied provisions.

9. A __?__ machine types news at a distance.

10. Far-off looking requires a __?__.

Words:

pantheism	omnibus	panhandle
panacea	panorama	pandemonium
Panhellenic	panoply	teletype
pantomime	omelet	telescope

PUZZLE 4

This time you must think up the word yourself — if you can. The *italicized* words offer a hint.

1. One's signature or *self-writing* is known by the term __?__

2. If *–cardia–* means *heart*, what is the word for *heart-writing*, i.e., a record of heart action __?__.

3. A large outlet for *water* — near which one should never park — is called a __?__.

4. A plant which generates electricity from *water*power is a __?__ plant.

5. Brakes which use a liquid to transmit pressure are known as __?__ brakes.

6. The term __?__ *dynamics* is applied to the science of the action and motion of *water* or other fluids.

7. *Hydrogen* is literally __?__ gas.

8. A flying machine which will land on *water* is a __?__.

9. A disease transmitted by mad dogs is called __?__ because it produces a terrific *water-fear*.

10. *Phonics* is the science of __?__s, especially vocal.

A FEW TEASERS

Perhaps, if you have studied these lessons carefully, you can break down even the more complicated words in the list below, whether you have seen them before or not.

1. preconvention activities
2. discursive remarks
3. a cursory inspection
4. inexplicable mystery
5. ultramarine (a color — telling where it came from)
6. coniferous (*coni-* = cone) trees
7. indestructible homes
8. unusual perspicacity
9. inconsistent ideas
10. unpremeditated joy
11. an improvident (cf. *provide*) person
12. semi-automatic machinery
13. indissoluble union
14. incontrovertible evidence
15. nonaggression pacts
16. nonintervention committee
17. photomicrograph
18. electrocardiograph (*-cardia-* = heart)
19. phonocinematograph (*cinema* = motion)
20. antidisestablishmentarianism (it has to do with an English controversy over disestablishing the church, i.e., separating church from state.)

WHY NOT?

The more you practice, the easier it gets. Watch for words which your magic key will unlock. The following are two examples of uniform lists, one of which is already familiar if you have mastered this appendix:

anterior events	coniferous
exterior appearance	luminiferous
inferior goods	melliferous
interior decorations	odoriferous
posterior view	soporiferous
superior qualities	vociferous

Why not compile similar lists? Begin with the *–tracts–* and the *–verts–*, using the patterns in Lesson III for a start. Or go exploring on your own and bring the *–therms*, the *–manias*, the *–phobias*, or the *–ologies* back alive. It's real sport.

NEW WORDS

Some are imported, like *panzer*. Many are new forms of established words, like *leftwardness*, or are combinations like *atombomb*. Others are imitative, like *squawkies* for the first talking motion pictures; and a few, such as *gobbledygook*, are metaphorical or onomatopoetic. UNESCO is acronymic. Creation of new words is governed to a large degree by the following principles:

1. A new word is desirable only if no existing word will serve as well as the best one that can be devised. Familiarity with all existing words for the purpose is expected.
2. Unless a new word has a clear-cut meaning like *snafu*,* it is in a class with the objectionable kind of slang.
3. The spelling should be logical in terms of derivation or meaning.
4. It is considered bad form to combine a Latin prefix with a Greek root or vice versa, as in *genocide*.

* Muddled, disordered — one of the most popular and creative of the new words which came out of the war.

APPENDIX TWO

THE TEACHING OF SPELLING
By Ethel M. Dunn

The teaching of spelling has never been reduced to a science; and it therefore offers a challenge to the very daring. Prominent educators disagree as to method and there seems to be no royal road to success. Everyone, however, agrees that good spelling is essential not only in order to be understood but to avoid misunderstanding.

There are a number of reasons for misspelling, and inappropriate phonetic drill seems to be one of the potent factors. It is true that our language is not entirely phonetic, but if students fail to recall the symbol or syllable in connection with the sound, chaotic spelling results. A second factor in this spelling handicap is the lack of precision in enunciation and pronunciation which leads to slovenly spelling. A third consideration is the lack of training in the perceiving of words. Pupils should be taught to observe the word in the whole, then divided into syllables; letter-by-letter observation is futile and invites failure. Fourth, general defects in sensory and motor mechanisms present real difficulties and require special methods of procedure.

The words themselves contain difficulties which should be recognized. The length of words is often a stumbling block, and attention should be given to the units within the word; there is a strong relationship between the sound and the written form; therefore both the oral and the visual forms should be presented.

Silent letters, especially the final *e*, the diphthongs *ie* and *ei*, and the final consonant before a suffix are difficulties that may be overcome by rules. This does not mean that the simple memorization of a rule is an "open sesame" to good spelling; it does mean, however, that a building up of precepts and concepts to form a definite rule is helpful.

The following suggested procedure for this type of study is helpful. First, have the students collect all words possible containing *ei* and *ie;* secondly, require them to copy these words and arrange in two categories, the *ie* words and the *ei* words; thirdly, by means of observation have the students discover that there is no common element in the *ie* list but that the *ei* words contain *cei;* fourthly, dictate words from each group separately; fifthly, combine words from each group and dictate; and last, form the rule.

Not all of our words are governed by rule and so must be taught by means of other methods. In teaching spelling, not more than one word should be presented at a time. The new word should be written on the board by syllables and pronounced clearly by the instructor; then the meaning should be explained if necessary; the difficulty present in the word should be observed and stressed (underlining is effective); the mental image should be stimulated by having the word erased and rewritten by the pupils; the word should then be written by all the pupils and checked by reference to the correct form on the board. Later the word should be used in original sentences contributed by the class. Three new words a day are sufficient for the average class, and more than five may lead to disaster.

Pupils should be taught to associate sound units with others already learned which require the same spelling response. They should also be taught to attend to the rhythmic patterns of word.

Word building by means of the use of roots, prefixes, and suffixes not only is an aid in correct meaning but also in correct spelling and thus a new avenue of approach gives variety to the spelling drill.

Word derivation is an interesting factor in the matter of correct spelling and helps to simplify whole word families.

Sometimes the telling of the story behind some of the silent letters or behind the use of the apostrophe guides the pupil in intelligent appreciation of spelling difficulties and thus eliminates some of the hazards.

Spelling difficulties, however, are many times an individual problem; therefore individual errors should be analyzed, and each student should be taught to attack his own weakness.

All learning should be stimulated by strong incentives, for only by eternal vigilance will progress be attained.

KEYS

Comprehensive Key to Pretests

Part One Unit 1

1. 4		1. 3	
2. 6		2. 10	
3. 5		3. 5	
4. 8		4. 13	
5. 1		5. 14	
6. 10		6. 12	
7. 12		7. 9	
8. 13		8. 1	
9. 14		9. 11	
10. 2		10. 7	
11. 9		11. 4	
12. 7		12. 8	
13. 11			

Part One Unit 2

1. 5		1. 15	
2. 9		2. 13	
3. 11		3. 7	
4. 2		4. 3	
5. 8		5. 9	
6. 14		6. 14	
7. 4		7. 4	
8. 13		8. 12	
9. 3		9. 2	
10. 7		10. 5	
11. 12		11. 8	
12. 1		12. 10	
		13. 6	

Part One Unit 3

1. 5		14. 18	
2. 11		15. 4	
3. 9		16. 7	
4. 17		17. 1	
5. 8		18. 21	
6. 22		19. 6	
7. 10		20. 12	
8. 16			
9. 19		1. 4	
10. 2		2. 6	
11. 13		3. 1	
12. 14		4. 2	
13. 3		5. 3	

Part One Unit 4

1. 3		14. 22	
2. 12		15. 27	
3. 15		16. 25	
4. 6		17. 5	
5. 20		18. 24	
6. 2		19. 17	
7. 19		20. 7	
8. 11		22. 18	
9. 1		23. 13	
10. 16		24. 14	
11. 9		25. 8	
12. 23			
13. 26			

Part One Unit 5

1. 8		1. 5	
2. 5		2. 13	
3. 14		3. 7	
4. 7		4. 2	
5. 3		5. 10	
6. 10		6. 14	
7. 12		7. 4	
8. 4		8. 1	
9. 13		9. 15	
10. 6		10. 8	
11. 9		11. 12	
12. 2		12. 9	
		13. 3	

Part One Unit 6

1. 3		1. 6	
2. 9		2. 10	
3. 13		3. 12	
4. 1		4. 1	
5. 2		5. 8	
6. 14		6. 11	
7. 7		7. 15	
8. 11		8. 7	
9. 5		9. 3	
10. 10		10. 4	
11. 8		11. 14	
12. 12		12. 2	
		13. 13	

Part One Unit 7

1. 10		14. 2	
2. 19		15. 23	
3. 6		16. 26	
4. 15		17. 9	
5. 1		18. 12	
6. 17		19. 27	
7. 3		20. 7	
8. 4		21. 25	
9. 20		22. 21	
10. 5		23. 13	
11. 22		24. 16	
12. 18		25. 11	
13. 24			

Part One Unit 8

1. 5		1. 13	
2. 10		2. 10	
3. 8		3. 5	
4. 15		4. 8	
5. 3		5. 12	
6. 13		6. 9	
7. 4		7. 1	
8. 9		8. 4	
9. 6		9. 6	
10. 11		10. 14	
11. 2		11. 3	
12. 14		12. 11	
13. 1			

Part One Unit 9

1. 14		1. 8	
2. 5		2. 13	
3. 8		3. 9	
4. 10		4. 15	
5. 2		5. 7	
6. 6		6. 1	
7. 13		7. 12	
8. 9		8. 4	
9. 7		9. 6	
10. 12		10. 14	
11. 1		11. 10	
12. 4		12. 11	
		13. 2	

Part One Unit 10

1. 10		1. 6	
2. 6		2. 9	
3. 8		3. 13	
4. 12		4. 8	
5. 2		5. 15	
6. 9		6. 3	
7. 4		7. 11	
8. 14		8. 2	
9. 3		9. 12	
10. 11		10. 5	
11. 1		11. 10	
12. 7		12. 1	
		13. 7	

Comprehensive Key to Pretests

Part Two Unit 1		Part Two Unit 2		Part Two Unit 3		Part Two Unit 4	
1. 10	1. 6	1. 3	1. 8	1. 9	1. 7	1. 8	1. 10
2. 4	2. 10	2. 14	2. 5	2. 15	2. 12	2. 13	2. 14
3. 5	3. 14	3. 5	3. 10	3. 11	3. 8	3. 5	3. 6
4. 12	4. 11	4. 9	4. 14	4. 13	4. 3	4. 15	4. 13
5. 7	5. 9	5. 1	5. 9	5. 8	5. 11	5. 9	5. 1
6. 15	6. 2	6. 15	6. 13	6. 3	6. 14	6. 2	6. 3
7. 2	7. 3	7. 8	7. 3	7. 1	7. 10	7. 12	7. 12
8. 14	8. 7	8. 13	8. 12	8. 5	8. 6	8. 14	8. 5
9. 11	9. 12	9. 4	9. 1	9. 7	9. 13	9. 10	9. 7
10. 13	10. 1	10. 7	10. 6	10. 12	10. 1	10. 1	10. 11
11. 6	11. 13	11. 11	11. 4	11. 4	11. 9	11. 3	11. 2
12. 1	12. 5	12. 2	12. 2	12. 14	12. 4	12. 7	12. 9
13. 8		13. 12		13. 2		13. 4	

Part Two Unit 5		Part Two Unit 6		Part Two Unit 7		Part Two Unit 8	
1. 6	1. 1	1. 5	1. 9	1. 3	1. 4	1. 7	1. 8
2. 9	2. 7	2. 10	2. 5	2. 8	2. 12	2. 12	2. 4
3. 5	3. 11	3. 14	3. 14	3. 13	3. 15	3. 4	3. 6
4. 12	4. 14	4. 11	4. 11	4. 9	4. 10	4. 11	4. 2
5. 7	5. 6	5. 3	5. 2	5. 1	5. 1	5. 3	5. 12
6. 11	6. 2	6. 9	6. 13	6. 6	6. 11	6. 10	6. 10
7. 15	7. 9	7. 1	7. 8	7. 12	7. 14	7. 1	7. 13
8. 4	8. 12	8. 13	8. 3	8. 10	8. 3	8. 5	8. 15
9. 10	9. 4	9. 7	9. 12	9. 11	9. 13	9. 14	9. 5
10. 14	10. 13	10. 15	10. 1	10. 14	10. 7	10. 2	10. 1
11. 1	11. 8	11. 2	11. 4	11. 2	11. 2	11. 9	11. 14
12. 13	12. 3	12. 4	12. 6	12. 5	12. 6	12. 8	12. 7
13. 2		13. 12			13. 9		13. 3

Part Two Unit 9		Part Two Unit 10		
1. 5	1. 3	1. 9	1. 6	1. 8
2. 8	2. 6	2. 6	2. 13	2. 1
3. 11	3. 1	3. 10	3. 7	3. 2
4. 1	4. 10	4. 1	4. 1	4. 10
5. 10	5. 7	5. 2	5. 8	5. 3
6. 3	6. 9	6. 7	6. 5	6. 9
7. 9	7. 2	7. 4	7. 9	7. 11
8. 2	8. 5	8. 5	8. 2	8. 4
9. 6			9. 10	9. 12
			10. 12	10. 5
			11. 14	11. 14
			12. 3	12. 6
				13. 15

Comprehensive Key to Pretests

Part Three Unit 1		*Part Three Unit 2*		*Part Three Unit 3*		*Part Three Unit 4*	
1. 5	1. 9	1. 14	1. 3	1. 5	1. 8	1. 10	1. 4
2. 8	2. 4	2. 10	2. 10	2. 1	2. 11	2. 8	2. 10
3. 2	3. 8	3. 3	3. 6	3. 9	3. 2	3. 13	3. 14
4. 13	4. 10	4. 12	4. 1	4. 7	4. 14	4. 11	4. 9
5. 10	5. 2	5. 1	5. 11	5. 13	5. 9	5. 5	5. 13
6. 14	6. 7	6. 4	6. 14	6. 3	6. 1	6. 12	6. 3
7. 11	7. 11	7. 15	7. 8	7. 14	7. 6	7. 15	7. 12
8. 9	8. 3	8. 9	8. 2	8. 11	8. 7	8. 3	8. 2
9. 12	9. 14	9. 13	9. 13	9. 2	9. 4	9. 1	9. 6
10. 1	10. 13	10. 8	10. 4	10. 15	10. 13	10. 7	10. 1
11. 3	11. 1	11. 11	11. 9	11. 10	11. 10	11. 14	11. 7
12. 6	12. 15	12. 6	12. 5	12. 6	12. 3	12. 6	12. 11
	13. 12	13. 2		13. 8		13. 9	

Part Three Unit 5		*Part Three Unit 6*		*Part Three Unit 7*		*Part Three Unit 8*	
1. 5	1. 5	1. 11	1. 4	1. 8	1. 13	1. 3	1. 8
2. 8	2. 10	2. 7	2. 3	2. 9	2. 5	2. 6	2. 10
3. *4	3. 13	3. 5	3. 10	3. 3	3. 8	3. 11	3. 2
4. 1	4. 7	4. 15	4. 2	4. 15	4. 2	4. 13	4. 14
5. 9	5. 1	5. 14	5. 14	5. 10	5. 14	5. 2	5. 7
6. 7	6. 11	6. 1	6. 7	6. 14	6. 11	6. 14	6. 1
7. 2	7. 3	7. 6	7. 11	7. 13	7. 1	7. 4	7. 13
8. 10	8. 8	8. 12	8. 1	8. 11	8. 6	8. 12	8. 3
	9. 2	9. 13	9. 13	9. 2	9. 3	9. 1	9. 11
1. 5	10. 12	10. 2	10. 12	10. 6	10. 9	10. 8	10. 4
2. 1	11. 4	11. 9	11. 8	11. 12	11. 12	11. 10	11. 9
3. 7		12. 3	12. 5	12. 1	12. 7	12. 15	12. 5
4. 2		13. 8		13. 5		13. 5	
5. 8							
6. 3							

Part Three Unit 9		*Part Three Unit 10*	
1. 4	1. 5	1. 10	1. 8
2. 12	2. 10	2. 3	2. 1
3. 9	3. 6	3. 11	3. 9
4. 15	4. 13	4. 13	4. 2
5. 7	5. 1	5. 4	5. 10
6. 1	6. 4	6. 14	6. 3
7. 11	7. 14	7. 5	7. 12
8. 14	8. 7	8. 15	8. 4
9. 8	9. 11	9. 6	9. 13
10. 2	10. 2	10. 1	10. 5
11. 13	11. 9	11. 7	11. 14
12. 5	12. 3	12. 2	12. 6
13. 10		13. 8	

DIVISION TEST KEYS

PART ONE

A.		B.		C.		D.		E.	
1.	12	1.	4	1.	10	1.	5	1.	3
2.	6	2.	7	2.	12	2.	10	2.	12
3.	1	3.	9	3.	1	3.	8	3.	10
4.	11	4.	1	4.	5	4.	1	4.	1
5.	3	5.	12	5.	9	5.	12	5.	8
6.	8	6.	5	6.	2	6.	9	6.	5
7.	10	7.	3	7.	7	7.	4	7.	2
8.	2	8.	10	8.	3	8.	6	8.	4
9.	7	9.	6	9.	8	9.	2	9.	11
10.	4	10.	8	10.	6	10.	7	10.	6

F.		G.		H.		I.		J.	
1.	9	1.	6	1.	5	1.	7	1.	10
2.	12	2.	11	2.	8	2.	10	2.	6
3.	5	3.	5	3.	7	3.	1	3.	12
4.	1	4.	1	4.	11	4.	12	4.	8
5.	7	5.	12	5.	1	5.	3	5.	1
6.	11	6.	3	6.	12	6.	9	6.	11
7.	3	7.	9	7.	3	7.	2	7.	2
8.	8	8.	2	8.	10	8.	4	8.	4
9.	10	9.	8	9.	4	9.	6	9.	3
10.	6	10.	7	10.	9	10.	11	10.	9

DIVISION TEST KEYS

PART TWO

A.	B.	C.	D.	E.
1. 3	1. 4	1. 12	1. 4	1. 8
2. 6	2. 9	2. 8	2. 9	2. 5
3. 10	3. 11	3. 2	3. 12	3. 11
4. 12	4. 12	4. 6	4. 1	4. 2
5. 8	5. 1	5. 9	5. 6	5. 7
6. 11	6. 2	6. 10	6. 11	6. 3
7. 1	7. 8	7. 1	7. 3	7. 9
8. 2	8. 5	8. 3	8. 10	8. 12
9. 4	9. 7	9. 7	9. 7	9. 6
10. 5	10. 6	10. 4	10. 2	10. 4

F.	G.	H.	I.	J.
1. 6	1. 11	1. 3	1. 11	1. 4
2. 3	2. 12	2. 9	2. 1	2. 8
3. 8	3. 5	3. 11	3. 12	3. 10
4. 1	4. 9	4. 1	4. 7	4. 12
5. 9	5. 6	5. 6	5. 9	5. 1
6. 12	6. 2	6. 4	6. 3	6. 2
7. 2	7. 10	7. 8	7. 10	7. 9
8. 10	8. 7	8. 2	8. 5	8. 5
9. 11	9. 1	9. 7	9. 8	9. 3
10. 5	10. 8	10. 5	10. 4	10. 7

DIVISION TEST KEYS

PART THREE

A.	B.	C.	D.	E.
1. 9	1. 3	1. 10	1. 5	1. 5
2. 6	2. 12	2. 12	2. 11	2. 1
3. 11	3. 6	3. 5	3. 7	3. 6
4. 12	4. 8	4. 11	4. 12	4. 12
5. 1	5. 4	5. 6	5. 1	5. 7
6. 7	6. 1	6. 8	6. 8	6. 9
7. 8	7. 9	7. 2	7. 9	7. 2
8. 10	8. 10	8. 7	8. 10	8. 3
9. 4	9. 5	9. 3	9. 2	9. 4
10. 3	10. 2	10. 4	10. 4	10. 10

F.	G.	H.	I.	J.
1. 11	1. 5	1. 6	1. 5	1. 3
2. 4	2. 9	2. 12	2. 10	2. 6
3. 6	3. 11	3. 1	3. 12	3. 2
4. 10	4. 1	4. 7	4. 1	4. 7
5. 1	5. 6	5. 2	5. 8	5. 10
6. 9	6. 7	6. 3	6. 9	6. 11
7. 2	7. 2	7. 10	7. 6	7. 4
8. 7	8. 10	8. 11	8. 3	8. 9
9. 5	9. 3	9. 4	9. 2	9. 5
10. 8	10. 8	10. 8	10. 7	10. 8

SUPPLEMENTARY TEST KEYS

PART ONE

A.		B.		C.		D.		E.	
1.	6	1.	5	1.	5	1.	2	1.	12
2.	12	2.	11	2.	12	2.	8	2.	9
3.	1	3.	1	3.	1	3.	4	3.	1
4.	9	4.	6	4.	9	4.	7	4.	7
5.	8	5.	8	5.	4	5.	11	5.	4
6.	3	6.	4	6.	10	6.	9	6.	11
7.	11	7.	10	7.	3	7.	6	7.	6
8.	5	8.	2	8.	6	8.	12	8.	3
9.	2	9.	7	9.	11	9.	10	9.	8
10.	7	10.	9	10.	7	10.	3	10.	5

PART TWO

A.		B.		C.		D.		E.	
1.	4	1.	9	1.	4	1.	12	1.	10
2.	12	2.	1	2.	12	2.	6	2.	6
3.	6	3.	7	3.	11	3.	4	3.	4
4.	2	4.	10	4.	9	4.	9	4.	9
5.	9	5.	2	5.	8	5.	7	5.	12
6.	11	6.	12	6.	1	6.	2	6.	2
7.	1	7.	8	7.	6	7.	11	7.	8
8.	3	8.	4	8.	3	8.	3	8.	5
9.	7	9.	11	9.	10	9.	10	9.	11
10.	8	10.	6	10.	7	10.	5	10.	3

PART THREE

A.		B.		C.		D.		E.	
1.	3	1.	7	1.	8	1.	11	1.	7
2.	12	2.	1	2.	3	2.	6	2.	12
3.	1	3.	11	3.	6	3.	8	3.	5
4.	9	4.	2	4.	2	4.	5	4.	2
5.	7	5.	4	5.	10	5.	12	5.	11
6.	10	6.	10	6.	12	6.	4	6.	8
7.	4	7.	9	7.	9	7.	9	7.	1
8.	6	8.	6	8.	1	8.	3	8.	6
9.	11	9.	3	9.	4	9.	10	9.	3
10.	2	10.	5	10.	7	10.	2	10.	0

āle, chăotic, câre, ădd, ȧccount, ärm, ȧsk, sofȧ

ēve, hẹre, ĕvent, ĕnd, silĕnt, makēr

īce, ĭll, charĭty

ōld, ŏbey, ôrb, ŏdd, sŏft, cŏnnect

fōōd, fŏŏt, out, oil

cūbe, ūnite, ûrn, ŭp, circŭs, menü

chair, go, sing

then, thin

natūre, verdure

zh = z in azure

LIST OF BASIC WORDS

This contains only the 25 basic words from each unit. The number denotes the page on which each is presented and defined. The system of respelling for pronunciation is used by permission of the publishers of Webster's Collegiate Dictionary, Fifth Edition, Copyright 1936, 1941, by G. & C. Merriam Company. Where two or more respellings are given, however, only the first has been transcribed.

abate (á·bāt′), 32
abet (á·bĕt′), 32
abeyance (á·bā′ăns), 154
abhor (ăb·hôr′), 4
abolish (á·bŏl′ĭsh), 32
abridge (á·brĭj′), 147
abrogate (ăb′rŏ·gāt), 234
abscond (ăb·skŏnd′), 176
abyss (á·bĭs′), 33
accelerate (ăk·sĕl′ēr·āt), 90
accessible (ăk·ses′ĭ·b'l), 104
accord (ă·kôrd′), 12
acquiesce (ăk′wĭ·ĕs), 147
acquire (ă·kwīr′), 4
acquit (ă·kwĭt′), 147
acumen (ă·kū′mĕn), 241
acute (á·kūt′), 69
adamant (ăd′á·mănt), 241
adapt (á·dăpt′), 4
adhere (ăd·hēr′), 53
adjacent (ă·jā′sĕnt), 69
admonition (ăd′mŏ·nĭsh′ŭn), 91
adorn (á·dôrn′), 53
adroit (á·droit′), 201
adulterate (á·dŭl′tēr·āt), 234

advent (ăd·vĕnt), 33
advocate (ăd′vŏ·kāt), 32
aesthetic (ĕs·thĕt′ĭk), 201
affinity (ă·fĭn′ĭ·tĭ), 111
affirm (ă·fûrm′), 4
affront (ă·frŭnt′), 111
aggravate (ăg′rá·vāt), 147
aggressive (ă·grĕs′ĭv), 208
agile (ăj′ĭl), 46
alacrity (á·lăk′rĭ·tĭ), 92
alibi (ăl′ĭ·bī), 128
alien (āl′yĕn), 128
allege (ă·lĕj′), 90
allegory (ăl′ē·gō′rĭ), 213
allergic (ă·lûr′jĭk), 208
alleviate (ă·lē′vĭ·āt), 234
alter (ôl′tēr), 53
altercation (ôl′tēr·kā′shŭn), 148
amenity (á·mĕn′ĭ·tĭ), 227
amity (ăm′ĭ·tĭ), 34
amorous (ăm′ō·rŭs), 185
amphibious (ăm·fĭb′ĭ·ŭs), 201
amplify (ăm′plĭ·fī), 234
anathema (á·năth′ē·má), 199
anecdote (ăn′ĕk·dōt), 34

anguish (ăng′gwĭsh), 128
animation (ăn·ĭ·mā′shŭn), 12
animosity (ăn′ĭ·mŏs′ĭ·tĭ), 111
annihilate (ă·nī′ĭ·lāt), 90
anonymous (à·nŏn′ĭ·mŭs), 242
antagonist (ăn·tăg′ŏ·nĭst), 55
apathy (ăp′à·thĭ), 55
aperture (ăp′ēr·tŭr), 55
appall (ă·pôl′), 90
apparition (ăp′à·rĭsh′ŭn), 128
apprehension (ăp′rē·hĕn′shŭn), 13
aquatics (à·kwăt′ĭks), 34
ardent (är′dĕnt), 140
aroma (à·rō′mà), 34
arrogance (ăr′ŏ·gặns), 177
ascertain (ăs′ēr·tān′), 126
assail (ă·sāl′), 53
assuage (ă·swāj′), 206
astute (ăs·tūt′), 185
atoll (ăt′ŏl), 199
atrocious (à·trō′shŭs), 155
audacity (ô·dăs′ĭ·tĭ), 177
audible (ô′dĭ·b′l), 25
augment (ôg·mĕnt′), 53
auspicious (ôs·pĭsh′ŭs), 220
austere (ôs·tēr′), 118
authentic (ô·thĕn′tĭk), 185
avarice (ăv′à·rĭs), 55
avert (à·vûrt′), 4
avid (ăv′ĭd), 25
avocation (ăv′ŏ·kā′shŭn), 241
badger (băj′ēr), 90
barrage (bà·räzh′), 199
belligerent (bĕ·lĭj′ēr·ĕnt), 156
benign (bĕ·nīn′), 140
bequeath (bĕ·kwēth′), 90
bereave (bĕ·rēv′), 234
bias (bī′ăs), 128
bigoted (bĭg′ŭt·ĕd), 236
bourgeois (bōōr·zhwä′), 215

brevity (brĕv′ĭ·tĭ), 13
brusque (brŭsk), 18
bucolic (bŭ·kŏl′ĭk), 215
bumptious (bŭmp′shŭs), 185
cache (kăsh), 13
cajole (kà·jōl′), 126
calorific (kăl·ŏ·rĭf′ĭk), 228
calumny (kăl′ŭm·nĭ), 177
candid (kăn′dĭd), 18
canine (kā′nīn), 25
capitulation (kà·pĭt′ū·lā′shŭn), 227
capricious (kà·prĭsh′ŭs), 104
captious (kăp′shŭs), 201
carcass (kär′kăs), 92
carnage (kär′nĭj), 154
cartel (kär′tĕl), 178
casualty (kăzh′ū·ăl·ty), 128
catalepsy (kăt′à·lĕp′sĭ), 128
catholic (kăth′ŏ·lĭk), 243
cavil (kăv′ĭl), 176
celestial (sĕ·lĕs′chăl), 18
chagrin (shà·grĭn′), 92
chaos (kā′ŏs), 13
chastise (chăs·tīz′), 53
chimerical (kī·mĕr′ĭ·kăl), 201
churl (chûrl), 55
citadel (sĭt′à·dĕl), 13
cite (sīt), 32
civil (sĭv′ĭl), 140
clairvoyant (klâr·voi′ănt), 129
clandestine (klăn·dĕs′tĭn), 229
clarity (klăr′ĭ·tĭ), 241
clement (klĕm′ĕnt), 236
coalition (kō′à·lĭsh′ŭn), 199
coerce (kŏ·ûrs′), 4
cogent (kō′jĕnt), 140
coherent (cŏ·hēr′ĕnt), 229
coincidence (kŏ·ĭn′sĭ·dĕns), 92
collaborate (kŏ·lăb′ŏ·rāt), 176

dilettante (dĭl'ĕ·tăn'tĭ), 227
diminutive (dĭ·mĭn'ṳ·tĭv), 25
dirge (dûrj), 41
discern (dĭ·zûrn'), 11
disconsolate (dĭs·kŏn'sȯ·lĭt), 118
discretion (dĭs·krĕsh'ŭn), 56
discriminate (dĭs·krĭm'ĭ·nāt), 91
disparage (dĭs·păr'ĭj), 177
disparity (dĭs·păr'ĭ·tĭ), 213
disperse (dĭs·pûrs'), 54
disrupt (dĭs·rŭpt'), 126
dissension (dĭ·sĕn'shŭn), 178
dissipate (dĭs'ĭ·pāt), 126
divert (dī·vûrt'), 97
divulge (dĭ·vŭlj'), 5
docile (dŏs'ĭl), 46
docket (dŏk'ĕt), 111
dogmatic (dŏg·măt'ĭk), 215
dourness (dōōr'nĕs), 227
droll (drōl), 118
dubious (dū'bĭ·ŭs), 25
duplicity (dū·plĭs'ĭ·tĭ), 129
eccentric (ĕk·sĕn'trĭk), 140
effeminate (ĕ·fĕm'ĭ·nĭt), 220
effervesce (ĕf'ēr·vĕs'), 235
effete (ĕ·fēt'), 215
efficacious (ĕf'ĭ·kā'shŭs), 215
effigy (ĕf'ĭ·jĭ), 111
effrontery (ĕ·frŭn'tēr·ĭ), 93
egregious (ĕ·grē'jŭs), 220
ejaculation (ĕ·jăk'ṳ·lā'shŭn), 41
elation (ĕ·lā'shŭn), 56
elicit (ĕ·lĭs'ĭt), 127
elixir (ĕ·lĭk'sēr), 178
elude (ĕ·lūd'), 54
emaciate (ĕ·mā'shĭ·āt), 127
emanate (ĕm'á·nāt), 177
emancipate (ĕ·măn'sĭ·pāt), 183
embezzle (ĕm·bĕz''l), 127
eminent (ĕm'ĭ·nĕnt), 46

emulate (ĕm'ṳ·lāt), 54
enhance (ĕn·hȧns'), 54
enigma (ĕ·nĭg'má), 178
ensuing (ĕn·sū'ĭng), 69
entice (ĕn·tīs'), 33
episode (ĕp'ĭ·sōd), 6
epitaph (ĕp'ĭ·tȧf), 41
epithet (ĕp'ĭ·thĕt), 93
epoch (ĕp'ŏk), 14
equitable (ĕk'wĭ·tȧ·b'l), 220
equivocal (ĕ·kwĭv'ȯ·kȧl), 220
err (ûr), 11
errant (ĕr'ȧnt), 69
erratic (ĕ·răt'ĭk), 186
escapade (ĕs'kȧ·pād'), 207
escarpment (ĕs·kärp'mĕnt), 227
esteem (ĕs·tēm'), 11
ethereal (ĕ·thēr'ĕ·ȧl), 236
evict (ĕ·vĭkt'), 11
evince (ĕ·vĭns'), 54
exaggerate (ĕg·zăj'ēr·āt), 97
exasperate (ĕg·zăs'pēr·āt), 127
execration (ĕk'sĕ·krā'shŭn), 148
exertion (ĕg·zûr'shŭn), 56
exhilaration (ĕg·zĭl'á·rā'shŭn), 241
exhort (ĕg·zôrt'), 127
exhume (ĕks·hūm'), 177
exigency (ĕk'sĭ·jĕn·sĭ), 241
exonerate (ĕg·zŏn'ēr·āt), 127
exorbitant (ĕg·zôr'bĭ·tȧnt), 69
exotic (ĕks·ŏt'ĭk), 201
expedient (ĕks·pē'dĭ·ĕnt), 220
expiate (ĕks'pĭ·āt), 183
explicit (ĕks·plĭs'ĭt), 201
extenuate (ĕks·tĕn'ṳ·āt), 206
extricate (ĕks'trĭ·kāt), 54
exuberance (ĕg·zū'bēr·ȧns), 178
exultant (ĕg·zŭl'tȧnt), 25
façade (fȧ·säd'), 129

facetious (fá·sē′shŭs), 104
facile (făs′ĭl), 104
fallacy (făl′á·sĭ), 141
fallible (făl′ĭ·b'l), 141
fastidious (făs·tĭd′ĭ·ŭs), 186
fatuous (făt′ụ·ŭs), 215
feign (fān), 33
felicitous (fē·lĭs′ĭ·tŭs), 186
ferocity (fē·rŏs′ĭ·tĭ), 99
fetish (fē′tĭsh), 199
fidelity (fī·dĕl′ĭ·tĭ), 154
fiend (fēnd), 34
filch (fĭlch), 11
fluctuation (flŭk′tụ·ā′shŭn), 141
forensic (fō·rĕn′sĭk), 208
formidable (fôr′mĭ·dá·b'l), 118
fortitude (fôr′tĭ·tūd), 99
fortuitous (fôr·tū′ĭ·tŭs), 221
franchise (frăn′chīz), 241
frugal (froō′găl), 46
fruition (froō·ĭsh′ŭn), 179
frustrate (frŭs′trāt), 33
fugitive (fū′jĭ·tĭv), 70
furtive (fûr′tĭv), 18
futile (fū′tĭl), 141
galvanize (găl′vá·nīz), 133
garnish (gär′nĭsh), 147
garrulous (găr′ụ·lŭs), 208
gestapo (gĕ·stä′pō), 199
ghastly (găst′lĭ), 18
gossamer (gŏs′á·mēr), 119
gratify (grăt′ĭ·fī), 133
gregarious (grē·gâr′ĭ·ŭs), 208
grotesque (grō·tĕsk′), 221
guile (gīl), 34
haggard (hăg′ērd), 25
halcyon (hăl′sĭ·ŭn), 243
harass (hăr′ás), 11
harbinger (här′bĭn·jēr), 41
hazard (hăz′ērd), 148

heinous (hā′nŭs), 186
heresy (hĕr′ĕ·sĭ), 154
hibernate (hī′bēr·nāt), 235
hilarious (hĭ·lâr′ĭ·ŭs), 104
hoary (hōr′ĭ), 18
homage (hŏm′ĭj), 179
homely (hōm′lĭ), 46
hostile (hŏs′tĭl), 46
humid (hū′mĭd), 47
hybrid (hī′brĭd), 112
hyperbole (hī·pûr′bŏ·lē), 227
hypocrisy (hĭ·pŏk′rĭ·sĭ), 179
ignominy (ĭg′nŏ·mĭn·ĭ), 242
illusion (ĭ·lū′zhŭn), 112
immaculate (ĭ·măk′ụ·lĭt), 47
immortal (ĭ·môr′tăl), 25
immutable (ĭ·mū′tá·b'l), 229
impale (ĭm·pāl′), 183
impasse (ĭm·pås′), 179
impeach (ĭm·pēch′), 183
impeccable (ĭm·pĕk′á·b'l), 215
impediment (ĭm·pĕd′ĭ·mĕnt), 6
impending (ĭm·pĕnd′ĭng), 70
imperative (ĭm·pĕr′á·tĭv), 119
impervious (ĭm·pûr′vĭ·ŭs), 229
impetuous (ĭm·pĕt′ụ·ŭs), 104
implacable (ĭm·plā′ká·b'l), 156
implicit (ĭm·plĭs′ĭt), 70
impromptu (ĭm·prŏmp′tū), 104
improvise (ĭm′prŏ·vīz), 97
impunity (ĭm·pū′nĭ·tĭ), 112
inadvertent (ĭn′ăd·vûr′tĕnt), 186
inane (ĭn·ān′), 141
inarticulate (ĭn′är·tĭk′ụ·lăt), 135
inaugurate (ĭn·ô′gụ·rāt), 235
incarnation (ĭn′kär·nā′shŭn), 199
incessant (ĭn·sĕs′ănt), 26
incinerate (ĭn·sĭn′ēr·āt), 183
incipient (ĭn·sĭp′ĭ·ĕnt), 141
incognito (ĭn·kŏg′nĭ·tō), 71

incongruous (ĭn·kŏng'grōō·ŭs), 221

incorrigible (ĭn·kŏr'ĭ·jĭ·b'l), 149

incredible (ĭn·krĕd'ĭ·b'l), 141

incriminate (ĭn·krĭm'ĭ·nāt), 97

incubus (ĭn'kū·bŭs), 200

incur (ĭn·kûr'), 33

indictment (ĭn·dīt'mĕnt), 149

indigent (ĭn'dĭ·jĕnt), 243

indignation (ĭn'dĭg·nā'shŭn), 71

indolence (ĭn'dō·lĕns), 142

indomitable (ĭn·dŏm'ĭ·tȧ·b'l), 26

ineffable (ĭn·ĕf'ȧ·b'l), 201

inert (ĭn·ûrt'), 70

inexorable (ĭn·ĕk'sō·rȧ·b'l), 149

inference (ĭn'fēr·ĕns), 142

inferior (ĭn·fẽr'ĭ·ēr), 70

infernal (ĭn·fûr'nȧl), 70

infinitesimal (ĭn'fĭn·ĭ·tĕs'ĭ·mȧl), 105

inflexible (ĭn·flĕk'sĭ·b'l), 119

infringe (ĭn·frĭnj'), 97

ingenious (ĭn·jēn'yŭs), 156

ingenuous (ĭn·jĕn'ū·ŭs), 236

inherent (ĭn·hẽr'ĕnt), 243

inimical (ĭn·ĭm'ĭ·kȧl), 186

innocuous (ĭ·nŏk'ū·ŭs), 186

innovation (ĭn'ō·vā'shŭn), 191

inquisitive (ĭn·kwĭz'ĭ·tĭv), 63

inscrutable (ĭn·skrōō'tȧ·b'l), 150

insidious (ĭn·sĭd'ĭ·ŭs), 105

insinuate (ĭn·sĭn'ū·āt), 97

insolence (ĭn'sō·lĕns), 71

insomnia (ĭn·sŏm'nĭ·ȧ), 213

instigate (ĭn'stĭ·gāt), 206

interim (ĭn'tēr·ĭm), 6

interment (ĭn·tûr'mĕnt), 154

intermittent (ĭn'tēr·mĭt'ĕnt), 135

intimate (ĭn'tĭ·māt), 55

intrepid (ĭn·trĕp'ĭd), 156

intricate (ĭn'trĭ·kĭt), 63

intrinsic (ĭn·trĭn'sĭk), 221

intuition (ĭn'tū·ĭsh'ŭn), 227

inundate (ĭn'ŭn·dāt), 148

inveterate (ĭn·vĕt'ēr·ĭt), 150

irascible (ī·răs'ĭ·b'l), 209

iridescent (ĭr'ĭ·dĕs'ĕnt), 229

irony (ī'rō·nĭ), 112

irresolution (ĭ·rĕz'ō·lū'shŭn), 142

iterate (ĭt'ēr·āt), 133

jargon (jär'gŏn), 149

jeopardize (jĕp'ēr·dīz), 98

jubilant (jōō'bĭ·lȧnt), 47

juvenile (jōō'vĕ·nĭl), 135

labyrinth (lăb'ĭ·rĭnth), 6

laconic (lȧ·kŏn'ĭk), 156

lambent (lăm'bĕnt), 193

lament (lȧ·mĕnt'), 33

languid (lăng'gwĭd), 119

latent (lā'tĕnt), 221

laudable (lôd'ȧ·b'l), 47

legitimate (lė·jĭt'ĭ·mĭt), 229

lenient (lē'nĭ·ĕnt), 47

lethargy (lĕth'ēr·jĭ), 99

levity (lĕv'ĭ·tĭ), 112

liberate (lĭb'ēr·āt), 61

livid (lĭv'ĭd), 26

logistic (lō·jĭs'tĭk), 201

loiter (loi'tēr), 11

longevity (lŏn·jĕv'ĭ·tĭ), 154

loquacious (lō·kwā'shŭs), 112

lucid (lū'sĭd), 18

lucrative (lū'krȧ·tĭv), 156

ludicrous (lū'dĭ·krŭs), 26

lugubrious (lu·gū'brĭ·ŭs), 193

luminous (lū'mĭ·nŭs), 47

lurid (lū'rĭd), 47

luscious (lŭsh'ŭs), 26

magnanimous (măg·năn'ĭ·mŭs), 105

magnitude (măg'nĭ·tūd), 105
malady (măl'a·dĭ), 35
malefactor (măl'ē·făk'tēr), 207
malicious (ma·lĭsh'ŭs), 19
manifest (măn'ĭ·fĕst), 39
manipulate (ma·nĭp'ū·lāt), 11
maritime (măr'ĭ·tīm), 243
martial (mär'shăl), 63
massive (măs'ĭv), 26
mature (ma·tūr'), 19
maudlin (môd'lĭn), 221
mediate (mē'dĭ·āt), 183
mediocre (mē'dĭ·ō'kēr), 202
meditate (mĕd'ĭ·tāt), 12
medley (mĕd'lĭ), 21
melancholy (mĕl'ăn·kŏl'ĭ), 63
mellifluous (mĕ·lĭf'lōō·ŭs), 105
menace (mĕn'ĭs), 39
mercenary (mûr'sē·nĕr'ĭ), 119
meretricious (mĕr'ē·trĭsh'ŭs), 221
metamorphosis (mĕt'a·môr'fō·sĭs), 142
meticulous (mē·tĭk'ū·lŭs), 105
metropolis (mē·trŏp'ō·lĭs), 191
migration (mī·grā'shŭn), 200
militant (mĭl'ĭ·tănt), 209
mirage (mĭ·räzh'), 155
miscreant (mĭs'krē·ănt), 155
missile (mĭs'ĭl), 6
mitigate (mĭt'ĭ·gāt), 206
mobile (mō'bĭl), 193
mollify (mŏl'ĭ·fī), 206
monotonous (mō·nŏt'ō·nŭs), 135
morbid (môr'bĭd), 113
morose (mō·rōs'), 156
mortality (môr·tăl'ĭ·tĭ), 191
motley (mŏt'lĭ), 19
mundane (mŭn'dān), 236
munificent (mū·nĭf'ĭ·sĕnt), 113
mute (mūt), 63

naïve (nä·ēv'), 193
nebulous (nĕb'ū·lŭs), 193
nefarious (nē·fâr'ĭ·ŭs), 193
negligent (nĕg'lĭ·jĕnt), 63
negotiate (nē·gō'shĭ·āt), 207
nether (nĕth'ēr), 237
niggardly (nĭg'ērd·lĭ), 135
nocturnal (nŏk·tûr'năl), 26
nomadic (nō·măd'ĭk), 47
nonchalance (nŏn'sha·lăns), 228
nonentity (nŏn·ĕn'tĭ·tĭ), 191
novice (nŏv'ĭs), 35
nullify (nŭl'ĭ·fī), 235
nurture (nûr'tŭr), 133
obeisance (ō·bā'săns), 71
oblique (ŏb·lēk'), 119
oblivion (ŏb·lĭv'ĭ·ŭn), 155
obnoxious (ŏb·nŏk'shŭs), 48
obsequious (ŏb·sē'kwĭ·ŭs), 150
obsess (ŏb·sĕs'), 98
obsolete (ŏb'sō·lēt), 237
obstinate (ŏb'stĭ·nĭt), 64
occult (ŏ·kŭlt'), 209
officious (ŏ·fĭsh'ŭs), 64
olfactories (ŏl·făk'tō·rĭz), 214
omen (ō'mĕn), 35
omniscient (ŏm·nĭsh'ĕnt), 120
optimism (ŏp'tĭ·mĭz'm), 228
opulence (ŏp'ū·lĕns), 105
ostensible (ŏs·tĕn'sĭ·b'l), 157
ostentation (ŏs'tĕn·tā'shŭn), 214
overture (ō'vēr·tŭr), 191
pacifist (păs'ĭ·fĭst), 214
pallid (păl'ĭd), 135
panacea (păn'a·sē'a), 214
pandemonium (păn'dē·mō'nĭ·ŭm), 99
panorama (păn'ō·rä'ma), 191
paragon (păr'a·gŏn), 200
paramount (păr'a·mount), 243

paraphrase (păr′a̓·frāz), 184
parley (pär′lĭ), 6
paroxysm (păr′ŏk·sĭz′m), 191
pastoral (pȧs′tȯ·ra̓l), 222
pathetic (pȧ·thĕt′ĭk), 26
patriarch (pā′trĭ·ärk), 200
penitence (pĕn′ĭ̆·tĕns), 41
pensive (pĕn′sĭv), 19
penury (pĕn′û·rĭ), 35
perceptible (pēr·sĕp′tĭ̆·b′l), 27
perfunctory (pēr·fŭngk′tȯ·rĭ), 230
perjury (pûr′jēr·ĭ), 192
pernicious (pēr·nĭsh′ŭs), 157
perpetrate (pûr′pĕ·trāt), 98
perpetual (pēr·pĕt′u̓·a̓l), 48
perplexity (pēr·plĕk′sĭ̆·tĭ), 41
pertinacity (pûr′tĭ̆·năs′ĭ̆·tĭ), 228
pervade (pēr·vād′), 39
perverse (pēr·vûrs′), 27
pessimism (pĕs′ĭ̆·mĭz′m), 228
pestilence (pĕs′tĭ̆·lĕns), 35
phlegmatic (flĕg·măt′ĭk), 215
pious (pī′ŭs), 135
pique (pēk), 184
placid (plăs′ĭd), 19
plagiarism (plā′jĭ·a̓·rĭz′m), 207
plaintive (plān′tĭv), 19
plausible (plô′zĭ̆·b′l), 20
plebian (plĕ·bē′ya̓n), 120
portentous (pōr·tĕn′tŭs), 222
posterity (pŏs·tĕr′ĭ̆·tĭ), 105
potent (pō′tĕnt), 20
potion (pō′shŭn), 41
precarious (prĕ·kâr′ĭ·ŭs), 64
precedent (prĕs′ĕ·dĕnt), 106
precipitous (prĕ·sĭp′ĭ̆·tŭs), 120
precision (prĕ·sĭzh′ŭn), 106
precocious (prĕ·kō′shŭs), 113
precursor (prĕ·kûr′sēr), 214
predatory (prĕd′a̓·tō′rĭ), 27

predilection (prē′dĭ·lĕk′shŭn), 192
preposterous (prĕ·pŏs′tēr·ŭs), 230
prerogative (prĕ·rŏg′a̓·tĭv), 99
presentiment (prĕ·zĕn′tĭ̆·mĕnt), 142
preternatural (prē′tēr·năt′ͧu·ra̓l), 216
prevaricate (prĕ·văr′ĭ·kāt), 133
primitive (prĭm′ĭ̆·tĭv), 27
procrastinate (prȯ·krăs′tĭ̆·nāt), 98
prodigal (prŏd′ĭ·ga̓l), 237
prodigious (prȯ·dĭj′ŭs), 150
profusion (prȯ·fū′zhŭn), 192
progeny (prŏj′ĕ̆·nĭ), 41
promiscuous (prȯ·mĭs′kŭ·ŭs), 237
promulgate (prȯ·mŭl′gāt), 12
propensity (prȯ·pĕn′sĭ̆·tĭ), 99
propitiate (prȯ·pĭsh′ĭ·āt), 148
propriety (prȯ·prī′ĕ̆·tĭ), 192
prosaic (prȯ·zā′ĭk), 113
prostration (prŏs·trā′shŭn), 142
protégé (prō′tĕ·zhā), 214
protract (prȯ·trăkt′), 148
protuberant (prȯ·tū′bēr·a̓nt), 136
provident (prŏv′ĭ·dĕnt), 136
proximity (prŏks·ĭm′ĭ̆·tĭ), 106
pseudonym (sū′dȯ·nĭm), 142
pugnacious (pŭg·nā′shŭs), 120
pulverize (pŭl′vēr·īz), 39
punctilious (pŭngk·tĭl′ĭ·ŭs), 120
pungent (pŭn′jĕnt), 27
pusillanimous (pū′sĭ̆·lăn′ĭ·mŭs), 194
quay (kē), 21
querulous (kwĕr′ͧu·lŭs), 121
quintessence (kwĭnt·ĕs′ĕns), 214
quisling (kwĭz′lĭng), 200
raconteur (răk′ŏn·tûr′), 242
rancor (răng′kēr), 106
rapture (răp′tͧur), 6

recalcitrant (rḗ·kăl′sĭ·trănt), 230
recede (rḗ·sēd′), 61
reciprocate (rḗ·sĭp′rṓ·kāt), 184
recompense (rĕk′ŏm·pĕns), 71
reconcile (rĕk′ŏn·sīl), 39
recondite (rĕk′ŭn·dīt), 222
rectify (rĕk′tĭ·fī), 184
recumbent (rḗ·kŭm′bĕnt), 194
recuperate (rḗ·kū′pēr·āt), 98
regal (rē′găl), 48
regale (rḗ·gāl′), 39
relegate (rĕl′ḗ·gāt), 184
relent (rḗ·lĕnt′), 12
relevant (rĕl′ḗ·vănt), 202
relinquish (rḗ·lĭng′kwĭsh), 61
reminiscence (rĕm′ĭ·nĭs′ĕns), 106
remnant (rĕm′nănt), 21
remonstrate (rḗ·mŏn′strāt), 61
rendezvous (rän′dḗ·vōō), 71
renounce (rḗ·nouns′), 133
repel (rḗ·pĕl′), 61
repose (rḗ·pōz′), 71
reprieve (rḗ·prēv′), 235
reprisal (rḗ·prīz′ăl), 106
reproach (rē·prōch′), 39
requisite (rĕk′wĭ·zĭt), 27
requite (rḗ·kwīt′), 62
resent (rḗ·zĕnt′), 40
respite (rĕs′pĭt), 155
restitution (rĕs′tĭ·tū′shŭn), 99
resurrection (rĕz′ŭ·rĕk′shŭn), 149
resuscitate (rḗ·sŭs′ĭ·tāt), 98
retaliate (rḗ·tăl′ĭ·āt), 98
retard (rḗ·tärd), 62
reticent (rĕt′ĭ·sĕnt), 136
retinue (rĕt′ĭ·nū), 71
retribution (rĕt′rĭ·bū′shŭn), 142
reverie (rĕv′ēr·ĭ), 207
revoke (rḗ·vōk′), 134
ribald (rĭb′ăld), 237

robot (rō′bŏt), 41
roguish (rō′gĭsh), 48
rueful (rōō′fŏŏl), 20
sacrilegious (săk′rĭ·lē′jŭs), 194
sadistic (să·dĭs′tĭk), 222
sagacity (sȧ·găs′ĭ·tĭ), 99
sage (sāj), 64
salient (sā′lĭ·ĕnt), 222
salubrious (sȧ·lū′brĭ·ŭs), 222
salvage (săl′vĭj), 12
salvo (săl′vō), 6
sanction (săngk′shŭn), 149
sanguine (săng′gwĭn), 157
sardonic (sär·dŏn′ĭk), 222
satiate (sā′shĭ·āt), 40
saturnine (săt′ēr·nīn), 222
scrutinize (skrōō′tĭ·nīz), 134
secede (sḗ·sēd′), 235
seclusion (sḗ·klōō′zhŭn), 100
sedition (sḗ·dĭsh′ŭn), 242
sequence (sē′kwĕns), 100
severity (sḗ·vĕr′ĭ·tĭ), 42
shambles (shăm·b′ls), 106
simultaneous (sī′mŭl·tā′nḗ·ŭs),
    113
sinister (sĭn′ĭs·tēr), 27
sinuous (sĭn′ū·ŭs), 202
skeptical (skĕp′tĭ·kăl), 136
solstice (sŏl′stĭs), 200
specious (spē′shŭs), 230
spontaneous (spŏn·tā′nḗ·ŭs), 121
stentorian (stĕn·tō′rĭ·ăn), 121
stigma (stĭg′mȧ), 107
stoical (stō′ĭ·kăl), 223
stratosphere (strā′tṓ·sfēr), 228
stratum (strā′tŭm), 100
strident (strī′dĕnt), 243
stringent (strĭn′jĕnt), 113
subsequent (sŭb′sḗ·kwĕnt), 20
subterfuge (sŭb′tēr·fūj), 143

subtle (sŭt''l), 113
succinct (sŭk·sĭngkt'), 194
succor (sŭk'ēr), 72
succulent (sŭk'ū·lĕnt), 209
suffuse (sŭ·fūz'), 235
sundry (sŭn'drĭ), 64
superannuated (sū'pēr·ăn'ū·āt'ĕd), 216
supercilious (sū'pēr·sĭl'ĭ·ŭs), 113
surfeit (sûr'fĭt), 192
surmount (sûr·mount'), 62
surreptitious (sûr'ĕp·tĭsh'ŭs), 136
taciturn (tăs'ĭ·tûrn), 216
tangible (tăn'jĭ·b'l), 223
tantamount (tăn'tȧ·mount'), 216
taut (tôt), 48
tempo (tĕm'pō), 242
temporize (tĕm'pō·rīz), 185
tenacity (tē·năs'ĭ·tĭ), 100
tentative (tĕn'tȧ·tĭv), 194
terminate (tûr'mĭ·nāt), 62
tether (tĕth'ēr), 40
tractable (trăk'tȧ·b'l), 244
tranquillity (trăn·kwĭl'ĭ·tĭ), 107
transfigure (trăns·fĭg'ûr), 134
transgression (trăns·grĕsh'ŭn), 42
transient (trăn'shĕnt), 121
traverse (trăv'ērs), 62
trite (trīt), 121
trivial (trĭv'ĭ·ăl), 121
truculent (trŭk'ū·lĕnt), 209
turbulent (tûr'bŭ·lĕnt), 209
tyranny (tĭr'ȧ·nĭ), 72
ubiquitous (ū·bĭk'wĭ·tŭs), 157
ulterior (ŭl·tēr'ĭ·ēr), 244
unctuous (ŭngk'tṵ·ŭs), 194
urbane (ûr·bān'), 223

usurp (ū·zûrp'), 185
utility (ū·tĭl'ĭ·tĭ), 143
vacillate (văs'ĭ·lāt), 134
vagary (vȧ·gâr'ĭ), 208
vague (vāg), 27
valiant (văl'yȧnt), 64
vanguard (văn'gärd'), 6
vanquish (văng'kwĭsh), 62
vaunt (vônt), 62
vehement (vē'ē·mĕnt), 48
venomous (vĕn'ŭm·ŭs), 114
veracity (vē·răs'ĭ·tĭ), 143
verge (vûrj), 72
versatile (vûr'sȧ·tĭl), 244
vertigo (vûr'tĭ·gō), 242
viand (vī'ȧnd), 7
vicious (vĭsh'ŭs), 136
vicissitude (vĭ·sĭs'ĭ·tūd), 192
vigilance (vĭj'ĭ·lȧns), 155
vindicate (vĭn'dĭ·kāt), 134
vindictive (vĭn·dĭk'tĭv), 48
virile (vĭr'ĭl), 114
visage (vĭz'ĭj), 72
vitiate (vĭsh'ĭ·āt), 134
vociferous (vō·sĭf'ēr·ŭs), 28
volatile (vŏl'ȧ·tĭl), 223
vulnerable (vŭl'nēr·ȧ·b'l), 48
wane (wān), 40
wanton (wŏn'tŭn), 20
wary (wâr'ĭ), 48
water-logged (wôt'ēr-lŏgd'), 122
weird (wērd), 20
wily (wīl'ĭ), 64
wizened (wĭz'nd), 114
wrest (rĕst), 40
zealous (zĕl'ŭs), 49
zenith (zē'nĭth), 21
zephyr (zĕf'ēr), 7